Oriental Women

by Edward Bagby Pollard

The ancient wooing of Rebekah is Isaac, though it is by no means typical in all its details, contains many elements that mark Oriental weddings..... The courage of Rebekah in consenting to mount the camel of a stranger and go into a far country to be wed is noteworthy. With all the apparent grace and gentleness of Rebekah, here was a pluck most commendable.]

PREFACE

The relative position which woman occupies in any country is an index to the civilization which that country enjoys, and this test applied to the Orient reveals many stages yet to be achieved. The frequent appearance of woman in Holy Writ is sufficient evidence of the high position accorded her in the Hebrew nation. Such characters as Ruth, Esther, and Rebekah have become famous. Wicked women there were, such as Jezebel, but happily their influence was not of lasting duration. No other ancient people so highly prized chastity in woman; motherhood was regarded as an evidence of divine favor, while barrenness was considered a curse. The home life was one of singular purity and sweetness. Idleness was deplored as a crime, and every child was taught to work with his own hands.

The deities of the Babylonians and Assyrians were feminine as well as masculine. Ishtar was the Venus of classical mythology--the goddess of love, and the Babylonian Hades was presided over by a feminine deity. Rank, however, determined social freedom; the woman of the lowest class might go and come at will, but the woman of the high class was condemned to a life of isolation. Woman's position of honor in Egypt is evidenced by the presence of temples and monuments erected to her memory. She assisted her husband in the management of his affairs, and was granted a part in religious worship.

In the countries in which Brahmanism and Mohammedanism is the prevailing religion, the position of woman is relatively low. The Hindoo woman has no spiritual life apart from her husband; she can only hope for ultimate happiness through a union with him. The harem prevails, and woman is the slave of man.

In contrast to the position of woman in these countries and in China is the position she holds in Japan. While not yet occupying a place of respect equal to that accorded her in the Occident, she is coming gradually to be regarded as she deserves. There yet remain the loose morals, characteristic of the Oriental nature, and it is still regarded as right and proper that a good wife should barter her chastity if it is necessary in order to save her husband the disgrace of imprisonment for debt. The higher classes, however, are coming to treat woman with a respect far higher than that usually accorded her in the Orient. The process of her elevation must of necessity be slow, for no great reform is accomplished by a coup d'tat, but only through the ameliorating effects of enlightenment and education, and this alone will accomplish the final emancipation of the woman of the Orient from her present condition of servitude. E.B. POLLARD.

I

WOMEN OF THE DAWN

The story of the first woman in the Hebrew Scriptures and Semitic myth is as familiar as a household tale. Jewish and Christian literature alike have frequent mention of the part she played in the race's infancy, though in the sacred writings themselves she is but rarely mentioned.

What the Book of Genesis furnishes upon the creation of the first woman may not be considered of great interest as a scientific treatise upon the first appearance of feminine life on the earth, but it is of marked importance as revealing the idea around which the life and character of the Hebrew woman were developed. Here we find a pure monotheism (the presence of no goddess at the birth of things), a high morality, the dignity of marriage and of motherhood, that give to the Hebrew women great advantage over their sisters of many another country.

Very early was it discovered, say the Hebrew records, that it is "not good for man to be alone." The method by which this fact was first made manifest is of no little suggestiveness. Would it be possible from the many creatures of earth, sky, and sea, already made, for man to find a companion in whom he might confide, with whom the long hours might be made more joyous? God tries the man whom he has made. Could he be satisfied with a creature of a lower order as fellow and friend? Could he, by subduing and having dominion, find in dog, camel, or favorite steed a sufficient helpfulness, a satisfaction for his human longings? No! As one by one the living creatures passed in solemn order before him, it was soon realized by the names that Adam gave them, that he found no true fellowship in all that earth-born throng. "And the man gave names to all cattle and to the fowl of the air, and to every beast of the field, but for man there was not found an helpmeet for him."

The epoch-making "deep sleep" that fell upon Adam, the taking of the rib, the making of the first woman, the closing again of the wound, and the presentation of a helpmeet for the man--all this is a familiar Scripture story. Whether it be intended to be literal history is of little moment here. Very beautifully have Matthew Henry and others, following the rabbis, commented upon the essential meaning of this narrative in suggesting that woman is not represented as taken from the head of man that she should rule over him; nor from his feet, to be trampled under foot; but she was taken from his side that she might be his equal; from under his arm that she might be protected by him; near his heart that he might cherish and love her. "This is now bone of my bone and flesh of my flesh: she shall be called Ishshah"--that is, if man is to be called Ish, woman shall be Ishshah, simply his equal.

It is not strange that there should have arisen many legends about this first Oriental woman. According to one of the Jewish stories contained in the Talmud, Adam was at first very huge. When he stood, his head reached to the very heavens; and when he reclined, he covered the earth with his gigantic form. But in a deep sleep which God caused to fall upon him, Eve was made from parts of all his members. After the creation of Eve, therefore, Adam was never again quite so large. Some of the Jewish rabbis taught that Adam, the first man, had in his body thirteen ribs,--one more than was possessed by any of his descendants,--and that this surplus bone became, in the hands of the Creator, the physical basis for the creation of the mother of all.

The thought has been suggested that as man was commissioned to subdue and have dominion over the beasts of the field and all the forces of Nature, the reason for woman's creation lies in her ability to tame man. Whether this be true or not, the student of Hebrew history will not lack ample evidence to show that to the women of Israel is due largely the place that their people hold in history as teachers of religion and morals; to them is due, also, that conservative quality which has made the Hebrews a peculiar and permanent people.

One of the old rabbis, commenting upon the Biblical account of woman's creation from the rib of Adam, remarked: "It is as if Adam had changed a pot of earth for a jewel." Good Dr. South, of pious memory, unaffected by the modern views of development, is credited with the remark that "Aristotle was but the rubbish of an Adam." If this be true, what must Eve have been!

About the beauty of the first woman, the Scriptures are silent, though, in Paradise Lost, Milton finds no hesitancy in creating her with surpassing physical grace, so that it was possible for her, like Narcissus, to fall in love with her own charms. Poets have not been slow to sing her praises:

"The world was sad, the garden was a wild And man the hermit sighed, till woman smiled."

The Hebrews called the first woman Eve--that is, living or expanded, "the mother of all living." But these Oriental records attribute to Eve the advent into the world of death and human woes. The discord that came from the apple once tossed into a famous company of frolicking Greeks cannot compare with that which grew out of the fatal fruit, forbidden to the primal tenants of the Garden of Eden.

"Earth felt the wound--And Nature from her seat Sighing through all her works, gave sign of woe, That all was lost."

The French saying cherchez la femme has been in some form upon the lips of men from the earliest dawn of time. "The woman which thou gavest me," is Adam's lame apology for his weakness, as in one brief sentence he shifts the blame with dexterity upon God--the giver,--and woman--the God-given.

In marked contrast with this dark view of the first woman's legacy to the world is the account of the first promise, the light that burst forth suddenly as through a rift in the overshadowing cloud: "The seed of the woman shall bruise the serpent's head." Thus Lamartine's remark that "woman is at the beginning of all great things," becomes as pertinent as it is true. It is impossible to estimate the effect upon Israelitish motherhood of the belief in that ancient promise that some mother's son should yet arise to crush the monster of evil that was loosed in the world. Many a Hebrew mother came to feel that her own babe might become the hero chosen to strangle the serpent. This thought made motherhood the more prized, it became the aim of every Hebrew woman.

What if we could reproduce the sensations of that mother-love when the first woman enfolded in her bosom the first infant born, and heard its first cry for a mother's care? Of much interest is the Hebrew narrative here; for when Eve beheld her firstborn son she is said to have made an exclamation which many Hebrew scholars interpret as meaning, "I have obtained the promised One," believing that the pledge of Jehovah concerning the woman's seed had even then been realized. But the first son was to bring pangs to his mother's soul by slaying the first brother. Who can adequately describe the effect which that first death must have had upon the maternal heart? Instead of the lost Abel came a new son to console the mother-heart, Seth, the good; and the struggle between good and evil goes on throughout the Hebrew records, woman usually taking her place with the forces that made for righteousness.

Concerning the first bad woman, Lilith, held by some to have been the wife of the first man, very curious are the legends. Later rabbinic literature is rife with these stories. Among the Babylonians and Assyrians, Lilith was a night-fairy, as the derivation of the name would indicate, though some derive it from lilu, the wind. Popular superstition among the Hebrews, either through inheritance from the early days before Abraham, their father, lived in the Mesopotamian valley, or through the contacts with this region during the Babylonian exile, looked upon Lilith as a female demon of the night. She was supposed to be especially hostile to children, and this is why the Latin translations of the Vulgate version of the Scriptures rendered the word as lamia, a hag or witch who was supposed to be harmful to the little folk-- though grown up people, also, might well beware of her baneful power. She is mentioned but once in Scriptures, and then in that highly graphic portrayal by the prophet Isaiah concerning the coming desolation that should soon befall the land of Edom, which was to become a place where "the wild beasts of the deserts meet with the wolves, and the satyr cries to his fellows, and Lilith (rendered in the accepted version, Screech Owl, and in the later version, Night Monster) takes up her abode."

It is Lilith's earlier history that is of especial interest, for, as runs the Jewish legend which one often meets in Talmudic literature, Lilith was the first wife of Adam, but becoming angered, she flew away and became a demon of the night. But the world will probably never concede that the first woman was a wicked one. The subtlety of an evil woman's charms is probably the underlying motive of the story of this "sweet snake of Eden," of whom Rossetti, in his Eden Bower, affirms consolingly, "not a drop of her blood was human."

"Who was Cain's wife?" is one of the perplexing questions asked by those who delight in hard sayings. The late Professor Winchell believed in a race of pre-Adamites, and many persons are committed to the theory of several centres of human origin. To those holding such views the question of Cain's marriage does not present particular difficulties. But those who hold to the theory that there was but one pair from whom all the family of mankind has sprung find difficulty in reconciling their theory with Biblical statements, and they are driven to acknowledging the necessity for marital relations between near kindred when the race was in its beginning--relations which would offend the best moral sentiment of to-day.

There is a curious passage in the Book of Genesis which tells of the marriage of the "sons of God" with the "daughters of men." Have we here the echo of that ancient tradition that once the gods and men intermarried and from the union the great heroes of the past were born? The close position of this statement concerning the "sons of God" and the "daughters of men" with the account of the great growth of evil in the world has led some to hold that these "daughters of men" were women from the unrighteous line of the murderous Cain, while the "sons of God" were men from the more upright family of Seth. Others, however, seeing also in close connection the statement that giants were on the earth in those days, find here a remnant of a very general tradition that from the gods had descended great heroes and giants who in past ages had fallen in love with daughters of human parentage. Since the Hebrews, however, were so strong in their monotheistic conceptions, this latter theory loses a great part of its force.

The state of society presented in the earliest Hebrew records indicates that the practice of polygamy was general. There are some who see indications among the Hebrew customs that there was a period, earlier than that of which any Hebrew records tell, in which polyandry and not polygamy was the fashion--when one woman had several husbands, rather than one husband several wives. The so-called Levirate marriage which was in vogue among the Hebrews is perhaps the strongest evidence that the customs of polyandry and mother-right were practised among them.

In common, then, with other peoples, the Hebrews practised polygamy; and while the influence of the best thought and teaching was, except in the earlier, patriarchal period, distinctly against it, the practice was still customary even down to the Christian era. The law of Moses, while not forbidding plurality of wives, discouraged the custom, and especially forbade the king from "multiplying wives."

The earliest example of polygamy of which the Hebrew records speak is that involving one of the most unique and interesting families of this early twilight of human existence. One Lamech, a descendant of Cain, is said to have married two wives, who bore the rather musical names of Adah and Zillah. And here we are introduced into the presence of a most remarkable household. For not only is Lamech to be awarded the distinction of having made the earliest attempt at verse which the Hebrew tradition has recorded, but Adah and Zillah became the mothers of a most talented family; the former of Jabel, "the father of such as dwell in tents and have cattle," and of Jubal, the inventor and patron saint of the harp and the pipe; while Zillah was the mother of Tubal-Cain, the first forger of implements of brass and iron. Lamech, the father, having doubtless received a sword from the forge of his son, used it in revenge upon an enemy, and gave utterance to the first recorded lines of poetry, which are possibly a fragment from what has been called The Lay of the Sword. It is a crude poem, dedicated by Lamech to his wives--for it was not uncommon among the early Semites to call the women to witness a hero's deeds of prowess:

"Adah and Zillah, hear my voice, Ye wives of Lamech, hearken to my speech, For I have slain a man for wounding me, Even a young man for bruising me. If Cain shall be avenged sevenfold, Truly Lamech, seventy and seven."

It is not to be wondered at that in the very midst of dry genealogical tables the writer of Genesis should have stopped for a moment to tell of this epoch-making household.

Whether the women of this unique family, Adah, Zillah, and her daughter Naamah, were equally gifted with the men of the household, we are not told; but surely there must have been some genius in those feminine members of the home, who were so closely connected with the beginnings, not only of the fine arts of poetry and music, but also of the industrial pursuits of cattle raising and of metal working.

The early Hebrews were nomads. At first glance it might appear that woman's part in such an order of society would be scant, and her life one of comparative inactivity. But this view would lead into error, for in the nomadic life, while the men were guarding their flocks from the depredations of hostile bands or from the ravages of wild beasts, the women were the home makers and the home keepers.

Mason, in his Woman's Share in Primitive Culture, commenting upon Herbert Spencer's division of the life history of civilization into the period of Militancy, and the later period of Industrialism, raises the question whether it may not after all be more in accord with the facts--at least in the early history of the race--to speak of a sex of militancy and a sex of industrialism. The Hebrew woman, from her place in the tent or seated about the tent door, not only tended the fire, but invented, developed, and carried on many a handicraft into which not until later the men themselves entered.

For centuries the story of the lives of the patriarchs has thrilled and edified many a young heart, but what of the credit due to the matriarchs? What part do we find them playing in the early life of these Oriental peoples! The patriarch was not only father of his family or clan, but was their king and high priest. Yet it would be a mistake to suppose that the mother of the family was not an important factor in that early society, as the lives of many a Hebrew woman will easily demonstrate. The names of Sarah, Rebekah, Rachel, Miriam, Huldah, and a host of others will readily occur to the mind of anyone at all familiar with the literature of the Old Testament.

A fair type of the life of the wife and partner of an ancient chief (sheik) of the higher order is found in that of Sarah, wife of the first and greatest Hebrew patriarch, "Abraham, the faithful." Living the life of nomad and shepherd, this pioneer of a new monotheism took his spouse away from the land of her fathers in the valley of Mesopotamia. Sarah's reverence for her husband became proverbial, and her conduct has been taken as the type of what was best in the domestic life of Israel--chaste behavior coupled with reverence. And Peter, known as the Apostle to the Hebrews, writing over two thousand years after the body of Sarah had been laid in its last home in the cave of Machpelah, gives a glimpse of the Hebrew conception of the ideal relation between husband and wife typified in Abraham and Sarah. While enjoining upon the women to whom he wrote the need of a "meek and quiet spirit," a spirit not discoverable in jewels and elaborate apparel, but in what he terms "the hidden man of the heart," he said: "For after this manner in the old time the holy women also, who trusted in God, adorned themselves, being in subjection unto their own husbands: even as Sarah obeyed Abraham, calling him lord; whose daughters ye are as long as ye do well." Thus did the virtues of Sarah impress themselves upon later generations. Sarah is not to be classed among the strong-minded women. Probably she was not virile in any true sense of the term, since in the traditions of her people she does not seem to have made for herself a place as leader that at all corresponds to the rank of her husband. He was to all Hebrews "Father Abraham," the first and foremost of his race; and no Jew could esteem his future life as giving promise of happiness unless his head might at length rest in Abraham's bosom. There is an ancient legend which says that Sarah, hearing of the plan of Abraham to sacrifice Isaac on the sacred spot of Moriah, died from the shock to her maternal heart. The father returned, bringing his only son alive with him, but Sarah had passed away. The narrative distinctly says that Abraham "came to mourn for Sarah and weep for her," as though the end had come during the absence of her husband. The Hebrew respect for women is illustrated in the costly burial accorded Sarah in a cave which was purchased from the sons of Heth--a place reverenced by the people of Israel for many centuries, because Sarah was buried there.

There is but one blot upon the life of this first mother of the Hebrews. Sarah was a faithful wife and devoted mother, but on at least one occasion she revealed a character capable of hasty, jealous, and cruel conduct. It is the time for the weaning of her only son--an occasion of more than usual interest in a Hebrew home. The family feast is at its height; Sarah discovers that her handmaid, an Egyptian woman, Hagar, whom she herself had given to Abraham as wife, for thus we may call her, was jesting at her expense. Quickly and hotly she demands that the bondwoman and her son Ishmael be immediately driven from the home, to which request Abraham reluctantly yields. Like most other women, Sarah, though now aged, could brook no rival in her home, and her womanly instinct at once discerned that only a step thus sharp and decisive would prevent, in the circle of domestic life, endless friction, more bitter than the sufferings occasioned by her cruel action.

Hagar in the thirsty wilderness, laying her perishing child under a bit of shrubbery and then departing a little distance that her mother-eyes may not behold the end, has powerfully awakened the imagination of the artist, as, indeed, she touched the heart of the Almighty, as the record tells us. For although Hagar wandered in the wilderness of Beersheba, the region of "the seven wells," no water had she found--so far was she from the life-giving draught; and yet was she so near--for lo! her eyes now fell upon a well of water, from which she and the lad quenched their mortal thirst. Thus was preserved him who was to become the father of the Ishmaelites, a people whose hand was to be against every man, and every man's hand against them. The breach that day in the tent of Abraham, between his two wives, one bond and the other free, was to be deep and abiding, as N. P. Willis, in describing Hagar's feelings in the wilderness, has written:

"May slighted woman turn And, as a vine the oak hath shaken off, Bend lightly to her leaning trust again? O, no!"

And an apostle versed in rabbinic lore uses the story of Sarah as typical of the abiding difference between the principles of law and the precepts of grace.

Probably no feature in the social life of a people is of so universal an interest as its marriage customs, and there is no courtship, either ancient or modern, which has more enkindled the imagination and awakened the interest of men than that between Isaac and Rebekah. The English prayerbook, in its ceremony of marriage, has chosen Isaac and Rebekah as the ideal pair to whose fidelity the young couples of the later years are directed for inspiration and example. It is a truly picturesque and even romantic story, which never loses its charm; and Rebekah, whether at the well or in her household, will always present a unique picture of womanly grace and beauty.

This ancient wooing of Rebekah by Isaac, though it is by no means typical in all its details, contains many elements that mark Oriental weddings. The prominence of the parents in the negotiations is characteristic. It cannot be said, however, that the choice of either Isaac or Rebekah was constrained.

When Isaac and his parents have reached the conclusion to which Richter has given voice--"No man can live piously or die righteously without a wife"--the faithful Eliezer is made to thrust his hand under the thigh of his master and swear that he will see that Isaac is wedded not to a daughter of the people around, but to a woman of his own kindred living in the regions of Aramea. This habit of marrying within one's own tribe became firmly fixed in Hebrew custom. The use of marriage presents, here so rich and costly, is almost as old as marriage itself; and how much Rebekah and Laban, her brother, were influenced by this manifestation of the riches of her wooer none can ever know. The part taken by Laban in this marital transaction is by no means unusual. Brothers in the East often played an important role on such occasions. When Shechem, the Hivite, wished to marry Dinah, daughter of Jacob, he consulted not only her father, but her brothers as well; and the brothers of the heroine of the Song of Songs are represented as saying: "What shall we do for our sister in the day when she shall be spoken for?"

The courage of Rebekah in consenting to mount the camel of a stranger and go into a far country to be wed is noteworthy. With all the apparent grace and gentleness of Rebekah, here was a pluck most commendable. We may say with Dickens: "When a young lady is as mild as she is game and as game as she is mild, that's all I ask and more than I expect." But it turned out to be but one of the many cases, since the world began, of "love at first sight"; and affection strengthened with the years! The frequent and cynical remark that marriage is after all but a lottery will probably long survive. Isaac did not act upon the sentiment expressed in the remark of Francesco Sforza: "Should one desire to take unto himself a wife, to buy a horse, or to invest in a melon, the wise man will recommend himself to Providence and draw his bonnet over his eyes." The daughters of Heth and of Canaan around him were not to his liking, and Providence seems greatly to have helped him in the emergency, for in the unseen Rebekah (whose very name means "to tie" or "to bind") Isaac found a lifelong blessing; and probably nothing could better disclose the wisdom of his matrimonial choice than the words of the Bible narrative, "and he loved her, and Isaac was comforted after his mother's death."

There is one blot upon Rebekah's record as a wife and mother, which, however, no less reveals a fault in Isaac's character as a father. It is a defect that was doubtless inherent in the ancient Oriental system itself. It was more usual than otherwise for mothers as well as for fathers to have favorite children. When both parents centred their affection upon the same child, usually a boy, it was ill for the rest; when mother and father were divided, it was ill for family felicity. Rebekah loved Jacob, the younger; Isaac loved Esau, the elder. And it is in this unfortunate distribution of parental affection that is to be found the beginning of a violent fratricidal feud, a long separation, as well as the causes which led to the bringing within the confines of Hebrew history two of the most important women of ancient Israel,--Leah and Rachel. Here again we find illustrated the fixed habit among the Hebrews to seek wives among their own people.

Among the Hebrews it was the custom that one who would acquire a wife must pay for her, either in money or in service. Usually, the young girl's consent was not thought to be a necessary part of the matrimonial bargain, and a father delivered a daughter to the purchasing suitor, as he might a slave that he had sold to the highest bidder. The woman herself played but a secondary part. It is thus quite plain that in this early day, marriage did not depend upon a contract entered into between one man and one woman, but between two or more men. And yet, in ancient Israel, while daughters were sold for wives,--or, to put it less harshly, given away for a consideration,-- there is no intimation that a wife was in any sense regarded as a slave; nor are there instances of a husband selling his wife for a consideration. Parents were usually the parties to matrimonial bargains. In the case of Jacob and

Rachel, however, we do not find the parents making the match, for the parents of the pair are widely separated. Jacob falls in love with Rachel at his first sight of her, as she, at close of day, leads the flock of Laban, her father, to drink from the open well hard by the dwelling. Laban readily agrees to surrender his daughter to Jacob,--who doubtless had no purchase money to procure a wife,--if the young man will serve him for seven years. But at the close of the stipulated period, the wily Laban falls back upon an unwritten law among the people of the day, that the daughters must be taken in marriage in the order of their seniority. Thus Leah, the elder sister, is accorded to Jacob, and seven years' additional service is necessary for the possession of Rachel. Persistence wins, and Jacob is at length in possession of both Laban's daughters, but the victory was the beginning of a life of struggle. Some one has remarked: "The music at a marriage always reminds me of the music of soldiers entering upon a battle;" it was so with Jacob. There must be a battle with Laban, the uncle and father-in-law, in which the daughters both take the part of the husband against their father, and agree to flee from that parent's house with the man to whom they had linked their destinies. There must be a battle with Esau, when mothers and little ones were to be exposed to great dangers and hardships; indeed, a long life of vicissitudes awaited the women whose lives were one with Jacob's, and contests between rival sons of rival mothers were to follow.

It has already been remarked that Sarah, wife of Abraham (whose name, Sarah, means "the princess"), occupies no such place in the imagination and tradition of the Hebrews as did Abraham, their father. It is around Leah and Rachel that the tribes of Israel group themselves, and the book of Ruth speaks of them as having built the house of Israel, and Leah and Rachel were the mothers of the twelve patriarchs for whom the tribes were subsequently named. Especially does Rachel occupy a high place, not only because she was Jacob's most favorite wife, but because of those personal qualities which more readily stirred the poetic and religious imagination of the people. The poet-prophet, Jeremiah, writing of the loss of life among the sons of Israel, because of the invasion and cruelty of Nebuchadnezzar, King of Babylon, represents the people's sadness at the terrible calamity as "Rachel weeping for her children because they are not"--an expression which may have been suggested by Rachel's early condition of childlessness, followed by the loss of both her sons, Joseph and Benjamin, in the land of Egypt. The expression has borrowed new force, because it is quoted as again exemplified in "the slaughter of the innocents" by Herod the Great at the time of the birth of Jesus.

II

ISRAEL'S HEROIC AGE

In the early history of the Hebrews, the people followed the free, roving life of the shepherd. In a climate where water supply was by no means sure, where a flowing stream which gave drink to the flocks to-day might be a rocky ravine to-morrow, families must needs have no certain abiding place. Woman the homekeeper must of course be affected by this Bedouin manner of life. Many daughters, like Rebekah and Rachel, were shepherdesses of their father's flocks of sheep and goats. When the Israelites went down into Egypt because the fertile valley of the Nile made famines less frequent than in the land of Canaan, they were somewhat ashamed, we are told, of the fact that they were shepherds, on account of Egyptian prejudices against that occupation, but in their native country they were proud of their occupation, and rather looked down upon merchantmen. The hated "Canaanite" became the synonym for "trafficker." It was the later exigencies of exile and dispersion that forced the Jews to buy and sell, and right well did they learn the lesson the world forced upon them. But in the beginning it was not so. And hence we find Israel, even after the twelve patriarchs had settled in the plains of Goshen, their Egyptian home, keeping their flocks and developing their home life in their own way in the kingdom of the Pharaohs.

Among the many notable women of Israel's heroic age, Miriam must not be forgotten. The romantic story of the hiding of her infant brother, in the rushes of the Nile, when King Pharaoh would have destroyed every Hebrew boy, is a familiar chapter. The sisterly tenderness and devotion which stationed the girl of twelve years to watch what might happen to the infant brother, to fight away wild beasts, and at length to direct the living treasure to the bosom of its own mother, is one of the best examples in literature of womanly tact and sisterly devotion.

The daughter of Pharaoh, a child of the Nile, comes down to the sacred stream to wash her garments or bathe her body in the saving water, and quickly, indeed quite willingly, falls into the well-wrought plan of Jokabed, the mother of the child Moses, and Miriam, the sister--a counterplot to that of the princess's father, and so ancient history is written with new headlines.

It is Miriam who enjoys the distinction of being the first prophetess in Israel, as her brother Moses is the first who was called a prophet, and her brother Aaron the first high priest. The part she took in leading the intractable people of Israel out of Egyptian bondage into the land of the Canaanites, must have been considerable, though according to the record she was nearing the century mark before the journeying began. As a poetess and musician, also, Miriam holds no mean place, for we are told that when her people had successfully crossed the arm of the sea, and Pharaoh's pursuing hosts had been cut off in the descending floods, Miriam organized the women into a chorus, and going before them with timbrel in her hand she led in voicing the refrain sent back in antiphonal strains to the song of the great camp, while her companions followed with timbrels and dances. This aged woman had music and patriotic fervor still present in her soul, as victory was assured to her people. The Hebrew song that grew out of this incident which is recorded in the Book of Exodus has been termed "Israel's Natal Hymn," a sort of poetic Declaration of Independence, and is far more majestic in its qualities than Moore's poem based upon the same event:

"Sound the loud timbrel; O'er Egypt's dark sea Jehovah hath triumphed--His people are free."

By a singular confusion, the Koran identifies Miriam, sister of Moses, with Mary, the mother of Jesus. This may be partly due to the fact that the New

Testament Scriptures as well as the Septuagint Greek translation of the Old spell both names alike, "Miriam."

But great women, like great men, sometimes make mistakes, and their blunders are often just at the point where they have achieved greatness. Miriam's distinction lay in her insight into the merits of her brother's mission and in her unselfish devotion to the cause to which he had been dedicated. Her greatest grief befell her by her unfortunate effort to break that very influence and to destroy his leadership, because she was displeased with a marriage he had contracted. She was smitten with leprosy, but the esteem with which she was held may be discovered when we read that the whole camp grieved at her calamity and consequent isolation from the people, and "journeyed not till Miriam was brought in again."

Miriam, the first prophetess and one of the strongest women that Israel ever produced, died during the wilderness wandering, and was buried in the region west of the Jordan. For many generations her tomb was pointed out in the land of Moab. Jerome, the Christian father, tells us that he saw the reputed grave close to Petra in Arabia. But, like the place of the entombment of her more distinguished brother, "no man knoweth it unto this day."

Among no people has the national consciousness been more thoroughly developed or more deeply seated than among the Hebrews. It is not to be wondered at, therefore, that among the women of Israel may be discovered the most ardent spirit of patriotism. Miriam's part in the founding of the Hebrew Commonwealth has already been noticed. When in the wanderings of the wilderness it became necessary to erect a temporary structure for the worship of Jehovah, the God of Israel, the women willingly tore their jewels from their ears, their ornaments from their arms and ankles, and devoted them to the rearing of the tabernacle. With their own fingers they spun in blue, purple, and scarlet, and wrought fine linen for the hangings and the service of their temple in the desert. In a theocracy, piety and patriotism were one. Not even the Spartan mother, who wished her son to return from the wars bringing his shield with him or being borne upon it, nor the women of Carthage, who plucked out their hair for bowstrings, could surpass the women of Israel in their sacrifices for national independence and political glory. In the days of Octavia, the ministers of Rome levied a tax upon Roman matrons to carry on a foreign war, and demanded a sacrifice of their jewels; and the Roman women thronged the public places, appealing to the high and influential in their vigorous protest against this taxation, and thus saved their ornaments. But the women of Israel did not need to be urged to tear off their ornaments and devote them to the common welfare. It was a woman who received the first recognition for services rendered the victorious hosts of Joshua, after the first campaign against the Canaanites had been waged. This was Rahab, a woman of Jericho, who, though her past life had been far from exemplary, seemed to see in the approaching Israelites a people of destiny. She therefore hid the Hebrew spies who had come to inspect the land, and, letting them down over the walls of the city, saved their lives. Thus did Rahab, the harlot of Jericho, preserve her own life when Joshua entered the city a victor; and, being admitted among the people of Israel, she became the ancestress of their greatest king, David, and, through him, the ancestress of Christ.

During that era in Israel's life, when the people were no longer merely an aggregation of shepherd clans, but had not yet been moulded into a national existence by a strong feeling of unity or the recognition of a common need, woman's life was exceptionally severe in its hardships and dangers. The unorganized tribes, engaged in their agricultural and pastoral pursuits, with hostile clans about them and hostile cities and strongholds as yet unsubdued, were subject to frequent incursions from bands of marauders and from armies of neighboring tribes, which would suddenly swoop down upon them like vultures on their prey. It was under such conditions as this that the women suffered untold indignities and misery. Kidnappers sold the women and children to slave traders of the coast, who carried them to Egyptian and Greek ports; so that even before the great dispersion of the children of Jacob which the kings of Assyria and of Babylonia brought about in the eighth and sixth centuries prior to the Christian era, the Hebrews were being scattered throughout the world.

It was in the period of transition and chaos which immediately followed the entrance of the people into the land of Palestine that Israel's most manlike woman appears as a veritable savior of her people. She is the second woman to whom the title of prophetess is accorded. The record reveals the fact that she was not only a woman strong in deeds of valor, but a leader in the religious life of Israel. The days were dark enough for the descendants of Abraham. For two decades now had Jabin, with his "nine hundred chariots of iron," struck with terror the ill-equipped, disorganized Hebrews. But there dwelt "under the palm tree" between Ramah and Bethel among the hills of Ephraim a woman who, by force of will and recognized wisdom, judged the people of Israel. "The inhabitants of the villages ceased, they ceased in Israel, until that I Deborah arose, that I arose a mother in Israel." It is from the sanctuary of this woman's mind and heart that deliverance from the king of the Canaanites is to break forth. She is called Deborah, i.e., "woman of torches," or "flames," either because she made wicks for the lamps of the sanctuary, or because of her fiery, ardent nature. Certainly there was warmth in her heart and fire in her love of her native land. She speedily sends for Barak, a chief man of Naphtali, and enjoins upon him to prepare an army of ten thousand men to meet Jabin's army, which is approaching under its captain Sisera, on the banks of the river Kishon. Barak hesitates, but at length answers: "If thou wilt go with me, I will go,"--so necessary did this strong, magnetic woman's presence seem for the enlistment of the people in the holy order of the enterprise. Deborah did not flinch in the presence of this challenge. The army is raised. The battle is joined, and Sisera's host is discomfited before Israel. The captain himself becomes a fugitive before the victors. But the end is not yet. Another woman appears upon the stage of this tragedy. The fleeing Sisera seeks shelter in the secret place of Jael's tent. Weary to exhaustion, the captain of the enemies of her people sinks down to sleep, the more profound because of the great draught of buttermilk or curds which Jael gave the thirsty man; and then with tent pin, a hammer, and an unquivering hand, Jael struck the sharp instrument through the sleeping man's temple and pinned him swooning to the dirt floor of her tent.

It was this bloody, but daring, deed which gave rise to one of the earliest of Israel's epic songs, the Song of Deborah. It is a remarkable poem, given in full in the Book of Judges. It sets forth praises to Jehovah for deliverance, and to Jael for the deadly stroke. A few lines from this epic, which many consider the earliest piece of Old Testament writing, will disclose the patriotic spirit of Israel's womanhood in those days of social and political disorder. The people are represented as crying out to the strong woman who lived under the solitary palm:

"Awake, awake, Deborah, Awake, awake, utter a song."

Deborah comes at the call of distress. The people are rapidly marshalled to her help. But some hold back:

"Why abodest thou among the sheepfolds, To hear the bleatings of the flocks? .... Gilead abode beyond Jordan And why did Dan remain in ships?"

The battle is joined. Canaan is worsted before the followers of the woman of the hour.

"The stars in their courses fought against Sisera. The river Kishon swept them away, That ancient river, the river Kishon. O my soul, march on with strength."

Then, turning upon the indifferent and laggard hosts that held back and refused to strike the blow for liberty, the poetess exclaims:

"Curse ye Meroz, said the angel of the Lord, Curse ye bitterly the inhabitants thereof, Because they came not to the help of the Lord, To the help of the Lord against the mighty."

Concerning the woman whose unfailing hand had struck the fatal blow, the poetess sings:

"Blessed above women shall Jael be, The wife of Heber the Kenite. Blessed shall she be above women in the tent.

"He asked water And she gave him milk, She brought forth butter in a lordly dish."

The tent pin has pierced the temples of the oppressor of Israel:

"At her feet he bowed, he fell, he lay down, At her feet he bowed, he fell, When he bowed, he fell down--dead."

Very dramatic do the lines become when, imagining the mother of Sisera waiting for her son to return victorious from the battle, and looking out through the lattice of her dwelling wondering at his long delay, she asks:

"Why is his chariot so long in coming, Why tarry the wheels of his chariots?"

But Sisera never returns to his maternal roof. For forty years did the people enjoy the freedom of Deborah's deliverance, the woman whose influence went out from "the sanctuary of the palm."

It is said of this period, commonly known as the Age of the Judges, that "every man did that which was right in his own eyes." This would be known in political theory as well as in practical government as nothing short of anarchy. And indeed, it was, for while each man did that which was right in his own eyes, the "right" of each was so frequently wrong, that social chaos reigned with almost unbroken sway. And while one woman of the period became a deliverer for four decades, for more than a century many women suffered untold misery for lack of unity among the tribes and leaders capable of bringing the life of the reign to rights.

It is often affirmed that sons more frequently inherit characteristics of their mothers, while to the daughters are bequeathed the traits of their fathers. An unnamed woman of this period of the political chaos, the wife of a certain Manoah, from the family of the Danites, was chosen to be the mother of a giant. Now, giants were rare in Israel, though in the earlier days of Palestinian occupation, Nephelim, and "the sons of Anak," are mentioned as among those enemies of the Hebrews. Their huge forms, it is written, were a menace to Israel's peace, and in comparison with these monsters her sons were said to be "as grass-hoppers." One day, as the story runs, an angel appears to this nameless, hitherto childless, wife of Manoah, and informs her that a son who is to be born, and nourished at her own bosom, is to have a remarkable history. She herself is to take care neither to drink wine nor any strong drink, for her son is to be dedicated to the abstemious life of the Nazarite. The woman is obedient to the angelic voice; and she with her husband offers up a burnt offering to Jehovah in grateful praise. The son is born. He is taught that no intoxicating draught shall enter his lips, nor should a razor touch his head, that his long-grown locks might speak outwardly of his vows. But wine is not the only temptation that is to beset this giant youth. The daughters of neighboring Philistia were to his eyes more than passing fair.

The influence of these young women, whose features, we may suppose, bore some characteristics of Grecian beauty,--as their progenitors had landed on the shores of Canaan from the island of Crete, gradually adopting a Semitic language and civilization,--was very potent over the heart of the muscular but susceptible young Hebrew. A love affair in which the long-haired Nazarite plays a prominent role will introduce us, somewhat at least, into woman's world of this disorganized period in the early life of Western Palestine at a day more than a thousand years before the Christian Era.

This affair of the heart was brought to light when one day the young man came in to tell his father and his mother that a fair damsel in Timnah, a city of the Philistines, had captured the very citadel of his being. Neither the protestations of his parents, nor their careful descanting upon the virtues of the daughters of his own people could move the young man. His heart was set. Neither parents at home nor the lion that met him on the way to secure his bride could thwart his firm-set purpose. Mother and father are for the moment forgotten, and the lion is torn asunder by the strong arms of this young giant. Every obstacle is surmounted and Delilah is in the arms of Samson.

Now, George Sand was doubtless correct in the rather prosaic remark: "It is not so easy to see through a woman as through a man." Samson did not quite penetrate the wiles of his lady love. Her beauty hid all else, and Samson fell. "The whisper of a beautiful woman," says Diana of Poitiers, "can be heard further than the loudest call of duty." The Nazarite vow, so strong and binding, became in Delilah's hands, as she held the shears, weaker than the withes she bound about the arms of the captured giant. Robert Burns has, in a characteristic fashion, given what might well be inscribed to Samson's memory:

"As Father Adam first was fooled, A case that's still too common, Here lies a man a woman ruled The devil ruled the woman."

Delilah, the Philistine, is to be contrasted with the typical Hebrew women, not only in the matter of feminine chastity for which they stand out among ancient women as preeminent, but also in that fidelity to husband and to native land which made the Hebrews the most stable and persistent race with which the world is acquainted.

In marked contrast with this witch of the Philistine plains, stands out the heroic daughter of Jephtha. Her purity, patriotism, and her deep respect for the sacredness of a religious oath, place her at the very opposite pole. "Great women," says Leigh Hunt, "belong to the history of self-sacrifice." If this be true, Jephtha's daughter must be enrolled among the great, as her heroic self-devotion shines through the dimness of ancient history. Her father was one of Israel's deliverers in the days of tribal division and political chaos. Returning from victory over the hostile Ammonites, Jephtha purposes to give, as sacrifice to Jehovah for bringing him success in arms, the first creature that comes forth to meet him as he turns his face homeward. It is his own daughter, his only child, going out to meet him with the timbrel and with dances. In his eyes a "very daughter of the gods, divinely tall, and most divinely fair." Will he break his vow? Will the young woman herself, this Hebrew Alcestis, shrink from the sacrifice? "My father, thou hast opened thy mouth unto the Lord, do unto me according to that which hath proceeded out of thy mouth."

For a woman to die childless in Israel was looked upon as a calamity, a mark of divine displeasure, and the daughter of Jephtha was a virgin. It is for this reason that she begged the coveted privilege of two months' respite that, with her maidens, she might withdraw to the neighboring mountain and there "bewail her virginity." At the end of the required period, returning to her father's house, she yields herself a sacrifice to the hasty but well-meant vow of her patriotic father. So deeply did her pure devotion to filial and patriotic ideals impress the daughters of Israel, that every year they went out to lament, four days, in honor of the daughter of Jephtha, the Gileadite, of whom N. P. Willis has drawn this appreciative picture:

"Now she who was to die, the calmest one In Israel at that hour, stood up alone And waited for the sun to set. Her face Was pale but very beautiful, her lip Had a more delicate outline and the tint Was deeper; but her countenance was like The majesty of angels!"

Among no ancient people was the love of chastity in women so thorough and imperative. There is probably no better illustration of this fact than in the very ingenious method by which the men of Benjamin obtained their wives, at a time when total extinction of the tribe seemed to stare them in the face. An aged Levite, with his wife, who had been unfaithful to him, but by his efforts had been reclaimed and with him was returning home, is passing through the land of Benjamin. When they reach the city of Jebus, afterward named Jerusalem, the famous centre of Israel's later life, no one offered the customary hospitality, so the man and his wife were about to lodge in the street, a disgrace to the city, according to the common customs of entertainment. It is then a temporary resident of the city invites the homeless ones into his house. When the Benjamites saw them go in, they took the woman from the house and shamefully maltreated her, leaving her helpless upon the steps till morning. The Levite, incensed at the terrible crime, took the woman, cut her in pieces and sent the fragments throughout the tribes, telling the story of the deed of some of the sons of Benjamin. It is pronounced by all the worst blot upon the land since the sojourn in Egypt. The whole people is aroused to anger. They collect men of war from the tribes, and go up to battle against their brethren of Benjamin, till the entire tribe seems about to be exterminated. Especially was the destruction of their women grievous. What must be done when the dust of battle has rolled away? Shall a tribe be lost to Israel? This must not be. The sacred number must be preserved. How shall Benjamin obtain wives, for all the rest of Israel had made a solemn oath that they would never give their daughters to the sons of Benjamin because of this horrible crime which had been so peremptorily punished. At length, the elders of all the people devise a plan. Marriage with the Gentile peoples is, of course, not sanctioned, and all the tribes of Israel have refused to give their daughters to Benjamin--there is yet a way out of the dilemma. Some one remembers that every year at harvest time there is given a feast at Shiloh, where many Hebrew damsels come together to enjoy the religious and festal dances. It is agreed that the sons of Benjamin shall hide themselves in the adjacent vineyards, and while the maidens are dancing, each man is to run out, seize a wife and make his way swiftly homeward. But what say the fathers and brothers of the purloined damsels to this high-handed procedure of the young men of Benjamin? The elders agree to step in then and to advise all to acquiesce in quietness, for the people had not violated their oaths. Their daughters had not been given to Benjamin; they were stolen! So Benjamin obtained wives and the tribal existence was preserved by the same method in which Rome was repeopled at the expense of the Sabines.

Israel holds a high place among the people of the earth because of the prevalence of piety among its women. Religion is deeply grounded in the intuitions and feelings of the race, and derives force, at least, from the sense of dependence upon higher powers, as Schliermacher has taught. Since women are far truer in their intuitions and feelings than men and the sense of dependence is more highly developed, it is not strange that women everywhere are more religious than men. Among the holy women of old none can be accorded higher place than Hannah, the mother of Samuel.

One may at first be astonished that childlessness is so frequently mentioned as characteristic of women in the Scriptures. Among them, Sarah, Rebekah, Rachael, the unnamed wife of Manoah, Hannah, and Elisabeth,--mother of John the Forerunner,--are all familiar examples. But barrenness was probably not more common among the Hebrews than among other peoples. Only, in Israel, childlessness was accounted a calamity, if not a direct visitation of the Almighty. Hence, every pious woman wished to be released from the curse. The women themselves ridiculed and ever despised those who were not blessed with offspring. Besides, every man among the Hebrews wished to live in his descendants. To die without children was to be "cut off" from the face of the earth, and to be forgotten. There was a yearning to live forever in the land.

The contrast between the great emphasis which the Egyptian laid upon immortality, the large place it held not only in their religious teachings, but in the development of their civilization, as modern excavations have revealed it, and the lack of such emphasis in the writings of the Hebrew Scriptures has frequently been noticed, and by many greatly wondered at. But the Hebrews gave little thought to immortality in the next world. Their prophets spent most of their time stressing the importance of righteousness in this life, and the people emphasized the earthward side of immortality--that is, one's power to live forever in one's posterity.

The writer in the one hundred and twenty-eighth Psalm expressed the common Hebrew conception, as, in recounting the blessings of a truly happy man, he said: "Thou shalt eat the labour of thine hands: happy shalt thou be, and it shall be well with thee. Thy wife shall be as a fruitful vine by the sides of thine house: thy children like olive plants round about thy table." Or as another psalmist, in the same spirit, prays: "That our sons may be as plants grown up in their youth; that our daughters may be as cornerstones, polished after the similitude of a palace." Many a time in the Hebrew Scriptures is this ideal prominent. For a psalmist again writes: "As arrows in the hand of a mighty man, so are children of the youth. Happy is the man that hath his quiver full of them. They shall not be ashamed, but they shall speak with the enemies in the gate." And when the prophet Zachariah foretells the coming glory of Jerusalem, which should supersede the then present distress, he gives as one item of blessing: "And the streets of the city shall be full of boys and girls, playing in the streets thereof."

It may therefore be readily surmised how a woman of Hannah's piety might feel in the thought of her condition of childlessness. And while the hardships of the barren woman in Israel could in no way compare with those of some other peoples, as in Australia, where the childless woman of the aborigines is driven out to a dire struggle for existence, yet the feeling that her God was, for some cause, against her and that her husband might in his secret heart despise her, must have been agony indeed. "The brain-woman," says Oliver Wendell Holmes, "never interests us like the heart-woman; white roses please us less than red." Hannah was pre 雖 inently a heart woman; the red blood of warm devotion coursed through her veins. When at length her prayers, made in bitterness of suffering, were answered, and heaven gave her a son, she named him Samuel, for, she said, "God hath heard," and dedicated him wholly to Jehovah, placing him at the service of the tabernacle. When the time came to wean the lad, she journeyed with him to Shiloh, the place of the sanctuary, with her offering, as the custom was, and "lent him" forever to Jehovah, her God.

"I think it must somewhere be written that the virtues of the mothers are occasionally visited upon their children, as well as the sins of the fathers." These words of Dickens suggest one of the occasions in which motherly virtues seem to have been visited upon the child, for Samuel became the earliest representative of a long line of prophets who, for many centuries, were the spiritual leaders of Israel. He was the father and founder of a "school of the prophets," the earliest theological seminary of which we have any record. The prayer of thanksgiving which the records say Hannah uttered when God blessed her with this precious gift of a son, influenced not only the famous Magnificat of Mary, when she was told of the birth of her greater Son, but also that of Zacharias when the birth of John the Baptist was predicted by the angel who talked with him in the temple.

History records several famous cases of friendship between men; that between David and Jonathan, and that between Damon and Pythias of Syracuse, have become proverbial. Fewer have been the friendship among women. Indeed, some have argued the impossibility of such friendships. But there is probably no more attractive story of womanly devotion in all the range of literature than that which tells of the love between Ruth and Naomi. The Book of Ruth is a beautiful idyll of early Hebrew life, and the heroine here stands the test. The scene is laid in the time when judges ruled in Israel; and in this, as in many instances in the early days of Palestine, an epoch was born out of a famine. Elimelech, with his wife, Naomi, and their two sons, Mahlon and Chilion, hunger-driven, set out for the land of Moab. Death lays its claim to the husband and father, and Naomi, with her boys, is left widowed in a strange land. Mahlon and Chilion, now grown to manhood, marry two daughters of Moab, by name Orpah and Ruth. A decade passes, and the sons themselves die. Bereaved and broken in spirit, Naomi at length turns her heart toward her native Judean hills. Finding her daughters-in-law inclined to follow her into the uncertainty of her future subsistence in her former home, Naomi counsels their return, each to her mother's house. "And they lifted up their voice and wept." Orpah reluctantly obeys, but Ruth cleaves to her mother-in-law, with those unsurpassed and memorable words, which the author of the book of Ruth throws into Hebrew measure:

"Intreat me not to leave thee, Or to return from following after thee; For whither thou goest, I will go; And where thou lodgest I will lodge; Thy people shall be my people, And thy God, my God. Where thou diest, will I die, And there will I be buried. The Lord do so to me, and more also, If aught but death part thee and me."

"Some women's faces are in their brightness a prophecy, and some in their sadness a history." As these two women stood with their faces set toward Palestine, upon one was written a history of sorrow; upon the other there fell the sunrise of a new day. In Ruth's determination to follow Naomi, even to death,--for "a woman can die for her friend as well as a Roman knight" when she has one, as Jeremy Taylor has declared,--the young widow of Moab began a new life, which was destined to make her the ancestress of Judah's royal house, the great grandmother of David the king.

As the poetic story of Ruth proceeds, it records several interesting ancient marriage customs among the people of Israel. In marked contrast with the Hindoo custom of condemning widows to a life of scarcely bearable hardships, the Hebrew law was so framed as to make widowhood as far as possible a temporary state. The custom of Levirate marriage enforced upon the brother or nearest of kin to the deceased husband the obligation of taking the widow of his brother to wife, in order that the brother might not be without heir and memory in the land. Ruth's deceased husband had rights in the ancestral estate, and the Hebrew law was careful that estates should not pass out of the hands of the original owners, if it were possible to prevent it. Ruth, the widow, suddenly appears at Bethlehem, the old home of her husband's people. It is the time of the barley harvest. Naomi plays the role of the scheming mother. She would have her beautiful young daughter-in-law find a husband among her kindred, that her lamented son might have an heir to honor his memory and that the portion of the estate which was Elimelech her husband's might be redeemed. The love plot sends Ruth into the field of Boaz, a wealthy farmer and near kinsman of Elimelech, to glean after the reapers, for no man was permitted by the law to deprive the poor of whatever pickings they might find when the reapers had passed. The quick success of the plot, the fascination that Boaz feels for the graceful but unknown woman, the command given the reapers to leave behind by purposeful accident a little more of the grain than was usual and be gracious to the girl; the invitation at mealtime to come and partake of the repast of parched corn with the reapers; the resolve of Boaz that should there be found no nearer kinsman--whose duty it would first be to take the young woman to wife--he himself would choose her. All these incidents pass in rapid and romantic succession. The observation is apparently true that "women are never stronger than when they arm themselves with their own weakness." Boaz at once pledged himself to be the damsel's friend and protector. The next of kin declines or waives his right to the young widow, for he does not care to redeem Elimelech's portion of the land, a necessary part of such a matrimonial transaction. Boaz therefore summons the young man, next of kin, who has declined to redeem the land of his deceased brother and raise up heirs for him, to appear at the gate of the city as the law required. Here ten elders sit to witness and make legal the transaction. The shoe of the refusing kinsman is taken from his foot, in the presence of the assembled people, and given to Boaz, symbolizing the relinquishment of all rights in the premises. Then follows the custom of spitting in the face of the "man with the loosed shoe," which became a term of reproach, and was applied to the man who refused to fulfil toward a deceased kinsman the duties of the Levirate marriage. Time passes and the aged Naomi, whose mother named her "winsome," forgets the bitterness of her later years as she holds in her arms the infant Obed, in whom she exultingly sees the pledge that the house of her son shall live on, and a prophecy that his name will become famous among his people. "And Obed begat Jesse and Jesse begat David," the king.

III

THE DAYS OF THE KINGS

As we pass out of the unsettled age of the judges into the period when the commonwealth of Israel began to take definite shape, we come upon a corresponding change in the life of the Hebrew woman. The heroism in female virtue was perhaps no less frequent, but when the "heroic age" is behind us there is less opportunity for women to stand out in so strong a glare. And, indeed, all through this history the remark of Ruskin is close to the truth when he says: "Woman's function is a guiding, not a determining one." While epoch-making women occasionally appeared in the earlier period, they became fewer and fewer as the social order became more settled.

It was not till the days of the kings that the Mosaic law, in the broadest sense of the term, could exert any very potential influence over the life and conduct of the people. In a disorganized condition of society, of which it was said, "Every man did that which was right in his own eyes," to enforce Mosaic precepts would have been an impossibility, even had the people at large been acquainted with that law. Now, the law of Moses became one of the most powerful factors in giving to the women of Israel the high place they held in the commonwealth. The fifth of the "Ten Words"--which commands were the very nucleus about which the whole law was developed--reads: "Honor thy father and thy mother, that thy days may be long upon the land which the Lord thy God giveth thee." Thus, in this, the very first law of the Decalogue respecting duties to man, the duty of honoring the mother was made equally imperative with that of showing honor to the father. And it may be truly affirmed that Israel's remarkable permanence and persistency as a people may be traced to its domestic health, and that this vigorous domesticity is due largely to a better understanding of the true relation of the sexes than is discoverable among any other ancient nation.

That honor for parents makes for the permanence of a people both reason and history affirm. Any nation which honors its ancestry will hold tenaciously to ancestral ideals. Notwithstanding China's limitations in other directions, that nation, because of its worship of the fathers, has lived through many centuries and seen more powerful nations rise and fall.

The position of Israel as a separate people abides in strength because both father and mother have for ages been respected; and even though most of her sons and daughters are no longer "upon the land which the Lord their God gave them," they are still holding with wonderful firmness to the faith and ideals of their fathers. The Mosaic teachings concerning woman are not a little responsible for this remarkable state of racial longevity. The Hebrew woman's standing before the law gave her great advantage over her sisters of the other Semitic and Oriental peoples. The Mosaic law tended greatly to lessen the inequalities and mitigate the hardships of womankind. Even a woman captured in war was protected against the caprice of her captors.

Under the law, her life was equally as precious as that of a man, and therefore the taking of a woman's life was punishable with the same severity as was the murder of a man. The law was especially solicitous of her welfare during the period of child bearing, and greatly lessened the sorrows and isolation of widowhood.

While divorces were given almost at the will of the man, yet he could not without formality at once eject the woman from his house. He must give her a "writing of divorcement," which set forth the fact that she had been his wife. Thus was she protected from subsequent suspicion that she had lived with a man unlawfully. Wives of bond-servants were to go out free with their husbands on the seventh year of service, unless the master himself had given the wife to his manservant, in which case the woman and her children still belonged to the master.

Daughters were allowed inheritance as well as sons, though in earlier times than those of the kings they did not inherit their father's property except there were no sons. Fathers were not allowed to discriminate against a firstborn son and pass the inheritance to another because the mother of the oldest child happened to have lost favor in his eyes.

Laws forbidding unchastity and vice were explicit and severe. One who had taken criminal advantage of another's daughter was to marry her and pay the father the usual dowry; if not, he was to be amerced fifty shekels of silver, the ordinary dowry of virgins. If a husband suspected his wife of being unfaithful to him, an elaborate, but not severe, ordeal was laid upon the woman, called "drinking the waters of jealousy." If she passed this examination successfully, her husband had no power further to punish her; if not, she was to suffer for her shame.

The widow and the fatherless were given special consideration under the law. In the feast days when the people's hearts were merry and they were rejoicing in the increase of their lands, the widow was not to be forgotten. In business transactions the people were to take heed that the widow suffer not injustice. Her garments could never be taken in pledge, and judges were enjoined to see that no violence was done to her rights. The fallen sheaf in the harvest field, the forgotten gleanings of the olive trees, the droppings of the vintage were not to be withheld from her.

How deep-seated this sense of obligation to the widow was in Israel may be discovered in the Book of Job. The friends who visited Job in his bewildering grief could find no more probable cause for so severe a divine chastisement upon the arch-sufferer than that Job had neglected the widow or taken her in pledge. One effect of the attitude of the customary law toward widows is discovered in a most signal way in the Second Book of Maccabees, which relates that in the period of which it tells, about B.C. 150, it was customary to lay up large sums of money in the temple treasury for the relief of widows and of fatherless children.

Such women as Miriam and Deborah were factors to be reckoned with in the political movements of their times. So it was with the prophetesses generally, for just as the great prophets dealt with the politics of state, so a prophetess could not always escape the problems of statesmanship to which her time might give birth. Both prophet and prophetess were looked upon as the chosen spokesmen for Jehovah. Because of this, Huldah acted as a sort of prime minister and adviser of both king and high priests in their Jehovistic reforms during the reign of Josiah.

That women generally took a deep interest in political matters may be perceived in the way in which the exploits of David appealed to the imaginations of the women when Saul's star was setting and David's appearing above the horizon; for young women went out to meet the coming hero and king with musical instruments, singing a song whose refrain was:

"Saul hath slain his thousands, David his tens of thousands."

The power of the feminine idea may be forcefully seen in the very common conception of the nation itself as a young woman. Both prophet and poet--

and the prophets were usually poets--refer many times to the "daughter of Zion," meaning the people of Israel.

The prophet Jeremiah, foreseeing the coming destruction of the army of Babylon, says: "I have likened the daughter of Zion to a comely and delicate woman" who is about to be ravaged by the invader. And Isaiah, seeing the time at hand for the people to return from Babylonish exile, cries out: "Loose thyself, O captive daughter of Zion."

Affection for the native land was strong among the women as well as among the men. Lot's wife did not turn because of curiosity, but by reason of the strong attachment to locality; she looked back longingly toward her forsaken and burning home. The little Hebrew maid, torn by an invading army of Syrians from her native land, was quick to tell Naaman, the leper,--her new master,--of the virtues of her country and impelled him to seek out Elisha, the prophet of Israel.

The social position of Hebrew women was exceptionally free and independent. While a daughter's matrimonial plans were largely in the hands of father and brother, and wives were expected to look up to their husbands with all reverence, yet the recorded examples of independent action and influence among the women reveal a place of social equality and power, a lack of masculine restraint and domination that would do credit to more modern times.

Deborah accompanied, if she did not lead, the soldiers into battle and cheered them on to victory. The daughters of Shiloh, unaccompanied, were accustomed annually to attend festal dances in the vineyards of Benjamin. Women often went without escorts upon difficult and dangerous missions. Prophetesses frequently exerted not only a powerful but at times a decisive influence.

Marriage customs among the Hebrews in the days of the kings were not greatly different from those of other Oriental people of the same era. They differed but slightly from those of an earlier period. As a rule, marriage was not born out of impulse of the heart; though there were many marriages that surely ripened into love. If, as Jean Paul Richter says, "Nature sent woman into the world with a bridal dower of love," we have an explanation of the fact that there are many happy marriages in Israel, notwithstanding the fact that the arrangements continued to be largely in the hands of the parents. A daughter belonged to her father till of age: after this she could not be betrothed except by her own consent. Among the Hebrews betrothal was of the nature of an inviolable contract, and could be annulled only by divorce. If not in early days, yet in the later periods of Hebrew history there were writings of betrothal which set forth the mutual agreements between the parties. Later, there followed the marriage contract, also in writing. The amount paid for a maiden came to be at least two hundred denars, and just one-half as much for a widow. The father was to provide dowry according to his ability, and an orphan girl's dowry was bestowed by the community.

The marriage ceremony consisted of leading the bride from her father's house to that of the bridegroom. At which time there was a season of festivity and rejoicing. The marriage of a maiden usually occurred on Wednesday evening, that of a widow on Thursday. The "children of the bride chamber," the name by which the invited guests were called, made merry at the "marriage feast," which was always provided and lasted several days. As the procession passed along, going from the bride's to the bridegroom's house, people along the route might join in the festivities.

Grains of corn, nuts, and other edibles were the confetti tossed good-humoredly at the bridal pair. It became the custom, which still exists among Jews to-day, to break a glass bottle at Hymen's altar to indicate that the former life is no more, and that the bride has entered upon a new estate. Among the Hebrews the married woman was better protected in her rights than among most people of ancient times. While her property was usually under control of her husband, yet the dowry came to be considered her own, whether it be money, property, or jewels. A husband could not compel his wife to remove from the land of her fathers; and in many ways her individual rights were protected. Woman's inferior position in Greece was one element in the decline of that remarkable country; the defilement of the womanhood of Rome hastened the downfall of that city's power; but the protection given to Hebrew wifehood and widowhood became an element of great strength in the life of Israel.

The Greek attitude toward woman could probably be reflected in the old saying: "A woman who is never spoken of is praised most." In the period of Rome's decay women became immodestly conspicuous in the social and public functions of the day. As opposed to both these conditions the Hebrew, the wise man in the Proverbs, calls her a virtuous woman whom her husband can praise in the very gates.

Edersheim calls attention to a suggestive custom which sprung up from the slight difference of sound in the words for "find" in two passages of Scripture concerning women, both of which occur in the wisdom writings. The first of these reads: "Whoso findeth a wife, findeth a good thing." (Proverbs 18: 22.) The other, "I find more bitter than death the woman whose heart is snares and nets." Hence arose the habit of saying to a newly married man, "Maza or Moze?" "Have you found a 'good thing' or a 'bitter'?"

The tendency in Israel continued to restrict marriage to one's own tribe. The law of inheritance gave force to this custom. Those very near of kin were thus regarded as most eligible for wedlock. Jacob married two of his first cousins. A similar situation is seen in the marriage of Abraham and Sarah, of Isaac and Rebecca. Each husband, under specially trying circumstances, had claimed that his wife was his "sister," and so she was,--for in the patriarchal form of society all who belonged to the same family or clan were brother and sister,-- but not in the strict sense which the word was intended to convey. While brothers and sisters of the whole blood might not marry, yet it would not have been regarded as altogether out of place for half-brothers and sisters to marry, especially if they had a different mother.

The story of Amnon and Tamar not only throws light upon this point, but illustrates how brother and sister by the same father as well as the same mother stood in a greatly different relation, the one to the other, in the matter of brotherly protection from that of half-brother and half-sister.

Amnon, son of David, fell desperately in love with his half-sister, David's daughter, Tamar. By a cunningly devised plot Amnon succeeded in bringing the beautiful damsel into his chamber. When Absalom, Tamar's brother and half-brother to Amnon, heard that his sister had thus been dealt with, he felt himself under obligation to defend her honor, by slaying his half-brother, which he did at a feast given during the season of sheep shearing, when the king's sons were all making merry.

The remark of Frances Power Cobbe is as true in Israel as elsewhere. "A man may build a castle or a palace, but poor creature! be he as wise as Solomon or as rich as Croesus, he cannot turn it into a home. No masculine mortal can do that. It is a woman, and only a woman,--a woman all by herself if she must, or prefers, without any man to help her,--who can turn a house into a home." It was the Hebrew wife and mother who largely gave to the homes of the Israelites their peculiar quality. But it may be said it was seldom her necessity or her preference to set up a home without the presence of some son of Israel.

The birth of children was always considered an occasion for rejoicing. Hebrew women were, as a rule, active and strong, and natural in their mode of life. There are but two cases in all the Hebrew Scriptures of death at the time of childbirth. One is that of Rachel, who, when upon a fatiguing journey with her husband and family, gave birth to Benjamin and died; the other is the wife of Phineas, who, when she heard the sad news of the victory of the Philistines over Israel, the capture of the Ark of Jehovah, of her father Eli's and her husband's death in the battle, gave birth to a child whom the nurse called Ichabod, for said she: "The glory is departed from Israel." In the naming of her children the Hebrew mother thus often revealed a poetic imagination that is of a high order. In this the Hebrew language was helpful, for, as one has remarked of it: "Every word is a picture."

The bright eyes and graceful form of the gazelle suggested the name for a daughter of Tabitha, of which Dorcas is the Greek. Zipporah was a little bird; Deborah, the busy bee; Esther, a star; Tamar, a palm tree; Zillah, a shadow; Sarah, the princess; Keturah, fragrance; Hadassah, the myrtle. Thus, some resemblance or poetic association suggested to the mother, either at the birth of the child, or because of some fact or incident of later experience, the name the little one was to bear. Often there is a tragedy or a mother's sorrowful life history crystallized in a name. When Rachel, Jacob's favored wife, brought forth her second son amidst the suffering which was to take away her life, the woman standing by tried to comfort her in the fact that another son had been born to bless her. The mother, with her last faint breath, replied: "Call his name Benoni (son of my sorrow)." But the father, unwilling thus to perpetuate his wife's anguish, called him Benjamin (son of my right hand). When Naomi, the widow, bereft of her husband and sons, returns to her native Bethlehem after many years of absence and of sorrow, the women came out to meet her, saying: "Is this Naomi?" She answered them: "Call me not Naomi (pleasant or winsome), call me Mara (bitter), for the Almighty hath dealt very bitterly with me." So, among the Hebrews, names not only were given to both men and women at birth, but were frequently changed at some critical moment or because of some extraordinary experience in their life. Ordinarily, however, the favorite method of naming sons connected the boy in some way with his God; as when Hannah named her baby boy Samuel (God hath heard), and the name of Jacob (the supplanter), was changed to Israel (the prince of God). The girls seldom if ever bore names ending in el (God), ajah (Jehovah), but were called by some name of poetic association or natal experience. In no respect do the Hebrew mothers deserve greater praise than for their share in the upbringing of children. While the Jewish law placed the responsibility for the training of the Hebrew youth upon the father, a very large share of the responsibility fell upon the mother. With the Hebrew child, as with the children of all nations, it is impossible to say exactly where its education begins. The famous dictum: "If you would bring up a child in the way it should go, you must begin with its great-grandmother," finds special force among the Israelites. The women held an honored place in the education of the Jewish youth. Before the child could walk or could lisp a syllable, while still in its mother's arms, it would see her, as she passed from one room to another in the house, stop and touch the mesusah on the doorpost, and then kiss the finger that had thus come in contact with the sacred words of the law encased there. The little one would easily learn to put out its own tiny finger and touch the aperture of the sacred box on the doorpost, and then press it to the baby lips.

Here was the first lesson in the law of its fathers. Very early the mother took her babe to the temple, and offered a sacrifice for it. Especially was the birth of the firstborn significant, for the firstborn son belonged to Jehovah, just as the firstborn of the herd and the flock and the first-fruits of the ground. These must be sacrificed on the altar of the Lord. But, happily for the mother heart, the firstborn son might be redeemed by the sacrifice of a lamb, or, if the mother were poor, by a pair of turtle-doves or two young pigeons. So the young mother brought her boy to the altar, made her offering, and took her babe back to her bosom.

From the time of offering onward, the mother greatly aided in shaping the life of the young Israelite. In this training the sacred Scriptures played an important part. The rabbis, however, never regarded women as becoming masters of the intricacies of the law. It was a saying among them that "Women are of a light mind." This was doubtless an appropriate remark, for it is certainly true that much of the rabbinic lore is heavy, almost beyond expression. There were not a few women, though, who were well versed in the Scriptures and also in rabbinical teaching. The synagogues were open to the women, where they occupied seats partitioned from those of the men. The attendance of women upon the great feasts, where much could be learned of custom, tradition, and teaching, also gave them opportunity to be instructed in the religion of their fathers. The Christian apostle Paul congratulated his young friend Timothy, that from a babe he had known the Hebrew Scriptures, which he had learned from his mother Eunice and his grandmother Lois. These are typical mothers of the higher order; and while probably only the richer homes owned a copy of the entire Bible, most families possessed at least one or more scrolls containing parts of the sacred writings.

The strength of motherly devotion was nowhere stronger than among the mothers of Israel. The spirit of Rizpah was the spirit of most of them. For when seven of her sons, the sons of Saul, had been slain and their bodies exposed, in the revolution which brought David to the throne, Rizpah took a piece of sackcloth, and, spreading it upon a rock near by, guarded the bodies of her offspring from the beginning of barley harvest till the early rains: that neither birds might molest them by day nor beasts of the field by night.

Home life among the Hebrews of Palestine to-day is marked by much that characterized that life ten or even twenty centuries ago; therefore a few facts concerning the home life in the Jerusalem of to-day will teach us much concerning that of the past. Probably nine-tenths of the native homes of Jerusalem are unpretentious, unattractive, uncomfortable, and show signs of poverty. The people have learned the fine art of economy in house room. Father, mother, and the multitude of little ones with which the Jewish home is usually blessed do not find it difficult to be tucked snugly away in two or three rooms. These give ample space for cooking, dining, sleeping, and performing the necessary labor of domestic life; besides furnishing opportunity for the hospitality for which the East is still justly noted. Call any time you will, on any business bent, and your hostess, if there be no servant, will, before you are permitted to mention the matter of your call, bring to you a glass of wine or perhaps a cup of coffee to refresh you. This, too, though the family be poor and it be deprivation for even this repast to be served to the guest. And though you know of the sacrifice the hostess makes, you must not refuse, lest you offend and wound the spirit of hospitality at its very heart.

The brunt of the work of the house falls, of course, upon the wife and mother. And it is doubtful if the place of the woman of the Palestine of to-day, even among the Jewish families, is as high as in the days of Israel's independence and power. While great respect is shown the father as head of the family, the mother is often scarcely more than the servant of her children.

The sons especially do not give her the respect that was once her unquestioned due. The girl is from her birth looked upon and treated as inferior to her brothers. Patiently, all women of the Orient seem to bear this inferiority--a sort of penalty they must pay because Heaven made them women and not men. The young girl's matrimonial prospects are never in her own hands. She tamely submits to arrangements made for her, and, without test or questioning, assumes that her husband is her superior in all things.

Education among the girls of modern Palestine has been almost hopelessly neglected--except as teachers from England and America have been able to supply the deficiency or overcome the indifference. There is little wonder that home life is unattractive and the housekeeping miserable with so little possibility for the women to catch even a glimpse of the higher things that elevate and refine. Sometimes the Jewish girl is a wife as early as ten or twelve, and frequently at the age of fourteen. Thus home life is often rendered unhappy and divorce frequent. Physical, mental, and moral anguish follow in the wake of many of these early marriages. The young Jewish maiden's life is cheerless before her wedlock, as she is shut out from the joys of social gatherings; and, after marriage, cheerlessness gives way to impenetrable gloom. To say that there are no happy marriages would be wide of the mark. But divorces are sadly common among the Jews of Palestine to-day; the husband having almost unlimited power to break, under very slight provocation, the bond that binds him to his wife. The rabbi must of course confirm the dissolution of the bond, and thirty piasters is the price. The effect of this custom upon modern Jewish womanhood in the venerated land of Rebekah and Rachel is most unhappy.

Home life in ancient Israel was singularly sweet, pure, and industrious. The family was both the social and the religious unit. Idleness was considered a curse; and every child was taught to train his hands as well as to cultivate his heart.

The occupations of women were numerous and varied. Everywhere in the East needlework was and is highly prized. Mothers set their children at it at a very early age and great skill is often attained. The poorer women frequently earn with their own fingers the amount of their marriage portion; and in the hours of seclusion wives of the harem have always found embroidery and other forms of rich needlework a common pastime for the empty hours.

While working in skins, clay, and in metals was reserved for the men, the Hebrew women were very largely the producers of the food and the wearing apparel. They assisted in the cultivation of the fields, were the millers, grinding with their primitive stone mortar and pestle, the bakers, the weavers and spinners, making use of the hand spindle which may be seen in Syria and in Egypt to-day, though in the latter country the men shared with the women the skill in this handicraft. Among the Hebrews, as with the Greeks, Clotho is a woman.

We find the virtuous woman, as ideally drawn in the Book of Proverbs, to be one who finds good wool and flax and works willingly with her hands; distaff and spindle fly at her finger's bidding, so that her whole household sits doubly clothed in scarlet, and even fine linen is wrought in her house, and rich girdles go out to the merchantmen. She makes the field and vineyard turn out profitably and imports her food from afar. Whether as shepherdess, gleaner, or the maker of food stuffs or textiles, the Hebrew woman may justly hold a place of respect among her sex.

Among the amusements in which women specially engaged, those of music and dancing should be given first place. These often had a religious or semi-religious character. Women did not usually sit down, or rather recline, at banquets with the opposite sex. Their songs and dances were generally among themselves; dancing with the opposite sex was unknown. Instrumental music frequently accompanied their singing, a sort of tambourine or hand drum being a favorite instrument. Women played an important part also in mourning customs. Professional female mourners were hired to go up and down the highways, wailing piteously as part of the funeral rites. The prophet Nahum in predicting the overthrow of Nineveh uses a figure suggested by frequent observation of mourning: "Her maids shall lead her, as with the voice of doves, tabering upon their breasts."

The religious status of woman is one of the most significant facts in Israel's history. Passing out of the patriarchal stage of life, when the father was high priest in his home, into a more complex existence, it is not surprising that woman's place should become subordinated. Besides this, the Hebrew worshipped no goddesses, except in times of religious lapses. The women of Israel, however, are often found engaged in sacrifices, prayers, and active service to their God Jehovah.

While only the men were required to attend the annual feasts, the attendance of women in large numbers is often recorded. Their presence seems to be presupposed in the accounts of Hebrew worship; though for them the annual religious pilgrimages to Jerusalem were not obligatory.

In the temple worship they had a separate court, further removed from the inner precincts of the holy altar than the court of the men. And while they might join in the eating of some sacrificial meals, the sin offering was only to be partaken of by males. The official duties of the sanctuary were performed by men, but there were "serving women" who performed certain menial tasks about the sacred enclosure. When the temple ritual became elaborated, women were among the singers in the temple choirs, and they often aided in the music and by singing and dancing in times of great national rejoicing. And it is not without its suggestiveness that the Hebrews spoke of a divine revelation as Bath Kol, or "daughter voice."

In the days when religious secretism became popular in Israel, and the people began to divide the exclusive adoration they had hitherto given to Jehovah and to worship other gods and even goddesses, women became prominent in idolatrous rites. Jezebel, who was a worshipper of the Phoenician goddess Ashtoreth, not only became the patron of the priests and puppets of the Baal cult, but endeavored to break down Jehovah worship by the destruction of his prophets. Maachah, the mother of King Asa of the southern kingdom of Judah, introduced the worship of the Assyrian goddess

Astarte. Devotion to Ishtar, the chief goddess of Babylon became the fashion in Jerusalem in the days of Jeremiah the prophet, who tells of Hebrew women kneading dough and baking cakes in shape of the silvery moon in honor of the "queen of heaven," Ishtar, the moon goddess; or perhaps, as some hold, this was the worship of the planet Venus, for similar offerings were made in Arabia to the goddess Al-Uzza, who was represented by the star Venus; and the Athenians too, we are told, offered cakes of the shape of the full moon in honor of Artemis.

During the period of the Babylonish captivity, before the final fall of Jerusalem, Ezekiel rebukes the women of Jerusalem for worshipping Tammuz, the Babylonian Adonis, who had been taken to the under world; for, says the prophet, "There sat the women weeping for Tammuz," the departed husband of Ishtar.

There was never among the Israelites that reverence for women, akin to awe, which was manifested among the Teutonic tribes--a reverence which made women natural oracles. Doubtless in Israel, as everywhere, the instinctive, intuitive nature of women was discovered by the men of Israel as in other parts of the world. But women as oracles are isolated and exceptional. There were witches, who were under the ban. The highest spiritual influence and leadership in Israel was that of the prophet, for he was regarded as the mouthpiece of God, and, though of a far higher order, corresponded to the oracle among heathen peoples. Could a woman hold this place of dignity and power? The first person of this class mentioned in the literature of Israel is Miriam the prophetess. In the days of political confusion, before the time of the monarchy, Deborah the prophetess arose; and it was Huldah the prophetess who directed the reforms instituted by King Josiah, when the worship of Jehovah was purified, the temple repaired, and Mosaism restored to power. Just as there were false prophets in the days of religious decline, so there arose false prophetesses, like Noadiah, who attempted to thwart the reforms of Nehemiah and put his life in jeopardy. In the early days, the counterfeit of the prophetess, namely, the witch and sorceress, was not unknown in the land of Palestine. The law, however, was very stringent against such persons, though King Saul himself once went disguised to consult the Witch of Endor. Scripture says: "Thou shalt not suffer a sorceress to live." These are the words which were thought to give sanction to the burning of witches in New England a century or more ago.

In writing of the women in the days of the kings, one naturally turns to the days of David, the first who brought Israel to a state of political stability. The familiar saying, "The great men are not always wise," is well illustrated in the matrimonial experiences of King David. Many times was he married. Four of the wives of David are worthy of note. The first may be called his wife of youthful romance, Michal, Saul's daughter; the next, Abigail, the wife of manhood's admiration; the third, Bathsheba, the wife of lustful passion; the fourth, Maachah, the wife of old age's sorrow, for she bore unto him Absalom, the rebel. It was a giddy and dangerous height to which David the youth had suddenly arisen when the people were giving him, because of his prowess in slaying Goliath of Gath, greater honor than the king. Even the young Princess Michal could not disguise her admiration for the new and youthful hero. But he must slay one hundred Philistines if he is to possess Michal, says Saul, thinking David would lose his life in the attempt. But the young man slew two hundred, and claimed his bride. While her father was plotting the life of his young rival, Michal was plotting more skilfully to save it; for, overhearing her father give orders that her husband and lover should be slain, she let him down from the window, substituting for her absent lord an image resting in her bed, beneath the covering, in such wise as to support her statement to the messengers, who came to take him before Saul, that David was sick. Michal, having to make choice between her father and her husband, chose the latter; and though she was long separated from him while David warred with Saul, when at last David reigned he sent and recovered her, his first love, and Michal became his wife again.

But there were women of affairs in Israel, as well as women of sentiment and devotion. The story of Abigail, wife of Nabal, and how she became espoused to David, is a pleasing chapter of woman's power to excite the admiration of a manly heart by combining the grace and the tact of the womanly character with worldly wisdom and courage. It is one of the finest illustrations recorded of woman's independence in the land of the Hebrews. The story of Bathsheba's marriage to David is well known. Falling in love with Bathsheba's beautiful form, the king plotted the life of her husband, put him in the front rank in the battle, and, when he fell, took her to his own house as wife. And while Maachah became the mother of a son who was to be a very thorn in the heart of his father, the wickedness which brought about the marriage to Bathsheba became the cause of the bitterest expression of penitential anguish in all the range of literature. For an ancient tradition, embodied in the introduction to the fifty-first Psalm, affirms that that poem of heart-stinging grief was written when Nathan the prophet had shown King David the heinous blackness of his sin toward Uriah the Hittite.

Diplomatic marriages were not uncommon in the ancient commonwealth of Israel. They were not provided for in the law of Moses. Indeed, they were distinctly prohibited both by the genius of that law and by its positive enactments. And yet, no less influential a name than that of Solomon might have been quoted as giving sanction to this method of assuring national peace.

Even modern governments might be cited--not only of the East, but of the countries of Europe--as pernicious examples of the very ancient custom of cementing political friendship by the interchange of daughters. The Tel El Marna tablets present a number of illustrations of diplomatic correspondence between Oriental kings concerning daughters who had been given as wives to brother monarchs as a seal of friendship. Now this well-nigh universal custom of diplomatic marriages, though discouraged by the law of the Hebrews, spoken against by their prophets, and forbidden by the very genius of their religion, was not uncommon in the land of Israel. Saul, the first king, can scarcely be said to have welded the tribes into a stable and recognized nationality. David, his successor, was a warrior, who depended for his successes more upon military prowess than upon the skill of diplomacy. The third King of Israel fell heir to a nation made by the master hand of his father. The Hebrews were now recognized by contemporary peoples as a great nation, and, being respected for their power, peace reigned in Palestine. Solomon, a man of peaceful temperament, resolved to sway the sceptre and enhance his influence by the arts of diplomacy rather than by the instruments of war. Among these arts was that of knowing how to be wisely and numerously wed. He it was who introduced the harem, in the modern meaning of the word, into Palestine.

The living wives--in number seven hundred--that are said to have been possessed by King Solomon shows that the prayer made by the people when first they sought a king "like all the nations" had been answered. Here was the beginning, as some of the prophets thought, of Israel's subsequent disaster and final undoing as a kingdom. To them Jehovah was the one unifying cause, the great power that was to preserve their national integrity, their very existence as a people. To admit foreign wives into the palace, bringing with them their gods, and becoming perchance the mothers of their future kings was to defile the religion of the realm at its heart, to undermine the worship of Jehovah in the house of him who should be its main defender. In the life and reign of King Solomon we have the strange contradiction which is not infrequently discovered between theoretical wisdom and practical folly, between private life and public conduct. No man of ancient days appears to have understood woman better than Solomon, nor said more wise things concerning them. His dealing with the rival claimants of a certain baby, his wisdom in answering the hard questions of the Queen of Sheba have made his name famous. And yet it was his lack of practical wisdom in arranging his own household that sowed the seed of discord and dissolution which were later to cause great distress and at last disruption.

IV

THE ERA OF POLITICAL DECLINE

Altogether the most glorious reign in all the history of the Hebrew commonwealth was that of Solomon. David his father's military prowess and his own skill in diplomacy had brought peace with foreign nations, and rapid internal development. But even now germs of decay were perceptible. The custom of diplomatic marriage with daughters of heathen kings, the incoming of luxury, which was destined to undermine the social, political, and religious hardihood which had previously characterized the people, were destined powerfully to influence the life and character of Hebrew women. For here, elements of weakness will often first show themselves. It was inevitable that with the harem should come immorality, luxury, effeminacy, and the encroachments of foreign influence, through the women of many lands bringing their forms of worship and also their deities with them. It was in anticipation of all these dangers that the law forbade the king to "multiply wives to himself." It will be remembered that it was the increased taxation necessary to keep up such an establishment as that which Solomon brought into being in Israel that led at his death to a disruption of the kingdom into two antagonistic parts. It was the violation of this law that later led the northern kingdom of Israel into one of the bitterest struggles, one of the most cruel wars of extermination, ever enacted among a people which has suffered many grievous national experiences. King Ahab married a Princess of Phoenicia, the daughter of Eth-baal, King of the Zidonians. With her came her worship of Baal, the very name of which divinity was imbedded in the name of her father, Eth-baal.

For force of character, Jezebel is probably unexcelled in the Scripture records. But that character was, unfortunately, villainous. Moliere affirms that "It is more difficult to rule a wife than a kingdom." Ahab must have found it so, and surrendered both enterprises to Jezebel. When--like the famous miller of Potsdam who would not part with his mill even to the great Frederick--Naboth refused to sell the vineyard which was so coveted by the king, Jezebel says tauntingly to the disappointed, fretting husband: "Dost thou rule over the Kingdom of Israel?" This Lady Macbeth cries: "Give me the dagger." She prepares a great feast, invites Naboth as a guest of honor, accuses him falsely and has him killed. Triumphantly she now can present her husband with the much-coveted vineyard. Her horrible death in the revolution which the fast-driving Jehu led is held up by the prophets as a warning to subsequent generations, for, unburied and eaten by dogs,

Jezebel's body was cast away, so that none could afterward honor her memory or say: "This is Jezebel." And in the same revolution, by a Nemesis so common in history, Jezebel's son Joram was slain in the field of Naboth. That her name made a deep impression upon the Hebrew mind, however, may be seen in the fact that in the book of Revelation, written nearly ten centuries afterward, an heretical and idolatrous influence is referred to as "that woman Jezebel, which calleth herself a prophetess to teach my servants to commit fornification and to eat things sacrificed to idols."

In marked contrast with the motherly devotion which generally characterized the "daughters of Rachel" stands out the example of Athaliah the unnatural; since she was the daughter of Jezebel, the fact is not strange. To the truthfulness of the remark of La Bruye that "Women are ever extreme, they are better or they are worse than men," history has often testified. The woman who is usually satisfied to sit behind the throne has occasionally had ambitions to sit upon it. So it was with Athaliah. The law of the Hebrews, while it made provision for inheritance of daughters along with the sons, does not contemplate the dominion of a queen. Only one woman ever sat upon the throne of the Hebrews.

When King Ahaziah, the reigning King of Judah, had been slain by Jehu in a revolution directed against Joram, King of Israel, and all the seed royal, Ahaziah's mother, seized with ambitions to be herself the sovereign, proceeded to put to death all the possible heirs to the throne. Fortunately for the Davidic dynasty, however, a sister of the dead king rescued one of his sons, an infant, from the bloody massacre, and hid him in one of the apartments of the temple. When the proper time came, the high priest Jehoiada brought forth the lad, now seven years of age, and with the aid of mighty men, proclaimed him king. Athaliah was surprised and overwhelmed and was slain; but she had given Judah six years of unrighteous government.

The religious influence of Jezebel in the northern kingdom and of Athaliah, her daughter, in the southern was of greater consequence in the shaping of the history of the times than their lack of moral worth. Jezebel was an ardent worshipper of Baal; indeed, she was the patroness of Baal's prophets, the very bulwark of idolatrous practices in Israel. Over against her stood the prophet Elijah, the representative of what was apparently a lost hope. Jezebel had driven the prophets of Jehovah into the dens and caves of the earth. It is commonly thought that while men have more vices than women, women have stronger prejudices. But here is a woman of whom it may be stated--altering a remark made concerning Nero--"There is no better description of her than to say she was--Jezebel."

The Baal worship which she would foster, and did greatly succeed in fastening upon Israel until its overthrow by Shalmaneser, King of Assyria, was a debasing nature-worship, which tended to destroy manhood and drag womanhood into shame. And while there was set up no material monument of her power in Israel, yet it required generations for the pernicious influence of her life to die away. If, as Dean Stanley suggested, that Hebrew epithalamium, the forty-fifth Psalm, was written in honor of Jezebel's marriage to Ahab, none of its ideals concerning the new-made queen was ever realized in Israel. She must stand in the history with Jeroboam whose constant literary monument is disclosed in the oft-repeated words, "He made Israel to sin."

In contrast with the proud and cruel queen whose aim had been to slay Elijah and all who stood for Jehovah worship are certain obscure women who protected and comforted the prophet. "You will find a tulip of a woman," says Thackeray, "to be in fashion when a humble violet or daisy of creation is passed over without remark." We shall not fall under the implied condemnation by forgetting the nameless widow of Zarephath who, though found gathering a few sticks to make a meal of the last handful of flour and a little oil left in the cruse, yet when asked took the fleeing Tishbite into her frugal home and shared with him her poor repast. For fully a year did Elijah live under the widow's roof, and the meal in the barrel wasted not, nor did the oil in the cruse fail, till the famine was broken by the coming of the long delayed rains.

A people's religion will register its mark quickly upon its women. A most suggestive Semitic conception is found in the use of the figure of marriage to describe the relationship between a people and their god, or perhaps more accurately, between a land and its governing divinity. This entire conception finds its best illustration in the term Baal, which means husband, or lord. The god was conceived of as father and the land as mother of the people and of all the products of the soil.

The influence of the Baal cult upon Israelitish society, especially upon woman, cannot be understood without reference to the nature of that worship. Picture before your mind's eye the rustic prophet Amos, with wandering staff in hand, impelled by a divine impulse, making his way northward, and carrying a divine message to the people. He reaches Bethel in the southern part of the kingdom of Israel--a city that from time immemorial had been a sanctuary. He is shocked at the terrible orgies practised about the altars there in the name of religion; at the unbridled passion and lewdness in the name of the god and goddess of fertility, Baal and Ashtoreth; at the men and women revelling in shame, that the increase of the land might be celebrated and productiveness symbolized.

It is while looking upon such a scene of bestialized worship and debauched womanhood that Amos cries out in prophetic grief:

"The virgin of Israel is fallen, She shall no more rise. She is forsaken upon her land There is none to raise her up."

The domestic life of the prophet Hosea furnishes perhaps the best illustration of the condition and dark possibilities of womanhood in Israel during this era of religious lapse and of consequent moral decay. When religion sanctions prostitution at the altar, profligacy is not unnatural. Hosea had married one Gomer, daughter of Diblaim. Soon she forgets her marriage vows and gives herself to a life of shame. Hosea, not then a prophet, more than once tried to reclaim the erring wife of his love; but she again falls into evil ways. His home is destroyed; and as he thinks of the meaning of this fatal blow to his domestic happiness, he can but see in it a divine call to go forth to correct a condition of society which could foster such vice and make such sorrows possible. The whole meaning of his ministry, as he starts out with his children as object lessons of his and the people's great humiliation, is but an enlarged reproduction of his own bitter experience.

That the god and his land were related as husband and wife, was a very familiar conception in Israel, as well as with the nations round about. Even Isaiah proclaimed that the land of the Hebrew should be called Beulah, that is, "married," a land wedded to Jehovah, in pure and abiding love. But it remained for the worship of Baal, which means both "lord" and "husband," to fasten upon Israel the basest practices between the sexes, as a part of the worship of the god to whom the land was married.

Hosea sees in his own poignant grief an epitome of Israel's relation of apostasy from Jehovah. She should have been a wife of purity, keeping her covenant vows with her Lord, but instead, she had gone away to consort with other gods and was playing the harlot against her first love. Repeated efforts had failed to reclaim her, and now she is given up to horrible vice as she sacrifices her virtue at the altar of Baal. It is a fearful arraignment, hot with his own experiences and saturated with tears. The words of Hosea are themselves the best representation of society of the day, as we speak under the figure of his own bitter grief:

"Plead with your mother, plead, for she is not my wife and I am not her husband. Let her therefore put away her whoredoms out of her sight and her adulteries from between her breasts." This is the earnest plea for a purified Israel and a redeemed womanhood.

The day is to come, says the prophet with the broken heart, when "she shall follow after her lovers but she shall not overtake them. Then shall she say, I will go and return to my first husband; for then was it better with me than now." "For she did not know," says Hosea for Jehovah, "that I gave her corn, and wine, and oil, and multiplied her silver and gold, which they prepared for

Baal." And looking forward to a day when the sensual worship of Baal which so debauched womanhood, should be no longer known in Israel, the prophet, again as the mouthpiece of Jehovah, still carrying out the same figure of wedlock, says to Israel: "And I will betroth thee unto me forever; yea, I will betroth thee unto me in righteousness, and in judgment, and in loving kindness, and in mercies. I will even betroth thee unto me in faithfulness; and thou shalt know Jehovah. And it shall come to pass in that day that I will hear, saith Jehovah, I will hear the heavens, and they shall hear the earth; and the earth shall hear (with) the corn, and the wine, and the oil."

It was only after the destruction of Jerusalem by Nebuchadnezzar in B. C. 586, and the consequent exile of the Hebrews, that this nature worship which so endangered womanly virtue was exterminated.

During the long, synchronous reign of Uzziah, King of Judah, and of Jeroboam II., King of Israel, in the eighth century before the Christian era, prosperity both at home and abroad had given the people of both kingdoms great wealth. The Syrians had for a long series of years been a breakwater against the growing power of Assyria. In the meantime, there was unsurpassed opportunity for internal development, commercial expansion, and the accumulation of wealth. Riches had led to luxury, and commerce had made the people more hospitable to foreign ideals, both social and religious.

It was in the reign of Uzziah's successor, Jotham, that a new and eloquent voice was lifted up on behalf of reform, calling the people back to the ideals of the fathers and of the prophets. This new force in Jerusalem was the young Isaiah, whose striking vision in the year King Uzziah died caused him to give up a profane life for the prophet's office; and upon none of the Hebrew prophets do the condition and character of woman seem to have made so deep an impress. Among the very earliest of his public utterances, so far as they have been preserved to us, is that severe arraignment of the women of Jerusalem for their wanton haughtiness, their wasteful extravagance, their love of show, their self-indulgence and vice. Thus in detail does the prophet draw for us the moving picture of female pride: "Moreover, the Lord saith:

Because the daughters of Zion are haughty, and walk with stretched forth necks and wanton eyes, walking and mincing (or tripping delicately) as they go, and making a tinkling with their feet: therefore, the Lord will smite with a scab the crown of the head of the daughters of Zion, and the Lord will discover their secret parts. In that day the Lord will take away the bravery of their tinkling ornaments (anklets) about their feet, and their cauls (net works), and their round tires like the moon (crescents), the chains (or ear pendants), and the bracelets, and the mufflers, the bonnets (head tires), and the ornaments of the legs (ankle chains), and the headbands, and the tablets (or smelling boxes), and the earrings, the rings, and the nose jewels, the changeable suits of apparel (festal robes), and the mantles, and the wimples (probably, shawls), and the crisping pins, the glasses (hand mirrors), and the fine linen, and the hoods (or turbans), and the vails. And it shall come to pass that instead of sweet smell (of Oriental spices) there shall be stink; and instead of a girdle, a rent; and instead of well set hair, baldness; and instead of a stomacher, a girding of sackcloth; and burning instead of beauty. Thy husbands shall fall by the sword, and thy mighty in the war. And her gates shall lament and mourn; and she being desolate, shall sit upon the ground."

In this period, the women as they went along scented the air with the perfume from the boxes that hung at their girdles; they lolled idly and luxuriantly upon ivory beds and silken cushions sprinkled with perfume, and they gossiped to the sound of music.

In predicting the great disaster and slaughter that were to come upon the people through the Assyrian invasion, made successful by the effeminacy of the people, the prophet discloses not only the dire extremity to which the people were to be reduced, but reveals the feminine ideal among the Hebrews, already alluded to in this volume, namely, that which makes motherhood the aim of every Hebrew woman and the absence of it a calamity. In that day seven women shall take hold of one man, saying, "We will eat our own bread and wear our own apparel; only let us be called by thy name, to take away our reproach." Widowhood and celibacy were equally sources of deepest grief among the women of Israel, and both were to be among the results of the luxury and vice of the land.

Woman, as well as man, in this era of decay, had fallen into the habit of the most cruel covetousness, and, when occasion offered, the rich and powerful women oppressed the poor. The herdsman-prophet Amos, coming from his home in the rural districts of Judah, was shocked at the corruption into which even the women of Samaria, the capital of the northern kingdom of Israel, had fallen, and so, with a rustic boldness that would not mince matters of such grave concern, he compared the women to the fat cattle of the land of Bashan, saying to the wives and mothers of the corrupt and luxury-loving city: "Hear this word, ye kine of Bashan, that are in the mountain of Samaria, which oppress the poor, which crush the needy, which say to their masters, Bring and let us drink!"

In the age of decline, it is a noteworthy fact that not a woman appears to have lifted up prophetic voice against the moral and religious decay. Prophets there were, but apparently no prophetesses, except those whom Jeremiah rebukes with scathing earnestness,--women who prophesied according to their own feelings and desires rather than in harmony with the eternal principles as applied to the then present conditions. Indeed, in the entire period of decline which preceded the fall of Samaria in B.C. 722 and of Jerusalem in B.C. 586, no prophetess appears in the record, except that Isaiah speaks of his wife as the prophetess. This involves an entire change in the meaning of the word.

But there were patriotic women, just as there were patriotic men, during the days of decline. There was no greater suffering than that of women when they saw the Babylonian soldiery laying Jerusalem in ashes. Hugging their babes to their breasts, some were hewn in pieces, while others suffered shameful indignities and were led away among the captives, to sojourn in a strange land. The prophets had foreseen the coming anguish of the women; and when Jeremiah foretold the restoration of Israel to her land, he proclaimed that the eyes of Rachel, which had wept for her children "because they were not," should at length be dried, and her mourning turned into rejoicing. Thus the picture drawn in that elegiac poem--the greatest of all Hebrew threnodies, known as the Lamentations of Jeremiah--when he saw the sacred city in ruins, was reversed:

"How doth the city sit solitary That was full of people! How is she become as a widow! She that was great among the nations, And princess among the provinces, How is she become tributary!

"She weepeth sore in the night And her tears are on her cheeks: Among all her lovers She hath none to comfort: All her friends have dealt treacherously with her, They have become her enemies."

This was but the enlargement and national application of the distress experienced by the women of Israel during the siege and final overthrow of the city in which all Jewish hopes centred.

Of the Hebrew women during the period of the exile, we know comparatively little. And yet no woman of later Biblical Judaism made so deep an impression upon the Jewish mind as did Esther. By her beauty and the wise cunning of her uncle, she became the wife of King Ahasuerus, the famous Persian who attempted to measure arms with the Greeks--an effort which turned out so disastrously for the gigantic but undisciplined Persian army. The story of Vashti's deposal, because she refused to lend herself to the immodest proposal of the king, befuddled by the wine of banqueting and revelry; of the subsequent selection of Esther as queen; of her entreaty for her people, against whom a deep-laid and cruel plot was soon to be executed,--is a familiar narrative.

That a Jewish woman should have been elevated to such a position in the Persian palace seems so improbable that some have been inclined to doubt the accuracy of the story which the Book of Esther records, especially since profane history tells of but one wife of Ahasuerus, Amestris. But the argument from silence is always precarious. Vashti and Esther may easily have been extra-legal wives of the king, even though Amestris were his only legally recognized wife. The well-known custom of Oriental monarchies makes such a view highly probable. At all events, there stands the well-known feast of Purim, the "festival of the Lots," as a monument in Jewish religious life of the substantial accuracy of the events recorded in the Book of Esther.

The power of Esther's life and of her service to her people in exile may be in a measure estimated by the fact that no book in all the Bible was so much copied, or was so generally in possession of the Jewish families as that of Esther. Indeed, it was asserted by Maimonides and believed by many that when at the coming of Messiah all the rest of the Old Testament should pass away, there would still remain the five books of the law and the Book of Esther. Written as it was, upon separate scrolls, it was in thousands of Jewish houses. Even at the present day rolls containing Esther are the prized possession of Jewish families; and these are sometimes even now passed down from parents to their children upon the wedding day. On the day of Purim, the book is read in public as a part of the service, that the way in which Esther became the savior of her people may never be forgotten. The power of Esther's story over the Jewish mind has seemed the more remarkable, since it is the single book in the Hebrew Canon which does not contain the name of God. But on the other hand, there is no Hebrew writing that is so intense in its national spirit; none which breathes and burns so deeply with the characteristic genius of "the peculiar people."

There was perhaps no time in the history of the Hebrews when social life received a more severe shock than during the days of the reforms instituted by Nehemiah about the middle of the fifth century before Christ. When the Jews returned from their exile in Babylonia many of them married women of gentile blood and religion, daughters of those who had peopled the land of Palestine during the exile. Children of Jews were being born and taught heathen language and heathen worship by their mothers. Nehemiah, under appointment as governor, when he saw that Jews had married "wives of Ashdod, of Ammon, and of Moab," commanded that all foreign women be immediately divorced, and that only Jewish women should be taken for wives. Great was the temporary suffering involved, to be sure, but the aim in view, namely that of keeping the people henceforth free from idolatry seemed to justify even so drastic a measure. A grandson of the high priest, himself in priestly line, had married Nicaso, daughter of Sanballat, the Horonite, the very crafty and troublesome ruler of Samaria. When Nehemiah demanded of him that he give up his wife he refused. The governor accordingly expelled him from Jerusalem, chasing him out of his presence, as the Biblical narrative informs us. Josephus says that when the people demanded that he give up his alien wife or his priestly office,--as the law flatly forbade priests from having foreign wives,--he decided first in favor of his office. But when Sanballat, his father-in-law, heard of it, he told him not to move hastily, but if he would keep Nicaso his wife, he, Sanballat, would build him a temple of his own, so that he might be not only a priest, but high priest, and Nicaso's husband at the same time. This appealed to Manasseh's judgment, and he chose the plan of his father-in-law. Thus was built the temple on Mount Gerizim, which became thereafter the centre of Samaritan life and worship. It was concerning Mount Gerizim that the Samaritan woman at the well spoke when she said to Jesus: "Our fathers worshipped in this mountain; and ye say that in Jerusalem is the place where men ought to worship."

The suffering of the women during the grievous persecution of the Jews under Antiochus Epiphanes, "the illustrious"--nicknamed Epimanes, "the madman"--was frightful in the extreme. Some men, but fewer women, yielded to the pressure of the effort to destroy the Jewish religion by forcing the Greek pantheon, Greek games and theatre, and the Greek culture upon the Jews. The struggle into which the people were plunged brought the self-sacrifice of the women into prominence. A typical case of suffering is given in the Second Book of Maccabees. King Antiochus had laid hold of a mother and seven sons, and commanded that they violate their law by eating swine's flesh. The eldest was first put to the test. He refused to obey. The king commanded that the tongue of him who spoke thus defiantly should be cut out, his limbs mutilated, and his living body roasted in hot pans, and that his mother and her younger sons should witness the awful sight. One after another the sons were cruelly dealt with and slain. Each one was given opportunity to save his life by eating the forbidden flesh, but each refused. At length the youngest only remained. The king appealed to the mother, standing by, to advise her boy to obey and save his life. But the sturdy Jewish mother turned to this son and strengthened him in his determination to die rather than prove faithless to the religion of his fathers by obeying the merciless tyrant. He too was then murdered, even more cruelly than the rest. And at length, the mother herself lost her life upon the same altar of faithfulness, rather than transgress the law. Of such sturdy stuff were the Jewish mothers of this awful period made. There is little wonder that the sons of such women succeeded in winning their independence and in setting up again a Jewish state, which had been suppressed for more than four centuries.

A look into this period would be incomplete without reference to one of the apochryphal or deutero-canonical books of the Old Testament, highly prized by the Jews as containing a picture of pious home life among the Jews in the captivity. A devout Jew, as the story goes, with his wife Anna and his son Tobias were among those whom Shalmaneser, King of Assyria, had taken captive from the land of Israel and placed in the city of Nineveh when Samaria fell about B. C. 722. Loyal to his religion, Tobit, even in exile, refused to eat the bread of the Gentiles; but by dint of hard work and fidelity he at length became purveyor to the king. By the revolving wheel of fortune, Tobit is at length reduced to poverty. Here Anna his wife, with devoted womanly faithfulness, comes to the rescue with her skilful fingers, weaving and spinning for a livelihood; for her husband was now both poor and blind. One day Anna, wearied and provoked, reproaches her husband for his blindness-- such calamities were esteemed a divine curse in Israel, whereupon Tobit prayed that he might die. On the self-same day, a young Jewess, Sara, daughter of Raguel, a captive in Ecbatana of Media, was offering up a similar prayer that the end of her life might come. For her father's maid had charged her with killing her seven husbands, who had died one after another, each on the very first night of the wedding feast, though the strange deaths had been the work of Asmodeus, the evil spirit, who was not willing that the maiden should wed. Now these two widely separated and unrelated prayers were to be brought together into one romantic story by the help of an angel, who becomes a guide to the son of Tobit, young Tobias, who is about to start out in life in quest of a fortune. The angel guides him to Ecbatana, bids him make the eighth to offer marriage to Sara, whose seven husbands had perished on the nuptial night. Though Tobias had never seen the young woman before, he was to her the next of living kin and so should be (according to the Mosaic law) the one to offer his hand to the youthful, much-married widow. Would the young Tobias prove strong enough bravely to face the record of the seven deaths? The angel here comes to the rescue, and calls Tobias's attention to the heart and liver of a great fish which had been caught in the Euphrates as the two had journeyed together from Nineveh to Ecbatana. These, burned with perfumes in the bridal chamber, drove the evil spirit Asmodeus away, and the marriage festivities went on merrily. The life of Tobias had been saved. He takes his newly wedded wife back to his father's house in joy and triumph, cures his father's blindness by the same magic charm which had saved his own life in the bridal chamber, and peace and wealth and long life follow in rich profusion.

This story is chiefly of interest to us as it shows the continuation, even into the period of exile, of the Levirate marriage custom. While the story of the marriage of Sara, daughter of Raguel, is a Jewish romance, the literature of the inter-biblical period is not without its tragedies, in which woman plays an important role. Among these is the well-known story of Judith and Holofernes.

Many Jewish women have passed into literature and art. Rebekah at the wellside, Miriam watching by the reeds or singing of victory with timbrel, Ruth gleaning in the field of Boaz, Delilah the voluptuous, and Athaliah the monster, have exerted their influence both upon the makers of art and writers of drama, but probably no Hebrew woman before the birth of Jesus has made a deeper impress upon the imagination of men than Judith, the beautiful woman and patriot of Bethulia. A woman once saved the city of Rome from overthrow. Several times in the history of Israel was it given to a woman to be the deliverer of the people. The names of Deborah, Esther, and Judith have come down the centuries as those of women who risked their lives for the salvation of their people from the enemy, and succeeded because of their tact and prowess.

The story of Judith and Holofernes is told in the apocryphal Book of Judith. The Assyrians are at war with Israel, whose cities are being besieged and wasted in the merciless onslaught. Holofernes, the Assyrian general, at length lays siege to Bethulia in his onward march to the holy city of Jerusalem. The people are reduced to straits most direful and bitter. Women and little ones perish in the streets, and the people cry out to their leaders to sue Asshur for peace. The rulers, thus urged, promise within five days to yield to their besiegers. It is then that Judith, wealthy and pious, a widow of the city, comes forward to strengthen the fainting heart of the governors and to bid them trust God and stand firm. She promises, in the meantime, that she herself will aid them. Praying earnestly that God will help her in her purpose, she lays aside the habiliments of widowhood, and, arraying herself in garments of gladness, goes forth with her maids to the camp of Holofernes. Charmed with her beauty and grace, the Assyrian gives a feast, to which the bewitching Judith is invited. Holofernes makes merry, and, drinking to drowsiness, lies down in his tent to sleep. Others depart in the night, leaving him and the Jewess alone. Seeing her opportunity, Judith seizes the scimiter that hung on the pillar of Holofernes's bed, and, laying hold upon the hair of the sleeping man's head, severed it from his body, and made her way in the darkness back to the city. In the early morning a sally was made from the city gates, and the Assyrians, finding their captain headless, were thrown into utter confusion and completely routed. Thus did Judith become the deliverer of Israel. The women of the city ran together to see her who had been their savior, made a great dance for her, sang her praises, and bestowed their benedictions, placing garlands of olive upon her brow.

Portia's shrewd dealing with Shylock, the Jewish money lender, called forth the frequent applause of the onlookers: "A Daniel come to judgment, yea, a Daniel!" It is in the History of Susanna, an apocryphal addition to the canonical Book of Daniel, in which the great prophet is presented in the role of arbiter. He appears in a cause against a woman, Susanna, a Jewish lady of great beauty, the wife of a wealthy and distinguished Hebrew whose home was in Babylon. Susanna excited the amours of two judges, elders of the people, who were frequently at her husband's home; but she spurned all their advances, till, angered and resentful, they united in a plot to destroy her, and accused her of unfaithfulness to Joachim, her husband. The penalty for adultery was death, and the people crowded to the trial; for if there was conviction, stoning would follow. The two elders, standing, with their hands upon the innocent woman's head, tell the story agreed upon, how they saw the wife of Joachim in the very shameful act of which they accused her; and the assembly, believing the testimony of the two elders and judges of the people, condemned Susanna to death. At this juncture, the young man Daniel appears upon the scene, much as Portia in the trial of Antonio, and, by adroitly cross-questioning the two witnesses separately, involved them in contradictions, revealing the cowardly plot against the virtuous woman and convicting them of false witnessing. And since the law of Moses prescribed the same penalty for those who bore false testimony as that which would have come to the accused, the elders were put to death, and Susanna was given honor before all the people. This is but one of the many examples in Hebrew history which reveal the unusually high moral character and purity of life that prevailed among the Hebrew women.

It is one of the noteworthy and distressing facts of late Jewish history that in the later teaching of the rabbis woman is placed upon a distinctly lower plane. Her inferiority to man is frequently emphasized. And yet there was one factor which came into the life of Judaism, after the Babylonian exile, which gave to Jewish women an advantage which they had not previously enjoyed. It was the establishment of the synagogue. The secondary place given to women in the temple worship has already been referred to. The man, as head of the family, was representative of the family and responsible, therefore, for the performance of the ceremonies required of every Hebrew household. With the destruction of the temple and the dispersion of the Jews, the temple rites were rendered impossible. When the synagogue arose to fill the vacancy made by these conditions, women were given a place in attendance at the instruction given in these new centres of Jewish life. And while they were never strictly considered members of the congregation, yet, seated in a separate part of the room, they heard the Scriptures read and expounded;

and it was not unknown for women even to read on the Sabbath as among the seven appointees for the day. The Torah, or law, however, was considered rather too sacred and important to be committed to their exposition.

Judging from a remark in the Halacha it is just to infer that in the days when the Jews had become dispersed throughout the Roman world, there were two facts that had a very powerful influence upon Jewish women, one of them of Hebraic, the other of Greco-Roman origin. For the Halacha, in speaking of the women leaving their homes, said that there were two causes which took the women away from their domestic duties: one was the synagogue, the other, the baths,--not, indeed, an altogether uncomplimentary comment upon the women of the times, for it would seem they believed in the oft-coupled virtues of cleanliness and godliness.

From the days of John Hyrcanus, the influence of the Jewish rulers had been decidedly in favor of Hellenic culture. Thus the revolution brought about by the Maccabean revolt seemed about to be undone by the successors of the Maccabees. Jewish independence had been won in an effort to resist Antiochus Epiphanes and others in their attempts to destroy Judaism by making the Greek religion and customs prevalent throughout Palestine. Would the sons and successors of the sturdy Maccabeans give away the fruits of the hard-won victory? When to Alexandra was bequeathed the government by her husband, she decided to espouse the cause of the Pharisaic party, who hated the encroachments of foreign influence. But, alas, for the queen's inability to cope with a situation so strained! In her effort to appease the opposite party she put weapons into their hands, which were soon turned against her. As an old woman of seventy-three, she saw her two sons in bitter contest, at the head of opposing forces, each trying to rule over a tumultuous, faction-torn nation. She passed away, deploring a condition which she was utterly unable to correct. It was not till Pompey brought his Roman legions to the gates of Jerusalem, and set up the Roman eagles in the holy city itself that intrigue and battling for the Jewish throne was brought to a close. Then Jewish independence was no more.

A great granddaughter of Alexandra was destined indirectly at least to play a prominent role in later Jewish history. This was Mariamne. Herod, afterward known as the Great, had hoped by marrying this descendant of both the contending Jewish parties, to unite the influence of the two branches of the Asmonean house. In this, however, Herod was disappointed, and he proceeded to accomplish by force what he had hoped to do by wiles. In the frightful war of extermination waged by Herod against the whole Asmonean line, which he feared might endanger the rulership secured to him by the Roman power and his own political prowess, there figured a Jewish woman who, because of her sagacity, is not to be passed over in silence. She was Alexandra, a granddaughter of the queen of the same name. When Herod attempted to place in the office of Jewish high priest a young man who would be simply a tool for him, Alexandra advocated the candidature of Aristobulus,--her son and a brother of Mariamne,--who by birthright was in line of official succession. Alexandra shrewdly wrote to Cleopatra that the wily woman of the Nile might use her influence with Antony to force Herod to terms. Herod was compelled to yield and appointed Aristobulus, but determined that Alexandra as well as the new high priest should be put out of the way. One day after both Herod and Aristobulus had been enjoying a banquet given by Alexandra, Herod successfully plotted the killing of the high priest in a fishpond attached to the house of feasting, Herod's minions holding him playfully under the water until he was drowned. But Alexandra was not so stupid as to fail to take in the situation. Through Cleopatra she again succeeded in forcing Herod upon the defensive. Being summoned to appear before Antony, Herod succeeded, however, in again ingratiating himself with the Roman, and he returned as strong as ever to Jerusalem.

But his return was not altogether happy; for on his departure, he had given command that should his interview with Antony be ill-fated, Mariamne, his Jewish wife, should be slain, that no other man might have her for wife. The secret leaked out, and came to Mariamne's ears. She violently resented the treatment of Herod and on his return reproached him for his cruelty; but the insanely jealous and wily Herod was not to be changed by reproaches. On his absence from home on the occasion when he went to meet Octavius, the new star which arose on Antony's downfall, Herod again commanded that both Mariamne and Alexandra be put to death should he not return alive. Mariamne on his return received him with cold resentment. With the help of Herod's mother and sister the estrangement became more and more bitter. The king's cupbearer was bribed by them to declare that Mariamne had attempted to poison her husband. The jury, as well as the evidence, being well-arranged before-hand, the unfortunate Mariamne was led away to execution in B.C. 29, to be followed next year by Alexandra, who had watched her opportunity and, taking advantage of an illness of Herod, had attempted to gain possession of Jerusalem and overthrow the reign of Herod. It was a bold stroke for a woman. It failed, and she was executed. With her death the line of Asmonean claimants to the throne was ended.

But the end of this chapter in which womanly hate and intrigue played so prominent a part was not yet. When Herod's sister, Salome, who had taken so large a part in the death of Mariamne, saw Herod's sons return from their studies in Rome, with the looks and royal bearing of their mother, Mariamne; when she perceived the people's joy at their likeness to the late Jewish queen who had been so cruelly murdered, her jealousy became most bitter, and she began to plot against them as she had against their mother. Herod for a time seemed unmoved and married one of them to Berenice, Salome's own daughter. This only intensified Salome's hate; and step after step of domestic hatred and unhappiness led at length to the order by Herod that the two sons of his Jewish wife, Alexander and Aristobulus, should be strangled at Sebaste, where years before their mother Mariamne had become his bride. No wonder Augustus C鐚ar could utter his famous pun in the Greek language which may be reproduced in the words: "I would rather be Herod's swine than his son!"

This was the same Herod who issued an edict that rent the heart of many a mother "in Bethlehem and in all the coasts thereof," a command which sent Mary, the mother of the infant Jesus, into exile with her newborn Son, whose coming into the world was destined to open a new volume, as the narrative passes from Hebrew to Christian womanhood.

Among the Semitic peoples it is not usual, certainly in strictly historic times, to find women holding the first place in the seat of government. Semiramis in the prehistoric period of Assyria is a noteworthy exception to the general custom; and queens sometimes ruled among the Arabians, and "the Queen of Sheba" in southern Arabia became famous. But the common Semitic conception that the king was son and special representative of the deity made it more difficult for women to hold the sceptre. Among the Hebrews there is no instance of a woman being legally recognized as queen. Deborah, before the days of the kingdom, "judged Israel" by virtue of her prophetic character and her ability as a woman of affairs, and Athaliah was enabled to usurp the throne through the murder and banishment of male heirs to the crown. In speaking of her reign it was said that she was the only woman who ever reigned over Israel. There is, however, one other woman who held the Jewish sceptre. After the bloody struggle led by the Maccabees, the Jews at length obtained their liberty from the yoke of the Seleucid kings. Israel then enjoyed about a century of independence. During this period there arose one woman who for nine years ruled the nation. This was Alexandra, the widow of Alexander Janneus, whose unhappy reign came to an end by strong drink, B. C. 78. The conception of the government as a pure theocracy where the king reigned as representative of Jehovah himself rendered it impossible for women to be recognized as lawful sovereigns. The second Psalm, which seems to be a sort of coronation ode, written at the time of the incoming of a new king, expresses the relationship between Jehovah and the earthly ruler:

"The Lord said unto me, Thou art my Son, This day have I begotten thee."

Even wives of the Kings of Israel, as a rule, are not called queens, though Jezebel,--the Phoenician wife of Ahab,--king of the Ten Tribes, is a notable exception. This may be accounted for, however, by the fact that she was not an Israelite and worshipper of Jehovah, but a devotee of Ashtoreth, the queen divinity of Phoenicia; and withal she was a far stronger, more aggressive personality than her inefficient husband. It is of interest to observe also that Jezebel is called queen only in connection with her sons. The idea of queen-mother is far more common among the Hebrews than that of queen-wife. Mothers of kings were given especial honor. King Solomon takes his seat upon his throne and sends, not for his wife to sit by his side, but for Bathsheba, his mother, whose adjacent throne is set at the king's right hand. Asa, in his religious reforms, removed his mother from being queen because she had set up an image or sacred pillar in honor of Baal worship. Jeremiah the prophet called upon the King of Israel and his queen-mother--who seems to have been most active in opposing the prophet's proposed policy in submitting to the Babylonians without a struggle--to humble themselves, because their crowns were even then toppling from their heads. Thus the semi-royal character of the mothers of the kings is evident. This will account, at least in part, for the wording of the chronicles of the kings of Israel and Judah, for this is the set formula: "And A----slept with his fathers, and B----, his son, reigned in his stead. And his mother's name was M----. And he did that which was right (or evil) in the sight of the Lord."

Thus is the importance of the queen-mother constantly emphasized in the Hebrew records.

V

THE BABYLONIAN AND ASSYRIAN WOMEN

Archeology here puts on her apron, takes her pick and spade in hand to help us uncover the story of the woman of Babylonia and Assyria. Skulls, jewels, cylinders, tablets, monuments, mural decorations must be brought to light after their long sleep beneath the surface of the ground. As alive from the dead these come forth to tell, at least in broken story, of those women who helped to make the valley of the Tigris and Euphrates among the most noteworthy spots upon the face of the Eastern world.

What we may know concerning the women of this early Assyro-Babylonian civilization may be derived in part from the Greek annalists who taught the world to write history, but chiefly from the discoveries in modern excavations. And even with these sources at our command, we shall find that many things which we would like to know about Assyrian and Babylonian women are still obscure.

The Sumer-Accadian question shall not disturb us here. That there was a non-Semitic people living in the region of the Euphrates and the Tigris, and that they developed a civilization from which the Babylonian and Assyrians later borrowed, seems clearly established. What the Sumerian and Accadian women left to their Semitic sisters who came at length into the ancient heritage, it would now be impossible to say with any degree of certainty.

The ancient mythology and the epic poems of these people contain many female characters, which may throw some light upon woman's place in their civilization. A people's mythology is the dim daguerreotype of their childhood thinking. Fortunately for us, the last fifty years have brought to light a whole series of epic poems from early Babylonian life, some of them in fragmentary form, others more or less well preserved. In nearly all these the feminine character has its place.

It will be remembered that in the Hebrew account of the creation no female divinity plays a part. In the kindred Semitic accounts from Babylonia and Assyria, however, Tihat, or Mummu Tohat, becomes the primeval mother of all things. She was chaos--corresponding to the Hebrew Teh, or "abyss." And thus, from the womb of dark chaos, with the ocean as father, came the divinity, the sun, moon and stars, earth, man, everything. But, strangely enough, after the birth of the first gods from chaos, a strife arose between them and their mother Tihat. It is, however, the old story of light's struggle with darkness. Anu would decide the dispute, but Tihat declares that the war must go on. Marduk, the god of light, becomes the special champion of the forces arrayed against primeval darkness, and Tihat is vanquished and cut asunder. From one part he makes the firmament of the heaven, to which the gods of the heavenly lights, sun, moon, and stars, are assigned, and from the other half he fashions the earth.

So, also, in the story of the Deluge, the Babylonian Noah, called Sa-Napishti, takes his wife with him into the ark; and when the floods subside and the ship rests, stranded upon the land, Ishtar, the goddess of the rainbow, greatly rejoices as she smells the sweet incense that arises from the grateful altar of Sa-Napishti. The god Bel is persuaded never again to destroy the earth with a flood, and so takes Sa-Napishti and his faithful wife by the hand, blesses them, and at length translates them to paradise.

One of the most prominent heroines of early Babylonian epic is Ishtar. Indeed, there are many variant stories concerning her. Ishtar's descent into Hades is, in fact, one of the most important legends of Oriental mythology. She is the goddess of love, corresponding to the Canaanite and Phoenician divinities Ashtoreth and Astarte. She is the Aphrodite, the Venus of classic myth. Earlier she did not hold power over men's minds. She was a goddess of war, and the earlier warriors honored her as their patroness. It was Esarhaddon who enlarged the honors paid her; and he is said once to have interrupted his scribe, while reading of two important expeditions of arms, to send and fetch The Descent of Ishtar into Hades.

This romantic story of adventure on the part of the goddess is well set out in early Assyro-Babylonian literature. Tammuz, the young husband of Ishtar, has been cut off by the boar's tusk (of winter). Ishtar mourned incessantly for her lover, but in vain. She resolved to rescue him if possible from the realm of shade, the kingdom of Allat, whence he had gone; for, though god he was, he must keep company with all the rest whom death claimed. Only one method of restoring him to the realm of life was possible. There was a spring which issued from under the threshold of Allat's own palace. One who could bathe in and drink of these wonderful waters would live again. But, alas! they were zealously guarded; for a stone lay upon the fountain, and seven spirits of earth watched with assiduous care lest some might drink and live. Of these waters Ishtar resolved to go and fetch a draught. But no one, not even a goddess, can descend into this Hades alive. So we read: "To the land from whence no traveller returns, to the regions of darkness, Ishtar, the daughter of Sin, has directed her spirit to the house of darkness, the seat of the God Iskala, to the house which those who enter can never leave, by the road over which no one travels a second time, to the house the inhabitants of which never again see the light, the place where there is no bread, but only dust, no food, but wind. No one can see the light there, ... upon the gate and the lock on all sides the dust lies thick." But Ishtar, in her quest of love, is nothing daunted by the difficulties or the forbidding aspects of her task. She descends to the gates of Allat's abode and knocks upon them, calling commandingly to the doorkeeper to unlock the bolts: "Guardian of life's waters, open thy doors, open thy doors that I may go in. If thou do not open thy gate and let me in, I will sound the knocker, I will break the lock, I will strike the threshold and break through the portal. I will raise the dead to devour the living, the dead shall be more numerous than the living." The porter goes and tells his mistress, Allat, of the imperious demand of Ishtar. "O goddess, thy sister Ishtar has come in search of the living water; she has shaken the strong bolts, she threatens to break down the doors." Allat treats her with contempt, but finally commands her messenger: "Go, then, O guardian, open the gates to her, but unrobe her according to the ancient laws." Since men come naked into the world, they must go out unclad, and the older custom among the Babylonians was to bury the dead without clothing. Ishtar is stripped of her garments and jewels, and at each successive gate more of her ornaments were appropriated. First went her crown, for Allat alone was queen in that gloomy realm; then her earrings, her jewelled necklace; then her veil, her belt, her bracelets, and her anklets. When through the seventh gate she passed, all her garments were taken away; and Allat commanded her demon Namtar-- the plague devil--to take her from the queen's presence and strike her down with disease of every sort. Meanwhile, in the upper world all are mourning because of her absence; for, as goddess of love and procreation, all nature was perishing, and there was no renewal. All the forces of the upper world, therefore, united to bring her back to light; for the world would be depopulated and barren, if some means were not found to restore her.

Here the supreme god Hea comes to the rescue, for he alone, as controller of the universe, can violate the laws which he himself has imposed thereon.

Hea commands that Allat give life again to Ishtar by the application of the water of life to her. She was informed that power over the life of her consort Tammuz was given into her hands. The water of life was poured upon him, he was anointed with precious perfumes and clothed in purple. Thus "Nature revived with Tammuz: Ishtar had conquered death."

That the Babylonian Hades was presided over by a queen; that the real sceptre in the underworld was swayed by a woman is a matter of some significance. In the old Norse mythology the goddess Hel, without a husband, ruled in the abode of Hell, or the place of death. Among the Greeks, Persephone divided with her husband, Pluto, the control of the underworld. With the Babylonians it is the goddess Allat whose power controls the realm of the dead; and even her scribe, contrary to what we might expect, was also a woman, whose name was Belit-Iseri. Allat, the mistress of death, is not represented as an attractive woman, but ill shaped, with the wings and claws of a bird of prey. She goes to and fro in her realm, exploring the river which flows from the world to her own abode. A huge serpent is brandished in each hand, with which, as "an animated sceptre," she strikes and poisons those against whom her enmity is directed. The boat in which she navigates the dark river has a fierce bird's beak upon its prow, and a bull's head upon its stern. Her power is irresistible; and even the gods cannot invade her realm except they die like men, and graciously acknowledge her supremacy over them. Just as the dead eat and drink and sleep, so does Allat. Her daily portion, as with other divinities, comes from the table of the gods, brought by her faithful messenger, Namtar. Libations poured out in sacrifice by the living also trickle down to her through the earth. Thus Allat lives and reigns in the land from which no traveller returns, a kingdom into which twice seven gates open to receive the dead; but none opens for their release.

Professor Peter Jensen, of Marburg, Germany, has raised the question: Why in the realm of the dead is the power of woman so important, and even monarchical in character? He answers it by the very simple explanation that just as the Hebrews personified their Sheol, and the North Germanic nations their Hel, so the Assyrians and Babylonians regarded their country of the dead as a person. And that since names of places and lands are of feminine gender, in Assyrian thought as in the Hebrew, the land of the dead was conceived of under the form of a woman. Whether this be the true explanation or not, certain it is that the female principle played an important part in the religious thinking of the Assyro-Babylonian peoples.

It is not difficult, therefore, to perceive that women would hold an important place in Babylonian and Assyrian religious life, and in the Phoenician cult. When the goddess plays an important part in religion, especially when the renovative and procreative powers of nature are worshipped, woman will naturally find a place. While the Hebrews have their prophetesses, the religion of Babylonia and Assyria has its priestesses as well as prophetesses.

No account of the women of Assyria would seem complete without reference to the legend of Semiramis and her wonderful exploits. And as is the case with much of the history of the dawn of nations, we are indebted to the Greeks for preserving for us the story of this superlative queen. Ctesias, Diodorus, Herodotus, Strabo, and others tell her story or mention her achievements. This remarkable woman was said to be the daughter of Derceto, the goddess of reproductive nature and of a youthful mortal with whom she had fallen in love. The babe was exposed by its mother, but was found and cared for by a shepherd named Simmas. Having developed into a very beautiful damsel, she won the hand of Oannes, Governor of Syria. In the war against Bactria she so distinguished herself for bravery, disguising herself as a soldier and scaling the wall of the besieged capital, that the King Ninus, founder of the city of Nineveh, took her to be his own queen. Soon Ninus died and Semiramis became sole ruler of the realm. Unbounded ambition, coupled with surpassing genius, caused her to undertake the labor of eclipsing the glory of all her predecessors. She built cities, threw up defences, conquered kings, and extended her territory in every direction. She made the city of Babylon one of her capitals, fortifying it with gigantic walls of sun-dried brick, cemented with asphalt. She built wonderful bridges supported by huge pillars of stone. Diodorus Siculus, quoting Ctesias, thus describes her work upon the walls of the city of Babylon: "When the first part of the work was completed, Semiramis fixed on the place where the Euphrates was narrowest, and threw across it a bridge five stadia long. She contrived to build in the bed of the stream pillars twelve feet apart, the stones of which were joined with strong iron clamps, fixed into the mortises with melted lead. The side of these pillars toward the run of the stream was built at an angle, so as to divide the water and cause it to run smoothly past and lessen the pressure against the massive pillars. On these pillars were laid beams of cedar and cypress, with large trunks of palm trees, so as to form a platform thirty feet wide. The queen then built at great cost, on either bank of the river, a quay with a wall as broad as that of the city and one hundred and sixty stadia long, that is, nearly twenty miles. In front of each end of the bridge, she built a castle flanked by towers, and surrounded by triple walls. Before the bricks used in these buildings were baked, she modelled on them, figures of animals of every kind, colored to represent living nature. Semiramis then constructed another prodigious work: she had a huge basin, or square reservoir, dug in some low ground. When it was finished the river was directed into it, and she at once commenced building in the dry bed of the river, a covered way leading from one castle to the other. This work was completed in seven days, and the river was then allowed to return to its bed, and Semiramis could then pass dry-shod under water from one of her castles to the other. She placed at the two ends of the tunnel, gates of bronze, said by Ctesias to be still in existence in the time of the Persians. Lastly, she built in the midst of the city the temple of the god Bel."

It will be seen from such a paragraph as this just quoted how Semiramis anticipated much of the best work of engineering of modern times. The mountains and valleys yielded to her daring when highways were to be built for the extension of her power and her commerce. In Armenia, Media, and all the regions around she exhibited her genius and prowess. Even Egypt and Ethiopia fell before her. Only when she undertook to carry her arms into far-off India did she meet with reverses. Stabrobatis, King of India, with the aid of elephants, utterly routed the army of the valiant queen, and she never again attempted an expedition to the Far East. As an example of what Semiramis thought of herself, we may quote the words attributed to her: "Nature gave me the body of a woman, but my deeds have equalled those of the most valiant men. I ruled the empire of Ninus, which reaches eastward to the river Hinaman (the Indus), southward to the land of incense and myrrh (Arabia Felix), northward to the Saces and Sogdians. Before me no Assyrian had seen a sea; I have seen four that no one had approached, so far were they distant. I compelled the rivers to run where I wished, and directed them to the places where they were required. I made barren land fertile by watering it with my rivers; I built impregnable fortresses; with iron tools I made roads across impassable rocks; I opened roads for my chariots, where the very wild beasts were unable to pass. In the midst of these occupations, I have found time for pleasure and love!"

What are we to think of this story of the very wonderful lady of the Orient of long ago? Did she ever live, move, and have her remarkable being? It is needless to reply that the story is purely legendary, that none of the modern excavations which have been so fruitful in character have confirmed the story of Ctesias. On the contrary, the monuments have as yet failed even to certify to the existence of such a woman. The fact that her birth is given as from a goddess, that at her death she was changed into a dove, and was thereafter herself worshipped as a goddess, is some evidence of the unreliable character of the narrative. A queen who bore the name of Sammuramat and lived between B.C. 812 and B.C. 783 has been discovered as a historical personage, a name that may possibly have influenced that given the great prehistoric queen. But the marvellous achievements attributed to Semiramis are discovered to be the work of man through a long series of years, and that, too, highly idealized in the numerous details.

That the imaginary queen, as the story goes, had a power over the minds of the people is evident from the fact that many later achievements of arms and of building were attributed to her. And yet, notwithstanding the mythological character of the story of Semiramis, there is reflected much truth concerning Assyro-Babylonian history in these legends. That so great achievements should have been attributed to a woman is evidence of a lack of that prejudice against woman which is discoverable among many Oriental people. In the region of the Euphrates and the Tigris, women had a noteworthy degree of independence, and in some respects a recognized equality. The legend could have developed only in such an atmosphere. The comparison of feminine and masculine virtues has been made time out of mind; the following words from Plutarch are, in this connection, of interest: "Neither can a man truly any better learn the resemblance and difference between feminine and virile virtue than by comparing together lives with lives, exploits with exploits, as the product of some great art, duly considering whether the magnanimity of Semiramis carries with it the same character and impression with that of Sesostris, or the cunning of Tanaquil the same with that of King Servius, or the discretion of Portia the same with that of Brutus, or that of Pelopidas with that of Timoclea, regarding that quality of these virtues wherein lie their chiefest point and force."

It is certain that if early Assyrian myth is to be consulted, the Assyrians had no hesitancy in recognizing the possibility of real greatness in woman's accomplishments and womanly genius.

While there are few queens of note among the prominent personages of whom we read upon the monuments, and while the name of no woman occurs in the Eponym Canon by which the chronology of the nation's life is reckoned, yet the place of woman among the Assyrians and Babylonians was one of greater privilege and honor than among most ancient nations. Those unsurpassed walls that protected the great city of Babylon and the hydraulic works which Cyrus, the conqueror of Babylon, was forced to capture before the city fell into his hands are attributed by Herodotus to a woman,--Queen Nitocris.

In the Code of Hammurabi, who was King of Babylon about B. C. 2250, the most ancient of all known codes of law, woman fares well for so early a period. One of these quaint laws reads: "If a woman hates her husband and says, 'Thou shalt not have me,' they shall inquire into her antecedents for her defects. If she has been a careful mistress and without reproach, and her husband has been going about and greatly belittling her, that woman has no blame. She shall receive her presents, and shall go to her father's house." "If she has not been a careful mistress, has gadded about, has neglected her house and belittled her husband, they shall throw that woman into the water!" Under this code, a man might sell his wife to pay his debts. For three years she might work in the house of the purchaser; after which she was to be given her freedom. Where the law of Moses says: "He that smiteth his father or his mother shall be surely put to death," Hammurabi's code enjoins: "Who smites his father, loses the offending limb."

From the many contract tablets that have been exhumed much fresh light has been thrown upon the social customs of the people in the valleys of the Euphrates and the Tigris. In Babylonia the woman did not suffer greatly before the law from the fact that she was the weaker vessel. Indeed, the scales were held quite evenly as between the sexes. A woman might hold her own property, appear in public, and attend to her own business. Frequently, Assyrian women are depicted upon monuments riding on the highways upon mules. Woman might even hold office and plead in a court of justice--so far did Babylonia anticipate the progress of modern Western ideas. Agreements have been discovered upon tablets by which it was covenanted between a man and his wife that should the husband marry another during the lifetime of the first wife, all the dowry of the first shall be returned to her and she shall be allowed to go where she pleases. The law concerning divorce, however, would seem to lack that fairness which characterizes many other regulations of social life. A man might divorce his wife by the payment of a pecuniary consideration; but if a woman undertook the initiative in annulling the marriage contract, she might be condemned to death by drowning.

In the formula for the exorcism used by the priests to break the spell the gods had sent upon one possessed or sick, we discover that despising the mother was regarded as being as culpable as dishonoring the father. "Has he perchance set his parents or relations at variance, sinned against God, despised father or mother, lied, cheated, dishonored his neighbor's wife, shed his neighbor's blood, etc. Indeed, an ancient law, which is thought to go back even to Accadian precedents, even gives to the woman, if she be a mother, greater honor than to the man for it is prescribed that if a son denies his father he is to be fined; if he denies his mother, he is to be banished."

It must be said, however, that the social freedom of the women depended much upon their social rank. The women of the lower walks of life were singularly independent for an Oriental community. Indeed, their liberty was practically unrestricted. They could be seen upon the public highways, with both head and face uncovered. They could make their purchases at the market place, attend to any business that they might find necessary, and visit the homes of their friends without restraint. While all women, whatever might be their rank, had the same standing before the laws of the land, unbending custom kept women of the highest plane of social life within the seclusion of the home. Even when allowed the privilege of being seen in public, they must go attended by eunuchs or pages, so that both seeing and being seen were difficult processes. Of course, in the highest lady of the land, the queen, was found the culmination of dignity and exclusiveness, and she was rarely seen by anyone except her husband, members of the royal family, and her servants. Thus rank, instead of giving freedom and enlarged powers, tended only to bring monotony and seclusion.

The women of the lower classes usually went with bare feet, as well as bare heads. With their long shaggy garments they did not present a very picturesque or attractive appearance. The truth is, the costumes of the people of Babylonia and Assyria were wanting in that grace and beauty which is discoverable among some other people of the Orient. The garments lacked that lightness of effect which flowing robes and drapery make possible. The designs and materials were stiff, and with the profusion of borders and fringes presented a heavy aspect. The women did not choose so to dress as to show their natural figure, but by concealing themselves in heavy and sometimes padded garments, their forms were far from beautiful, and contrast most unfavorably with the Greek and Egyptian grace of womanly dress and carriage. The women as well as the men used much embroidery, which was generally very heavy and often elaborate. Some of the designs were highly ornate and beautiful.

Of the education of women in Babylonia and Assyria little definite is known, except that it was common for women as well as men to read and write. Exercises and translations of school children have been exhumed from the mounds of ancient Babylonian cities. Dolls and other playthings of the children have also been brought to light, showing that the children of all ages have much the same tastes and occupations. Music, dancing, embroidery, besides reading and writing, were among the accomplishments of the girls of these lands.

Households were amply equipped religiously, for every home must be provided with some method of keeping itself free from the power of evil spirits. When all believe that the world is peopled with demons who are perpetually trying to ensnare men and bring them to ruin if possible, we might expect that the women would be especially superstitious and punctilious to the last degree in order that all evil spirits may be frightened from their dwellings. Hence, they hung amulets in almost every conceivable place. Talismans, statuettes of the dreaded spirits might be seen in every home. Every charm was used to thwart the enemies of human happiness in their attempt to destroy domestic peace, estrange husband from wife, drive the head of the family from his own roof, and send barrenness and blight in every quarter.

The ancient Babylonians had a queer way of marrying off their daughters, if we may believe Herodotus--which we do not. Not any period in the year might the maiden select as the time to become a matron, but only on one occasion during the year, and that a public festival, was marriage permitted. On this occasion, the daughters of marriageable age were put up at public auction. The crier took his place, while the young men who were looking for wives or the young men's parents who were to pay for them, stood about watching their opportunity to exchange their money for feminine values. It is said that the girls were put up for purchase, according to their beauty--the prettiest first, and so on to the end of the sale. Often the contest of buyers would run high in excitement, and large prices were offered for the coveted prize.

After the good-looking damsels were all sold at fair prices, then came the less attractive maidens, who, we are informed, were not sold, but offered as wives with a dowry, the proceeds of the beauties being used to add to the value of their less fortunate sisters. When the auction was over, the marriage followed, and the brides accompanied their new-made husbands to their homes. There was no escape from this method of wedlock. The procedure was not optional, but imperative. There was no marriage ring or bracelet to commemorate the event, but each new wife was given a bit of baked clay in the form of an olive. Through this model a hole was pierced so that it might be worn continually about the neck, and upon it were inscribed the names of the parties to the transaction and the date of their marriage. Several of these clay memorials have been found as mute witnesses of the days when girls were put up at the annual sale of wives in the month of Sabat and knocked down to the highest bidder.

Later, however, this custom gave way to one more rational, when marriage came to be considered both "an act of civil law and a rite of domestic worship." It became a contract entered into by two parties. A scribe must be called in to draw up the marriage bond. It is to be properly witnessed and filed away with a public notary for future reference. There is a long period of social evolution between these two methods of conducting marriage. And it is not to be supposed that all trace of bargain and sale have disappeared. Not at all. The following happy effort has been made at reproducing a scene which might have easily occurred between the father of a young man who seeks in marriage the hand of a certain damsel and the father of the girl at the home of the latter.

"'Will you give your daughter Bilitsonnon in marriage to my son Zamamanadin?' The father consents and without further delay the two men arrange the dowry. Both fathers are generous and rich, but they are also men of business habits. One begins by asking too much, the other replies by offering too little; it is only after some hours of bargaining that they finally agree and settle upon what each knew from the beginning was a reasonable dowry--a mana of silver, three servants, a trousseau and furniture, with permission for the father to substitute articles of equal value for the cash." There being no further obstacles the marriage is accordingly fixed for a day of the next week.

But does not the young lady need a longer time to prepare for an event of so great moment in her life? No, because she has been anticipating for some time that such a transaction will be effected by her parents; for has she not already arrived at the age of thirteen? She has therefore not let the past months slip idly through her fingers. She has been busy sewing, embroidering, and making other things of beauty and usefulness for her expected home. But nothing has concerned her more than to see that her own person shall be attractive to her new husband when the veil is lifted on her wedding day. Odors and ornaments ample have been provided.

Early upon the appointed day the friends may be seen moving toward the home of the bride-elect. The scribe who is to draw up the marriage contract is present ready to perform his important task. With his triangular stylus he indents the covenant in soft clay. This is to be inserted in an envelope also of clay that there may be a double impression of the words of the contract. This is to be carefully baked and filed away for possible future use--it may be to be found thousands of years afterward by some explorer digging in the ruins of a long buried city. The day has dawned beautiful, for the astrologer has said that all would be propitious. The hands of the bride and groom are tied together with a thread of wool, the customary emblem of the union into which they have now entered. The marriage contract is clearly read before the assembled company, and the witnesses make their mark upon the soft tablet, the dowry and other presents are given over. Prayer is made to the proper gods for the happy pair, and curses are invited upon any who shall undertake to annul the covenant or revoke the gifts.

Next comes the banqueting, of which the Assyrians were so fond. Music and dancing, jesting and telling happy tales, with eating and drinking, make up the round of merriment. At length the time comes for the bridal party to make its way to the home of the groom's parents. All along the way are signs of rejoicing, in which all are expected to join. The groom's house is reached, and here the festivities are resumed and carried on for several days, till all are fatigued and sated with mirth and quite ready to see the young couple settle down to their new life as home makers.

Polygamy was rare for the Orient, especially at so early a period; but where polygamy was practised at all, the harem existed. In Assyria, the king might have more than one legitimate wife, to say nothing of those who were not so ranked. Sargon had three lawful wives, for each of whom he erected a separate apartment in his royal palace of Dur-Sargina. Like Oriental houses generally, the several apartments are entered from a central court. The queen's apartments were usually rich in decoration and furnishings. The harem of Sargon's palace, which may be taken as typical, was entered by gates. One of these had upon the front two huge bronze palm trees, on each side one. Since the palm tree is emblematic of both grace and fecundity, the significance of its use is apparent. There were anterooms and drawing rooms, as well as bedrooms, for the use of the queen. These were plastered, and mural decorations were abundant, the designs being sometimes conventional, sometimes depicting religious ideas in symbolism. Of course, the winged bull and the winged lion, watchful guardians of Assyrian interest, were often painted upon the walls. The gods were favorite subjects. In the women's apartments were chairs, stools, tables, and the floors of brick or stone were covered with carpets and mats. The bed, more like a modern lounge, was raised upon wooden legs, and held a mattress and appropriate coverings, and placed in a highly ornamented alcove, gave to the bedroom an attractive air.

But how does the queen amuse herself? for long indeed must the hours often have seemed as she lived out her life a comparative prisoner. G. Maspero, the noted French assyriologist, has thus described the occupation of the queens, as they try to fill the idle hours: "Dress, embroidery, needlework, and housekeeping, long conversation with their slaves, the exchange of visits, and the festivals, with dancing and singing with which they entertained each other, serve for occupation and amusement. From time to time the king passes some hours amongst them, or invites them to dine with him and amuse themselves in the hanging gardens of the palace. The wives of the princes and great nobles are sometimes admitted to pay homage to them, but very rarely, for fear they should serve as intermediaries between the recluses and the outer world."

The kings of both Assyria and Babylonia were, as a rule, kings of insatiable conquest. Hence, much of the year was spent with the army in some distant territory, or, it may be, in lion hunting, a sport which had great attractiveness to a number of the kings. It will be thus seen how little the wives of the monarch enjoyed his real companionship. There was ample time for monotony, broken now and again by jealousies, followed by bitter hatred and deadly plottings. One wife would almost inevitably share more of the attention of the king than the rest. Those who had reason to believe themselves neglected would certainly be incensed against the more favored rival. The servants of the palace would often be drawn into the disputes, which sometimes had a tragic end. The whole harem, combining against a favorite, might, through the use of poison or by some other clandestine means, end the life of her who was so unfortunate as to be loved by the king beyond the measure thought by her rivals to be her due.

One happy effort tended to relieve at least a little the dull seclusion of the ladies of the harem. This was the planting of a garden in a court adjacent to the house of the women. Often these gardens would be most elaborate and beautiful. The hanging gardens of Babylon, accounted as among the Seven Wonders of the World, were built in honor of a favorite queen. The garden of the harem consisted of trees, such as the sycamore, the poplar, or the cypress, and other plants selected to please the eye of those whose seclusion must have made this suggestion of the country most grateful.

Feasting played an important role in the heyday of Nineveh's grandeur, as also in the Babylon of later days. The king has just returned from a great triumph in the Westland. The whole city is agog. For days the round of drinking and carousing has proceeded, till the whole city is drunken. The queen wishes to have a part in the expressions of victory and rejoicing. She, with some trepidation, invites the king to dine with her in her apartments in the harem. At the appointed hour all is arranged. The gorgeous couch the queen has prepared for the king to recline upon while he sips his wine scented with aromatic spices, the rich drapery of the couch, the small table near by, laden with golden and silver vessels of costliness and elegance, the slaves who attend upon the lord's wishes, the poet-laureate to sing the conqueror's praises in elaborate lines of flattery--all conspire to make the occasion one of great magnificence. Thus, from king and queen to the lowliest of the great city, the spirit of revelry, the love of carousal, and the habit of intoxication, took hold of the luxuriant capital. We recognize the appropriateness of the familiar words of Nahum, the Hebrew prophet of Elkosh, who had been an eyewitness of the growing effeminacy of the great Assyrian capital, Nineveh, when he foretold the fall of the once glorious city: "Behold, thy people in the midst of thee are women, the gates of thy land shall be set wide open unto thy enemies; the fire shall devour thy bars."

How did the ordinary housewife spend her time? M. Maspero attempts to reproduce the daily life of the Assyrian woman of about the eighth century before the Christian era in these graphic words:

"The Assyrian women spend a great deal of time upon the roofs. They remain there all the morning till driven away by the noonday heat, and they go back as soon as the sun declines in the evening. There they perform all their household duties, chatting from one terrace to the other. They knead the bread, prepare the cooking, wash the linen and hang it out to dry, or if they have slaves to relieve them from these menial labors, they install themselves upon cushions, and chat or embroider in the open air. During the hottest hours of the day they descend and take refuge indoors. The coolest room in the house is often below the level of the courtyard and receives very little light." Thus the Assyrian lady adapts herself as well as she may to her surroundings, which were usually very simple as to furnishings and such things as a modern inhabitant of the West would classify under the head of "comforts." An Assyrian housewife was usually satisfied with a few chairs and stools of various heights and sizes. There were few beds, except among the rich. The people generally slept upon mats, which could be folded and put away during the daytime. Taking care of the house was woman's work, unless the family was rich enough to own slaves to attend to the menial work of domestic life. The women had the care of the oven, which was usually built in one corner of the court, and the meats were cooked by them at the open fireplace. Care of the culinary work of an Assyrian home was no small task, for the Assyrians were good feeders,--and as for drinking, here they surpassed even their powers at eating. So the woman of the house would find it necessary to care for the wine skins and water jars that might be seen hanging about the porches to keep them cool.

The people along the waterways lived largely upon fish. These were caught in great numbers and dried. The industrious housewife would take these dried fish, pound them in a crude mortar, and then make them into cakes, which Herodotus tells us were almost the sole diet of those who lived in the lower or marshy regions of the Mesopotamian valley. Ordinarily, men and women partook together their daily repast from a common dish, into which all dipped, but on the occasion of great banquets it was customary for the women to be served separately.

VI

THE LAND OF THE LOTUS

"Concerning the virtues of women, O Cleanthes, I am not of the same mind with Thucydides, for he would prove that she is the best woman concerning whom there is least discourse made by people abroad, either to her praise or her disprise; judging that, as the person, so the very name of a good woman ought to be retired and not gad abroad. But to us Gorgias seems more accurate, who requires that not only the face, but the fame of a woman should be known to many. For the Roman law seems exceedingly good, which permits due praise to be given publicly both to men and to women after death." These words of Plutarch find application in the life of the women of the land of the Nile. There is no lack of praise for the Egyptian women both while living and after they had passed away, as the testimony of the monuments amply prove.

It should be remembered that the history of Egypt extends over a very wide stretch of time, and that changes are to be reckoned with even in a region where everything moves slowly. For this reason it is not always possible to say that this or that was true of the Egyptian women. For there were the ancient, middle and later kingdoms, with each of which came new influences, and these differed in many respects from the period of Greek or Macedonian power; and the Egypt of to-day is a very different Egypt from that of the Pharaohs and the Ptolemies.

There are many widely differing people in the land of the Nile to-day. The traveller finds great diversity of scenery and of social conditions, and one has said of this marvellous land as the great dramatist wrote of one of her most notable daughters:

"Age cannot wither her, nor custom stale Her infinite variety."

The oldest book in the world is an ancient Egyptian papyrus discovered by M. Prisse at Thebes. It goes back to a period probably not later than B.C. 3580, being a collection of didactic sayings, or precepts, of Phtahhotep, a prince of the fifth dynasty. What so early an Egyptian sage has to say concerning women should be of no little interest. In giving advice to husbands, he gives this counsel, which we might imagine a wise man of to-day might easily have written: "If thou be wise, guard thy house; honor thy wife, and love her exceedingly; feed her stomach and clothe her back, for this is the duty of a husband. Give her abundance of ointment, fail not each day to caress her, let the desire of her heart be fulfilled, for verily he that is kind to his wife and honoreth her, the same honoreth himself. Withhold thy hand from violence, and thy heart from cruelty, softly entreat her and win her to thy way, consider her desires and deny not the wish of her heart. Thus shalt thou keep her heart from wandering; but if thou harden thyself against her, she will turn from thee. Speak to her, yield her thy love, she will have respect unto thee; open thy arms, she will come unto thee."

Ancient Egyptian literature does not lack its reference to women. One of the most famous of the stories that have been presented to us from Egyptian sources is The Tale of the Two Brothers. This goes back to the day of Moses, and has suggested to many the Hebrew account of Joseph. It reveals the charms of her whose beauty the sea leaped up to embrace, and the acacia flowers envied. This romance, written for the entertainment of Seti II. when he was yet crown prince, and considered, by Mr. Flinders Petrie, to be connected with the ancient Phrygian of Atys, gives us an early illustration of the fact that many ills and many pleasures have been born to the race through love of a woman.

The women of Babylonia and Assyria enjoyed a measure of freedom that was exceptional for the Orient, and yet the Egyptian woman was more independent still. Indeed, the respect that was paid to womankind by the Egyptians is one of the fairest elements in the civilization of the valley of the Nile. Motherhood also was highly respected. But one illustration, referred to by Lenormant, will suffice to prove this statement. A woman while enceinte, condemned to death for murder or any other crime, could not be executed till after the birth of the child; for it was considered the height of injustice to make the innocent participate in the punishment of the guilty, and to visit the crime of one person upon two. And he adds: "The judges who put to death an innocent person were held as guilty as if they had acquitted a murderer."

Before the law woman's rights were respected. In the division of the paternal estate, the daughters shared equally with the sons, and were more responsible than the sons for the care of the parents. In worship, the queen is sometimes depicted as standing near her husband in the temple--behind him, to be sure, as the king was the head of the religion and indeed "son of the Sun," but with him, like Isis behind Osiris, lifting her hand in sympathetic protection and shaking the sistrum, or beating the tambourine to dispel all evil spirits, or holding the libation vase or bouquet.

The Egyptian woman, of the lower or middle classes at least, suffered no enforced seclusion. She came and went as her will led her, appearing in public without covered face, and chatting with acquaintances whom she met without having her conduct questioned or her modesty placed under suspicion. She might enjoy a banquet with the opposite sex, and at its close look upon the weird figure of a corpse carved in wood, placed in a coffin, which Herodotus says was carried around by a servant. As he shows the image to each guest in turn the servant says: "Gaze here and drink and be merry; for when you die such you will be." Thus was Epicurus anticipated in ancient Egypt. Dum vivimus, vivamus. The Egyptians generally, however, kept the next world always in view, and immortality played no small part in shaping the Egyptian life, both as to its men and its women. The Greek influence, which, after the days of Alexander, was destined to revolutionize Egyptian thought and custom, notwithstanding the efforts of the Ptolemies to win favor of the populace by revolutionizing the waning worship of Osiris, is illustrated in a poem written about one hundred years before Christ, a Lament for the Dead Wife of Pasherenptah. In this poem, the ancient hope of immortality is overcast, and the weeping spouse is enjoined:

"Love woman while you may Make life a holiday, Drive every care away And earthly sadness."

The first lady of the land was of course a queen. The queens of Egypt not unfrequently had a wide outlook upon the material progress of the people. This is well exemplified in the expedition of Queen Chuenemtamun of which we know from discovered monuments, which represent the ship being ladened with large and costly stores under her direction. Queen Hatshepsu fitted out a fleet of five ships and sent them to the land of Punt,--the southern coast of Arabia, or, as some suppose, the African coast south of Abyssinia,--that they might bring back scented fig trees which she would transplant in her gigantic orchard at Thebes. The tallest monolith in the world, of reddish granite and one hundred and eight feet high, said once to have been covered with a coating of gold, was the work of this famous queen.

In a few cases queens ruled in Egypt, wives of kings governed jointly with their husbands, and there are instances in which pretenders to the throne married women of royal lineage that their claims might have at least the show of being legitimate. This was the case with Piankhi, one of the Ethiopian dynasty of kings, whose wife Ameniritis is described as a woman of rare intelligence and of superior merit; one who, because of her rare strength of character and wisdom, exerted a powerful influence in the government and won for herself great popularity in Thebes and the entire region around.

A modern traveller may easily be reminded of the honor paid to women in ancient Egypt by visiting the sites where temples and tombs were erected in honor of some beloved wife and queen. The temple of Hathor at the modern Aboo Simbel, which was erected by the famous builder Rameses II. in honor at once of Hathor the goddess of love, and of his wife Nofreari. Six statues adorn the entrance to the temple. They are thirty feet high, and represent Rameses and his beloved queen, who appears under the favor of the goddess Hathor. On the brow of the goddess is the crown--the moon resting within the horns of a cow; she wears also the ostrich feathers, which are the sign of royalty. Their children, as often portrayed upon Egyptian monuments, have their places beside their parents: the daughters stand close to the queen; the sons, near to the father. About the sculptured forms is recorded in hieroglyphic characters the love which the king felt for his fair queen, whose name meant "beautiful and good." The temple and statues are hewn out of the living rock, and, on entering, there is the shrine of Hathor, "the supreme type of divine maternity."

There is a touch of romance here, for on the outer wall the inscriptions tell us that this temple was reared "by Rameses the Strong in Faith, the Beloved of Ammon, for his royal wife Nofreari, whom he loves"; while within the doorway of this same temple may be read the legend, it was for Rameses that "his royal wife who loves him, Nofreari the Beloved of Maat, constructed for him this abode in the mountain of the Pure Waters." Thus beautiful was the enduring love between this royal husband and his wife.

No period of ancient Egyptian history is entirely wanting in the names of conspicuous women. There is a legend that comes down from the days of the Ptolemies, to the effect that when King Ptolemy Euergetes started out upon his expeditions against Syria, the strong rival of Egypt for the supremacy over the East, his queen, the beautiful Berenice (a favorite name for princesses for two centuries), made a vow that if her husband should be permitted to return from his expedition in safety, she would dedicate her hair to the gods. Her prayer was answered; and, faithful to her solemn vow, she cut off her hair and hung "the beautiful golden tresses that had adorned her head in the temple, whose ruins still stand on the promontory of Zephyrium." But, alas! they were not long allowed to adorn the walls of the holy place, for some sacrilegious thief carried them away from the shrine. The priests were bewildered, the king was wroth, no one knew what to do. At length the astronomers came to the relief of all concerned by announcing that it could have been no ordinary thief who plundered the temple for the beautiful tresses, but that the gods themselves had taken them, and that the keen eye had only to be turned heavenward to discover a new constellation which they now separated from Leo. The king and all concerned were now reconciled and happy. The constellation shines on.

Among the most beautiful of ancient buildings is the temple of Denderah. While magnificent in itself, much of its interest to us here is due to the fact that it was erected and dedicated to the Egyptian goddess of love and beauty, Hathor, nurse of Horus, the son of Osiris and Isis; and further, that it was begun by that fascinator of kings, the notorious Cleopatra. On the outside walls of the temple are figures of this famous queen, and of Caesarion, her son by Julius Caesar. One would judge from these representations that Cleopatra's beauty was of the most voluptuous and sensual type, the features being not only full but fat, though regular. On her head is placed the horned disc,--in honor of Hathor,--the sacred vulture, and the horns of Isis. Thus have been perpetuated the personal and religious features of the most remarkable woman Egypt ever produced. Pascal's oft-quoted comment upon the beauty of this Egyptian character doubtless contains a modicum of truth: "If the nose of Cleopatra had been shorter, the whole face of the earth would have been changed." Cleopatra, however, whose charms subdued victors, was more a Greek than an Egyptian beauty. The women of the Nile country, however, were not lacking in personal grace and physical charm. Their complexions were dark, their features generally regular, and their bodies athletic, though not large.

One might judge from the paintings that have come down to us, which depict the form and vesture of the Egyptian woman, that she was greatly lacking both in grace of figure and in taste for arraying herself attractively. But we are not to be misled by the elongated, wiry-looking figures that the monuments portray for us. Some of the blame must, without doubt, be laid upon the Egyptian artist, who had little idea either of proportion or perspective.

Egyptian women spent much time upon their toilettes. Great attention was given to the care of the complexion. For this beautifying process a powder was used consisting of antimony and charcoal, powdered fine and applied with so much skill that the skin by contrast is made to stand out in soft whiteness. For this cosmetic regimen a mirror of highly polished metal was found to be of indispensable value. The finger nails came in for a full share of attention, henna being used to stain them. As for the feet, scarcely less care was given them, and anklets and toe rings frequently adorned them. Shoes, or sandals, seem never to have been in high favor in Egypt, and, even when clothed in the most costly apparel, women preferred to go with bare feet.

It would seem very difficult, to modern taste, to attain to real beauty by means of tattooing. But we have grounds for asserting that the Egyptian beauties, at least at a certain period of their national history, covered their forehead, chin, and breasts, and sometimes the arms, with indelible painting in color. They were fond of rouging their faces, especially the lips, and the eye was a feature to which much time and art were given. Large eyes were the fashion, as may be readily judged from the many pictures of ox-eyed maids which have been preserved. A band of black pigment almost entirely surrounded the eyes, and extended across the temples to the roots of the hair. By painting the eyebrows and eyelids, the eyes were made to appear not only larger but more brilliant.

The Egyptian woman was fond of the use of oil, which was rubbed generously upon the body. Perfumes also played an important part in her life. Women made and sold perfumes and used them profusely. They were exceedingly fond of flowers, especially if they were new varieties. Extracts and essences from sweet-scented plants were much sought after. Favorite shrubs and flowers were transported from distant lands and transplanted in the land of the Nile. This was often done upon a large scale. Even the liquors drunk at banquets were scented with sweet perfumes.

The women usually dressed in a long, close-fitting smock-frock, clinging closely to the body and reaching quite to the ankles. The shoulders and upper part of the breast were left uncovered, the frock being held in place by two straps running across the shoulders. But it is not to be supposed that the women of Egypt knew nothing of fashion; though it must be confessed that fashions changed slowly. And in this matter the men were as fond of fashion as the women; for they wore linen skirts usually reaching to the knees, although their length was regulated by the prevailing style.

Under the New Empire woman's dress did not leave both shoulders bare, as formerly, but covered the left shoulder; the right shoulder and arm being left free. At length drapery began to be more common, and instead of the heavy, straight garment of earlier days, graceful folds appeared. With the drapery came a lengthening of the skirt. When this change occurred only the priests retained the simple skirt of former days. Most men wore a double skirt, consisting of an inner short garment, and an outer. Indeed, the men seemed quite as fond of their costume as the women, and were more varied in their tastes, loving finery, and leaving it to the women to be more conservative in matters of dress.

From the paintings and the other representations that have come down to us, both the peasant maid and the princess wore the same kind of garments, so far as the cut of them is concerned. Mother, daughter, and maid were dressed much alike and without much variety of color. The rich often wore a profusion of beads.

There was no part of the Egyptian woman's toilet upon which so much care was bestowed as upon the hair. Indeed, the Egyptians prided themselves upon their coiffure. Herodotus is authority for the statement that there were fewer bald-headed people in Egypt than in any other country. Civilization, in the valley of the Nile, at least, did not seem greatly to increase the tendency to baldness. There were cases, but they were of the nature of a calamity. Woe to the physician whose skill did not succeed in checking the falling hair. Pomades of various ingredients were common remedies for this ill. Oil, dog's feet, and date kernels were considered of great virtue, as was also a donkey's tooth pulverized and mixed with honey. And there was no more direful or more frequent imprecation pronounced by an Egyptian lady upon her rival than that the hair of her whom she hated might fall out!

[Illustration 2: GHAWAZI After the painting by C. L. Muller The "dancing girls" known as ghawazi, are often in evidence. They clothe themselves in gay garments of various colors. Sometimes they are pretty and attractive specimens of female grace, but, as might be expected from their character and profession, they soon become coarse and repulsive. They may be seen at the public places, and their dances are indecorous and immodest. They play a leading role in those wild orgies known as Fantasia.]

Wigs were commonly used by women as well as by men of the Ancient Empire. There was a coiffure of straight hair down to the shoulders or to the breasts. Examples have been found, however, in which the wigs reached not so far, as is the case in the statuette of the Lady Takusit, which is now among the ancient ornaments in the Museum of Athens. She wears a wig of stiff curly locks in rigidly regular lines plastered closely to the head, reaching almost from the eyes in front to the nape of the neck, and hiding the ears. The plaiting of the hair became common in later times, the hair hanging stiffly over the shoulders.

This piece of statuary, that of Lady Takusit, or Takoushet, as it is sometimes spelled, one of the most perfect of its kind, shows a woman of good form and regular features, standing erect with one foot in advance, her right arm hanging gracefully by her side, her left pressed naturally against her bosom. She is dressed in the closely fitting skirt already described, supported by straps over the shoulders and reaching to a point just above the ankles. Her robe is richly embroidered with scenes of a religious character, and her wrists are adorned with bracelets.

Besides the ordinary hair dress of the women, the queen enjoyed the exceptional privilege of wearing a diadem or headdress, representing a vulture, which was the sacred bird of Egypt and was accounted the special protector of the king in battle. This royal bird is represented as stretching out its strong wings over the head of the first lady of the land.

The women were great lovers of trinkets and jewelry of all kinds, and the men were not far behind them in this. They put an ornament wherever it could be appropriately worn. And this ruling passion was even strong in death, for the dead were often literally loaded with jewels upon their arms, fingers, ears, brow, neck, and ankles. Favorite jewels, specially, were entombed with the dead. In the Boulak Museum has been preserved probably the most complete collection of funeral jewelry, that of Queen Aahhotep, mother of Ahmes, the first king of the eighteenth dynasty. The following are some of the womanly belongings buried with Queen Aahhotep: a fan handle plated with gold, a bronze-gilt mirror mounted upon an ebony handle, on which was a lotus of chased gold, bracelets of various designs, anklets, armlets, gold rings, ornaments for the wrist made of small beads in "gold, lapis lazuli, carnelian and green feldspar, strung on gold wire in a chequer pattern," and many other ornaments of fine gold, of chased and repouss?work of great value.

The women of Egypt to-day are dark in complexion and generally slender. The women of the poorer classes are ill kept and poorly clothed. They generally wear long, and frequently tattered, garments of blue and black cotton. Their feet are bare, but the love of decoration is manifest still; for, though they be dirty and begrimed through lack of care and suitable clothing, the silver anklets, the rings for their fingers and even for their toes, and the bracelets for their arms, tell the tale of their fondness for adornment. Mohammedanism has caused the universal use of the veil. A narrow strip of black is caught by a brass or silver spiral directly between the eyes. The falling veil, therefore, covers all the face below the eyes. Ladies of the higher classes wear transparent Turkish veils of costly material, and their costly silk garments are loaded with embroideries.

Mothers in Egypt carry their babes on their backs or shoulders. The mother holds fast to the feet or the legs of her offspring, while the child throws his hands about her head and seems well satisfied with his position. The tattooing, which we have noted as existent in early Egypt, is no longer general; it, however, may be seen to-day among the women of Nubia. Some of the Berber women not only are tattooed, but place blue lines on their under lip and on the cheeks and arms. The men, women, and children of that region are very dark. The women plait their hair into numerous tiny curls, which stay well in place, for the hair has first been soaked in castor oil, partly because of the aesthetic effect, and partly as a protection against the hot rays of the tropical sun. The dress of the younger women is very scant; the older females are generally clothed in long blue garments, which they gather about them in folds. The younger girls, however, with much unadorned innocence, wear simply a leathern girdle and a complacent smile, for the Berber women appear good-humored and happy. This costume, a girdle of leather, soaked well in castor oil and adorned with shells, worn by the younger belles of Nubia, is known as "Madam Nubia."

The "dancing girls," known as ghawazi, are often in evidence in the towns of modern Egypt. They clothe themselves in gay garments of various colors. Sometimes they are pretty and attractive specimens of female grace, but, as might be expected from their character and profession, they soon become coarse and repulsive. They may be seen at the public cafes, and their dances are indecorous and immodest. They play a leading role in those wild orgies known as fantasia.

The modern Egyptian water girl is often an interesting bit of humanity. Canon Bell thus describes her in his Winter on the Nile: "You may be accompanied, if you like it, by a little girl clad in blue, adorned with a necklace of beads, earrings and bracelets, and sometimes a nose-ring, carrying a water jar on her head, from which she will supply you at luncheon among the temples and tombs, for a small backsheesh. She will run beside your donkey for miles, and never seem tired, and if you will drink from her jar, of the same shape which you will see sculptured on the temple walls, will reward you with a sweet smile from her coral lips. And what teeth she and all the people have! I never saw teeth so regular and so white. They are like a string of orient pearls; and it is a pleasure when the lips part, and you see them gleaming white as driven snow."

In ancient Egypt the woman was queen of her own house, the real mistress of domestic life. When the husband was at home, he was looked upon rather in the light of a "privileged guest," and the housewife was the respected hostess, holding everything beneath her undisputed sway. In short, she was the very soul and centre of the domestic activity, rising early and stirring the household into life and movement.

Let us take a peep into an Egyptian home. Excavation has revealed that the palaces of the kings of Babylonia were built in a much more substantial and enduring fashion than were the temples of the gods. The reverse is true of Egypt. Egyptian temples were built not for time, but for eternity. The palaces, however, were of far lighter character, being erected of brick or undressed freestone, but rarely of granite or the more enduring materials. Eternity played an important part in the religious thinking of the Egyptians. This will account in a measure for the more enduring character of the houses of the gods. The dwellings of members of the richer classes were made up of an aggregation of houses, suggesting a miniature village. There were separate houses for the various members of the family: the master, the chief wife, the harem women, the visitors, and the several classes of servants. Storehouses were separate from buildings designed for habitation, and the several domestic offices had their individual buildings. The court, which every villa had, was planted with trees and flowers, and frequently was provided with a fountain and a pool. The women of the harem found opportunity for amusement in these beautiful courts. During the day these secluded beauties whiled away their time in gossiping, playing upon instruments, and indulging in the games in vogue. When night came they lay down to rest with their heads upon pillows consisting of a piece of curved wood, upon which was usually carved an image of the god Bisou, who guarded the sleeper. This little dwarf, a divinity with short legs and rotund stomach, drives away the demons who infest the night and are liable to injure the sleeping one, unless protected by this well-disposed and well-armed deity.

The wife in the average Egyptian home was the companion of her husband, assisting him to manage his affairs. She encouraged him in his own daily work, and there are pictures of wife and children, seemingly in a most interested mood, standing by while the husband and father is busily engaged in some engrossing occupation. Often the king will take his wife fully into his life. The queen is frequently pictured by the king's side in some public function. The wife of Amenophis IV., with the rest of the royal family, is represented, probably on some important state occasion, as standing upon the gallery of the royal residence and tossing golden collars to the people. Indeed, Amenophis IV. is discovered to have been most domestic in his tastes, giving his wife and daughters a place of respect and honor in his kingdom. Some of his monuments represent him riding in his chariot, followed by his seven daughters, who were his companions even in battle. Sometimes the queen of the Pharaohs is found riding in state processions in her own chariot behind that of her husband.

How did the average women of the Nile busy themselves during the long days? While they were not the hewers of wood, women were usually the drawers of water, as in Palestine and Syria. They were not idlers, though men did the spinning, weaving, and laundry work. In truth, as we have before stated, it was the daughter, or daughters, and not the sons who were expected to provide for their parents in times of want and old age. This did not permit women to be in any sense a dependent class.

The relation of the Egyptian woman to the practical affairs of life is significant and of great interest. It is in the matter of buying and selling that we perhaps have most frequent representations upon the monuments. And women as well as men are portrayed driving their bargains with the venders of all sorts of wares. Women both buy and sell in the public places. One has perfume of her own manufacture, upon the merits of which she glibly descants, even in terms poetic, as she thrusts the jars under the nostrils of the hoped-for purchaser. Women jewelers are discovered attempting to dispose of their rings, bracelets, and necklaces, while other women are trying to obtain goods at the lowest possible prices. "Cheapening" was fashionable even among the women of Egypt. Sometimes groups of women are represented as bargaining in the shops. Herodotus in his travels observed what to him was a striking contrast between the industrial and commercial customs of the Greeks and those of the Egyptians in that the men of Egypt worked at the looms and carried on the handicraft, while the women frequently transacted business. But it should not be thought that women did not weave. They often worked at the loom, and men as well as women bought and sold the ordinary commodities of life.

In the house Egyptian women not only engaged in weaving, spinning, and the making of fabrics generally, but they assisted in the curing of fowls, birds, and fish. Of this kind of food the Egyptians were very fond. When the husband, who was very partial to hunting, returned with the game he had killed or trapped, it was at once preserved for later use upon the table. Strangely enough, the cooks are usually represented as men, though the women were not strangers to the preparation of food for family use. The Egyptians laid much stress upon their dietary. They believe, Herodotus tells us, that the diseases men are heir to are all caused by the materials upon which they feed. Swine's flesh was, as with the Israelites, forbidden flesh, except upon certain extraordinary occasions. Their staff of life was bread made of spelt. Their drink was chiefly a beer made from barley. Salt fish, and dried fowls, such as ducks, geese, and quail, were eaten with great relish. Some birds, as well as some fish, were tabooed because of religious scruples.

The recreations that were allowable to the Egyptian women were quite numerous and varied. But dancing, singing, and performing upon musical instruments were their favorite amusements. The kettle drum and the castanet were in common use among them, and pictures of girls playing on the lute are not infrequent. A wall painting in a Theban tomb discloses the fact that dancing girls were often employed to afford merriment at the feasts. It was not against Egyptian etiquette for women to attend banquets, and they are often represented as drinking freely, even to drunkenness, lying about with forms exposed, and vomiting from overindulgence.

In this connection it is curious to note the relation of the women of Egypt to gymnastic feats. In the Turin Museum there is an example of a female acrobat, who is in the very act of performing with wonderful agility a very difficult feat. The young woman is nude, with the exception of a double belt, one thong of which encircles the waist, the other confines the hips. She is willowy in form and with great ease and grace she throws herself backward, apparently about to turn a somersault, but she keeps her feet upon the ground, and her hands almost touch her heels. Her hair flows out loosely as she seems about to whirl her lithe body through the air.

That the Egyptian women were pleasure-loving may be learned by many a monument. Portrayals of elaborate festivals have been unearthed, others are recorded by early historians. Herodotus gives a description of one of these in honor of the Egyptian Diana in the city of Bubastis. "They hold public festival not only once in a year but several times.... Now when they are being conveyed to the city of Bubastis they act as follows; for men and women embark together, and great numbers of both sexes in every barge; some of the women have castanets on which they play, and the men play on the lute during the whole voyage, the rest of the women sing and clap their hands together at the same time. When in course of their passage they come to any town, they lay their barge near to land, and do as follows: Some of the women do as I have described, others shout and scoff at the women of the place; some dance, while others stand and pull up their clothes; this they do at every town at the river-side. When they arrive at Bubastis, they celebrate the feast, offering up great sacrifices and more wine is consumed at this festival than in all the rest of the year. What with men and women, besides children, they congregate, as the inhabitants say, to the number of seven hundred thousand."

The law of Egypt prescribed that there should be in each family but one legitimate wife. From numerous representations upon the monuments it would seem that great affection usually existed between spouses. Marriage was termed "founding for one's self a home." Temporary or tentative marriages were often made for one year. After the expiration of the trial period, by the payment of a certain sum, the man might annul the agreement.

The Tel-el-Amarna tablets brought to light in 1887, furnish some very interesting and informing materials concerning diplomatic marriages. Many letters passed between the kings of Egypt and the rulers of the land of Mitanni, and other Asiatic provinces concerning the marriage of royal daughters to the King of Egypt or to the king's son. Even bargaining concerning dowry finds a place in this correspondence. Inquiries respecting the treatment of a daughter who has been given in marriage to a prince, complaints of the breaking of the marriage contract, and all conceivable complications which might grow out of these marital relations, are discussed.

In the days of the Ptolemies and in the Roman period, it became very common for men to marry their own sisters, especially in the royal families. This was true of Cleopatra, the daughter of Ptolemy Epiphanes and Cleopatra. She married first her brother Ptolemy Philometer, and later, a second brother Ptolemy Physcon. This was the Cleopatra who lived a century before the famous "witch of the Nile." She distinguished herself by her signal favoritism toward the Jews, who had then become very numerous in Egypt, giving great encouragement to Onias in his undertaking of the erection of a Jewish temple at Leontopolis in Egypt.

In modern Egypt, however, marriage with sisters has given way to marriage between cousins, which in current opinion is by far the best sort of wedding match. It is not strange that this custom of legalized incest, the marrying of sisters should have sprung up in a land where Osiris and Set were worshipped. For both of these gods were wedded to their sisters, Isis and Nephthys.

As among the Hebrews, it was a matter of congratulation and of great domestic happiness to possess children, and much rejoicing took place at the birth of a babe. The inscriptions of monuments and tombs would indicate, too, a very beautiful family life in Egypt. There was nothing that so tended to give domestic life this charm as the fact that the mother took complete charge of the child's upbringing. She was its nurse, feeding it from her own breast often till it reached the age of three years. In Eastern countries it is not uncommon to see children of considerable size thus taking nourishment. When the child was unable to walk, or when the journey was too great for the yet undeveloped limbs, the mothers carried their children upon their necks, as do the Egyptian mothers to-day.

Motherhood was much respected both by sons and daughters,--more than is true of the children of modern Egypt,--and the wise men and poets of the land wrote and spoke most tenderly and sympathetically of the maternal love. As one of them said: "Thou shalt never forget what thy mother hath done for thee. She has borne and nourished thee. If thou forgettest her, she might blame thee, she might lift up her arms to God, and he would surely hear her complaint." An utterance of an Egyptian sage, which bears the spirit of the words of the Hebrew wise man, who said: "Forsake not the law of thy mother. Bind it continually upon thy heart, and tie it about thy neck. When thou goest it shall lead thee, and when thou sleepest it shall keep thee. When thou awakest it shall talk with thee;" and again: "Despise not thy mother when she is old." Affection between mothers and their sons was very strong. Many of the inscriptions upon tombs, with the accompanying pictures, reveal the dead son and his mother, and not the son and his father. This is in accordance with the very common fact in Eastern lands, especially in this part, that brothers and sisters by the same mother were much closer to one another than brothers and sisters by the same father. It is quite evident that in early days in Egypt descent was always traced through the mother, and not through the father. When, in a remote period, marriage ties were loose or polyandry was practised, it was manifestly easier to trace the family lineage through the mother. In ancient Egypt, it is interesting to note that inheritance of property passed not from a father to his son, but to the son of his sister, or sometimes to the son of his eldest daughter.

When children were named they did not receive a family or surname. All names were individual, the gods coming in for their share of honor in the selection, as was very common among ancient people, among whom religion pervaded everything. The girls were frequently named, for poetic or imaginative reasons, after trees, animals, qualities of moral excellence, and the like. Such appellations as "Daughter-of-the-crocodile, Kitten," etc., were not infrequent; and even here we find a religious motive, for both the crocodile and the cat were worshipped in Egypt. Mummied sacred cats have been exhumed in great numbers in recent years, only to be ruthlessly turned into fertilizers by the unappreciative and practical Westerner. "Beautiful Sycamore" is also an example of a woman's name. "Darling" and "Beloved" were also favorite names, and "My Queen" is also found. From the number of instances discovered, it would seem--and not unnaturally--that women liked to be called after Hathor, the goddess of love.

How did the little girls amuse themselves in those far-off Egyptian days? The girl nature is the same the world over, and has not undergone any radical change since the very dawn of history. The girls, of course, played with dolls. These were made from cloth and were usually stuffed. Some of them had long hair. Figures resembling jumping-jacks, loosely jointed and manipulated with a string, were a means of merriment for the little ones. The nursery was also frequently brightened by the presence of flowers; and birds, some free and some caged, were common pets; cats, too, were everywhere, and the small donkey furnished much sport.

It may seem somewhat strange that in a land to which has often been attributed the invention of the art of writing, there should have come down to us no literature from the hand and brain of a woman. The secret of this is probably found in the fact that while women were respected and even esteemed as the equals of men, yet it was not considered worth while to educate them in a literary way. In some of the arts, however, such as music, women were skilled.

In modern Egypt the education of the women is sadly neglected. It does not compare with that given them in ancient times. Indeed, in Mohammedan countries, generally, woman is sternly thrust into a position of inferiority, even of degradation. The school provided for the instruction of the children in Egypt, as in all Mohammedan countries, is the kattub, which is to be found in most towns and even in some of the small villages. These schools are attached, when possible, to a mosque, and the instruction is religious rather than literary, for the teaching is limited to the Koran, and all instruction is in the Arabic language. The schoolmaster, who usually has an assistant, is himself very ignorant of all that the modern Western world would term "learning." Even the elements of a modern education are strangers to him. There are said to be about nine thousand five hundred of these kattubs in Egypt, and in them are enrolled one hundred and eighty thousand pupils. But the kattub is dark and unattractive. There are no seats or furniture of any kind. To an Occidental eye, the schoolroom is inconvenient in every respect, and withal quite unsanitary and forbidding. The teacher sits on a mat, cross-legged. In front of him are ranged two rows of children, both boys and girls, sitting sideways to the teacher. One would suppose, seated as the children are, that the dreary humdrum of the daily instruction was surely meant to go in at one ear and out at the other. But the pupils learn to repeat passage after passage from the sacred book of Mohammed. For the time is largely taken up reciting sura after sura from the Koran, and the most lengthy passages are well memorized, the master correcting the boy or girl whose tongue has slipped, or prompting one whose memory has failed him. As the singsong of recitation is rolled out in languid sweetness, the pupils sway their bodies back and forth, keeping time to the rhythm. There is no casting of eyes at the girls, no giggling, no crooked pins in use, in the kattubs. The pupils know the stern master is on serious business bent. Besides, he makes use of the principle of "the expulsive power" of preoccupation; for, while the memorizing and reciting of texts goes on, there are no idle hands for Satan to make busy. The teacher himself sets the example of industry, for his hands are engaged in weaving a mat, while his ear watches to detect the slightest lapse from correctness in the pupil's tongue. So, too, the boys and girls must be busied at some useful handiwork, such as plaiting straw. Thus, "technical training" goes hand in hand with the mental in modern Egypt. The number of girls in these schools, however, is comparatively small. There are hopeful signs in the matter of female education in the Egypt of to-day, for the government, seeing the need, has granted a double sum for every girl in attendance upon the kattubs.

Women of all lands have had an important place in the time of sickness and death. Egypt is no exception to the rule. There were doctors in this cultured land. Specialism was in vogue even in ancient Egypt. As the celebrated Greek historian again says: "Medicine is practised among them on the plan of separation; each physician treats a single disorder and no more." There were eye specialists, headache specialists, tooth specialists, intestine specialists, and so on to the end of the category of diseases. Some of their treatises, comments upon cases, diseases, formul? methods of physicians, both of Egypt and of other lands, have come down to us. And yet, it must be confessed that exorcism held an important place in the Egyptian practice of medicine; and the women were among the foremost believers in this magical method of effecting cures. The Egyptian lady is suffering from a most violent attack of headache. She sends for the physician. He presently arrives, with one or more servants or assistants, bringing with them his book of incantations, and a case containing his materia medica, which consists of a goodly supply of clay, plants or dried roots of all sorts, cloths, models in wax or clay, black or red ink, et cetera. A diagnosis of the case is hurriedly made.

Kneading some clay, with which various ingredients are mixed, this disciple of Aculapius, or rather of Imhotep, repeats the appropriate incantation several times, places the ball of clay under the head of the sick, and leaves, feeling sure that the inimical spirit which torments her will not be able to gain possession against the powerful charm.

In case of death in any household, the mourning was pronounced and pitiable. The part which women played in Egyptian funerals was not unlike that among the Hebrews and other Oriental peoples. "They were," says Maspero, in his Struggle of the Nations, "not like those to which we are accustomed--mute ceremonies in which sorrow is barely expressed by a fugitive tear. Noise, sobbings, and wild gestures were their necessary concomitants. Not only was it customary to hire weeping women, who tore their hair, filled the air with their lamentations, and simulated by skilful actions the depths of despair, but the relations and friends did not shrink from making an outward show of their grief nor from disturbing the equanimity of the passers-by by the immoderate expressions of their sorrow." "O my father!" "O my brother!" "O my master!" "O my beloved!" would be heard from the female voices standing around the dead. There was no superstition which prevented a fond embracing of the body of the loved one who had just passed away. Tears flow in great profusion, hair and garments are rent, and the women beat their breasts, and then depart from the house of death. "With nude bosoms, head sullied with dust, the hair dishevelled and feet bare, they rush from the house into the still, deserted streets." Friends and sympathizers join in their grief as they pass along, and follow the procession of mourning. Since the Egyptian believes that the spirit can survive only so long as the body lasts,--a sort of conditional immortality,-- the corpse must be embalmed. The method is determined by the rank of the deceased. If it be a princess who has passed away, the most elaborate and costly methods and materials must be used. Each toe and finger must be carefully and separately wrapped and cared for. Next comes the solemn funeral procession, with the noisy, heartrending hired mourners, the libations and offerings, the catafalque drawn by oxen, and at length the dead is laid away in the tombs. An important part of the Egyptian funeral is the banquet, in which the dead, through his representative, partakes; during the feasting, the almehs execute their death dances and sing their songs appealing to the living concerning death and the dead.

It is Nut, the goddess of heaven, who, during the journey of the soul, after it leaves the tomb appears from the midst of a sycamore tree, offering the spirit a dish containing loaves and a cruse of water, and if the soul accepts the proffered gift, he becomes the guest of the goddess. Beyond are dangers of every sort which only amulets and the most powerful incantations can dispel. If the soul can pass these--though many fall by the way--he is transported by the divine ferryman to the presence of Osiris, the great god. Maat, the goddess of Truth, stands by and whispers the proper confession into the ear of him whom Osiris questions, and the soul is passed on to the "Field of Beans," the place of the blessed, where feasts, dances, songs, and conversation are thereafter enjoyed.

Probably no Egyptian woman was ever more influential, for a period at least, than Queen Tyi, the mother of King Chuen-Aten, who is better known as Amenophis IV. His father, Amenophis III., was born, as the story goes, under conditions most auspicious. Ra, the great Sun god, who was considered to have been the father of all the Pharaohs, and the first sovereign of Egypt, as well as the creator of the universe, favored King Thothmes by giving to him the son for whom he prayed. Queen Moutemouait, wife of Thothmes, as she lay sleeping in her palace was suddenly aroused by seeing her husband by her side, and then immediately afterward the form of the Theban Amen. In her alarm she heard a voice telling her of the birth of a son, who should come to the throne in Thebes, and then the apparition "vanished in a cloud of perfume sweeter and more penetrating than all the perfumes of Arabia." The child whose advent was predicted became King Amenophis III., one of the most brilliant and successful kings of the eighteenth dynasty.

King Amenophis III. was wedded to a foreign wife, more than one in fact. Among the wives of his harem was Gilukhipa, or Kirgipa, a daughter of the house of Mitanni, between which and the Pharaohs of this epoch the Tel-El-

Amarna tablets reveal so voluminous a correspondence. There was also in his harem a Babylonian princess, and, most famous of all, a lady, probably of Semitic extraction, whose name was Tyi. This Queen Tyi became the mother of the successor to Amenophis III. Under the influence of the queen-mother, the young King Amenophis IV. resolved on extensive religious reforms. He determined to dethrone or degrade the former deities of Egypt and exalt the "Sun Disc." Asiatic influence was paramount. He changed his capital from Thebes to the site of Tel-El-Amarna, and erected there both palace and temple. He changed his name to Chuen-Aten (Glory of the Solar Disc). But during his activity as a religious reformer, his empire was falling away by the sad neglect of the foreign affairs to which his father gave so large and successful attention. At his death his work fell to pieces, and his reformation swung back. Even his sons who succeeded him undid his work, and his name comes down to us as "The Heretic King," being caricatured by artists of the period which followed his ephemeral undertakings.

A modern Egyptian woman, or perhaps more accurately an Arab woman, digging into a mound in Middle Egypt, not far from the Nile, for the purpose of getting some material with which to patch her hut, pulled out a piece of baked clay with some queer inscriptions upon it, which turned out to be the cuneiform characters of the Assyro-Babylonian writing. Further excavations revealed the record hall of Amenophis IV., long buried under the ruins of his short-lived city. This collection of documents and correspondence in the Assyrian language, which was the Lingua Franca of those early days, are the source of our most accurate knowledge of the marriages, domestic relations and diplomatic history of this period in Egyptian history; indeed, of the history of the surrounding peoples as far east as the Mesopotamian valley.

At least two Egyptian women emerge in the Hebrew records, one of whom would indicate a low degree of morals, if we may judge of Egyptian women of high standing of the period by this one. It is Potiphar's wife who fell so deeply in love with Joseph, the handsome young Hebrew slave whom Potiphar had bought and made a servant in his own household, that she sought to use her wiles to entice the youth from rectitude. At length failing in her purpose, she charged him with attempting to use violence upon her, and had him imprisoned, only to find that the young man was to come forth stronger at last and find an honored place in the annals of Hebrew life in the land of Egypt.

The other Egyptian woman of whom Hebrew history speaks is Pharaoh's daughter, who, bathing in the Nile, with her maidens, discovered the infant who was destined to lead Israel out of Egypt and become the chief power in moulding the Hebrew commonwealth. The young Egyptian woman who became a mother to the child Moses, gave him all the advantages of Egyptian culture, which for those days were by no means meagre, and so played no insignificant part in the making of a lawgiver, and through him, in the making of a nation, whose moral and religious influence was to be second to none in the history of the past.

Late Judaism came in contact with a number of Egyptian princesses, especially in the age of the Ptolemies. Among these are the Cleopatras, three of whom lived a whole century before the days when Mark Antony was led astray by the most celebrated of all the women of this name. One of these was daughter of Antiochus the Great and wife of Ptolemy Epiphanes. She being attracted by the value of the balsam and other products of Palestine, asked that the taxes of the land of the Jews be given her as her dowry. A second Cleopatra, daughter of the last, greatly favored, as we have already noted, the Jews in Egypt, according to Josephus, and was in turn greatly beloved by the larger number of the Jews of the Diraspora, or Dispersion, who had sought refuge and a livelihood in the rich region of Egypt.

The third Cleopatra, daughter of the last-mentioned and of Ptolemy Philometer, was married in B.C. 150 to Alexander Bala. His checkered career is given us by Josephus and in the First Book of Maccabees. Two other women of this name also appear in the history of the Jews, one a mother of Ptolemy Lathyrus, a woman of great force and determination, who expelled her son from Egypt and caused him to take refuge in the island of Cyprus. The last was wife of Herod the Great, and mother of "Philip the Tetrarch." The story of Cleopatra, the beguiler of Mark Antony, is too well known to need repeating here. The women of Egypt of the Macedonian and Roman periods, let it suffice to say, were a power in the affairs of those marvellous days.

The moral code of the Egyptians, theoretically speaking, was relatively high, though it cannot be said that the women well known in Egyptian history or presented in romance bore an exceptionally elevated character. But the best women of ancient days were not usually those whose names were furthest known or most widely heralded. According to the Greek legends, some of the queens were not slow to accomplish their purposes, regardless of the method or the cost. Queen Nitocris, of the fifth dynasty, the celebrated queen with the "rosy Cheeks," avenged the murder of her brother by inviting the conspirators against his life to a banquet hall lower than the Nile, and while they feasted turned in the waters of the river upon them.

The Egyptian religious life was shared in by priestesses. Their pantheon contained goddesses, who were highly honored. Women were considered to have souls as well as men, and as great honor was paid them in the rites accorded to the dead.

Sacred prostitution, which was so well known among the ancient Semites, was also practised in Egypt. Anthropomorphism was common there as elsewhere among early religionists. The gods were supposed to have their generation in the same manner as men. The male and female divinities therefore had their necessary part in the mysterious creations of nature. The female function in generation, however, was a purely passive one. Just as, according to the current ideas, the father was the sole parent of the child, the mother only furnishing carriage and nourishment for the infant, so the female principle in nature was receptive matter--"the lifeless mass in which generation took place."

"Women," says Frederick Shelden, "are compounds of plain sewing and deception, daughters of Sham and Hem." This morsel of wit is not true of the women of Egypt in ancient days. The women of the Nile were, as a rule, remarkably faithful to their obligations to their gods, as they conceived them, and often to their households and to society. They were limited, to be sure, in their outlook upon life and service, yet religious to a fault, and sometimes moral. It has not been long since there was exhumed in Egypt,--which has proved indeed the most fruitful of all fields for the arch 鑿 logist,--a remarkable prayer engraved upon the funeral shell of an Egyptian lady who lived in the age of the Ptolemies. It is a prayer, the sentiments of which show how some of the essential elements of a commonwealth life have been recognized by good men and women of all lands and of all ages. The prayer is as follows: "All my life since childhood I have walked in the path of God. I have praised and adored Him, and ministered to the priests, His servants. My heart was true. I have not thrust myself forward. I gave bread to the hungry, drink to the thirsty, clothes to the naked. My hand was open to all men. I honored my father, and loved my mother; and my heart was at one with my townsmen. I kept the hungry alive when the Nile was low." Here godliness, support of religious ideals and services, truthfulness, humility, charity for the distressed, honor to parents, and good citizenship, are recognized as the true conduct and held worthy of the consideration and reward of the gods.

Among the Christian women of western Egypt of to-day are the Coptic women. Christianity very early made wide conquests in Egypt, and while the Christian religion has revolutionized ideals and modified customs, it has never destroyed many of the social habits that have had racial sanction for centuries. The Christian church of Egypt is the Coptic Church, which has existed almost since the beginning of the Christian era. The women of this fellowship are of course very different in many respects from the other women of modern Egypt, notably the Mohammedans. Close to Heliopolis is pointed out a sycamore fig tree called the Tree of the Virgin. It is here, according to the Coptic legend, that Mary and Joseph rested with their infant son when fleeing from Herod. Not far away is a miraculous fountain, in which, as the story goes, Mary bathed the feet of the child Jesus. Having once been salt, the spring now became wholesome and sweet.

The Copts have preserved their early traditions, and their customs are in many respects in contrast with those of other people around them. It is the mother of the young man, not the father who usually makes the arrangements for their son's marriage. "She goes among her friends to find a wife for her son, and when after inquiry she discovers a girl whom she thinks in every way suitable, she informs her son, who is influenced by her opinion and commits the arrangements to her judgment. Sometimes the choice of the bride is left to women whose profession it is to select a fitting bride for the man who employs them, and to open the preliminary negotiations. There is naturally a good deal of risk in this; but as women are so entirely secluded in the East, as they are shut out from their legitimate place in society, such an arrangement becomes necessary, and so husband and wife are married without having looked into one another's face." But when once a Copt has chosen a wife, she is his forever. No divorce is permissible. They are one till death.

When the influences that had early gone out from Egypt and made for art and learning in all the lands about the Mediterranean began to return with compound interest from the shores of Greece to the land of the Lotus, the women as well as the men were destined to feel their power. Many a woman had her life lifted from the drudgery of the purely physical life into the higher atmosphere of intellectual pursuits and attainments. Especially marked was this in Alexandria where the great library and university were exerting a powerful influence, and Christianity was making its teachings felt in favor of equality of opportunity. In that great university town, the first Christian theological seminary was established, where both men and women might study the teachings of the Nazarene. Theological discussions at length became so general in Alexandria that some one has said that "Every washer-woman in the city was arguing the merits of homoousian and homoiousian in the streets."

It was in this later period of Egypt's history that there arose one of the most unique of all female figures. For, of all women who ever lived in Egypt probably none can be given so high a place for various attainments and virile powers as must be accorded to Hypatia. She was born of intellectual ancestry, her father being the mathematician and philosopher Theon, who lived in the fourth century of our era. She was a disciple of her father, and had probably been a student in the cultured city of Athens. Returning to her native city she became a lecturer on philosophical subjects, and was recognized as a leader in the neo-Platonic school of her day. She is said to have attracted students far and wide to her classroom, not by her rare intellectual gifts alone, but by her charm of manner, her beauty of person, her modesty combined with real eloquence. Not only in the classroom did she exhibit her power of persuasion and forceful speech, but in courts of law she proved a powerful advocate. Her very eloquence, however, was her undoing, for because of the strife that arose in Alexandria between Christian sects and aroused them to the white heat of controversy and hate, the gifted Hypatia lost her life in a manner most horrible. Torn from the chariot in which she was riding she was dragged to the C鍟areum--which had been converted into a Christian church-- stripped naked in the presence of a howling, fanatical mob, and then cut to pieces with oyster shells. A horrible blot is this upon Alexandrian life and a fearful comment upon the wild extravagances that were sometimes enacted while Christianity was disentangling itself from paganism.

Truly wonderful has been the life history of this land of the lotus flower. Once the seat of the highest learning, by its fertilizing Nile the feeder of the bodies as well as the minds of men; later, the home of Greek philosophy and of Christian theology--it is to-day little reckoned with, except as a prize for stronger powers. Some day its natural wealth may redeem it, and its women put off their rags, or their veil, and exert new power in the march of progress.

VII

THE WOMEN OF THE HINDOOS

The mother of the primitive Aryan or Indo-European stock would surely be an interesting character if we could with certainty reconstruct her from her descendants of the several branches of that family which sent out the Hindoo, the Persian, the Greek, the Roman, the Slav, the Scandinavian, the Teuton, and the Celt. The part these races have played in the world's drama would indicate that the womanhood of ancient Iran could not have been lacking in qualities that made both for endurance and for progress. The ancient Hebrew tradition that Japheth should be enlarged even to dwelling in the tents of Shem seems realized in this far-spreading Aryan family. It is interesting to note that the word for "daughter" in all the branches of this family of languages is the same; the two roots of which it is composed signify to draw milk, attesting not only to the primitive pastoral condition of the peoples, but also to the common occupation of the girl as milkmaid in the days before the several migrations took place. India is a populous country, there being two hundred and fifty million people living in Hindoostan. These consist of Hindoos, Mohammedans, Eurasians, Europeans, and Jews. There is considerable variety, therefore, of custom and condition among these millions. Among those who prefer this or that particular form of religion there is a sameness of social condition, though local peculiarities may be discovered. There is probably no country where the details of life are performed with such scrupulous regard for the prescriptions of custom and religion. The great religions to-day differ among themselves upon many points; but so far as their teachings concerning women are concerned, they are in wonderful agreement. The sacred books of India, the Vedas, and other writings, the code of Manu, for example, were vested with an authority that had untold influences in the shaping of woman's destiny in the land of the Hindoos. Originally, that is, in the earliest Aryan civilization,--for non-Aryan people preceded the coming of the people of western Asia,--women were held in esteem and exerted unusual influence. Some of the most beautiful hymns of this ancient period are products of women's genius. The great epics of Mahabharata and Ramayana, with their wealth of female character, belong to this early Aryan period. Considering her place in later Hindoo history, the great attention given to woman in the Hindoo literature is noteworthy. No country of the Orient can furnish a literature in which woman is given a larger place, or to which women have contributed more frequently. The names of Ahulya, Tara, Mandadari, Lita, Kunti, and Draupadi are familiar to students of this Indian literature. The Mahabharata and the Ramayana are the two most important of the ancient epics of India. Both give a considerable place to women. The chivalry of man and the virtue of women furnish here as elsewhere the base of legendary literature.

"The ideas of the human family are few," says Mr. E. Wilson, in Literature of the Orient, "when the world's great epics are compared, the same old story of human struggles and achievements are sung, though with variations. The same heroes and heroines occur again and again through the world's history; and although in literary merit, in the points of artistic proportions and movement, the great Epics of Greece and Rome, the Iliad, the Odyssey, the ﬃ eid, are found to surpass the Ramayana and the Mahabharata, yet the ideals of love, marriage, conjugal fidelity, are no stronger in the Western classics, and indeed the moral tone of the Eastern masterpieces is more elevated than that of the classic writings of Greece and Rome." Like characters appear in the great works. Not the least interesting of those in the Eastern epos is Krishna, the faithful wife of Arjuna, the Hindoo Hector, a heroine who may readily be compared with the devoted Andromache. The story of Arjuna bringing home Draupadi as a prize, and of his mother bidding him share her charms with his brothers, seems to point to a time when polyandry was practised in India. The method by which Draupadi chose her husband from among her five suitors reveals also an early Hindoo custom known as the Svayamvara. Those who seek the young girl's hand are invited to be present in some public place where the ceremonies may readily be carried out. The company forms itself into a ring; and the maiden, making the round of the circle, tosses a garland of flowers upon the head of the one whom she prefers. The marriage rite is then performed. Much bloodshed was wont to occur on such occasions, because of the disappointment of the unsuccessful suitors.

It is not to be supposed, however, that the choice was prompted by the impulse of the moment or by some sudden fascination. The girl usually knew the records of her suitors, and her selection was based upon previous acquaintance and deliberate preference.

Indeed, in marked contrast with the present customs of India, it seems clear that in early times brides, especially of the higher classes, not uncommonly made choice of their own spouses. This may be seen in the Hindoo story of the faithful wife. An early ruler of Madra, Ashvapati, a pious and virtuous king, was much beloved by his people. He was childless. Many years did he spend in prayer for offspring. The gods gave him a daughter, who grew up to be a woman of surpassing beauty; but, strangely enough, no prince sought her hand in marriage. Her father, therefore, according to the ancient Hindoo law, sent her forth to choose her own husband. At length she returned with the man of her love, Savitri:

"Carried in a fair, soft litter mid the peoples' welcoming, Came the queen and good Savitri to the city of the King."

Among the choicest women of early Hindoo epics is Sita, heroine of the Ramayana. The famous poet Valmiki is supposed to have been the author; but the poem in its present form is supposed to contain additions made even as late as the Christian era, though its earliest portions probably go back to a period as early as the third century before Christ. The Ramayana is accounted among the sacred books of India, and special spiritual considerations, such as forgiveness of sin and prosperity, are thought to be the reward of those who diligently study it. Sita, the heroine, is the wife of Rama, the son of Dasharatha, who had long mourned his childlessness. This Dasharatha, a descendant of the sun, lives in the city of Ayodhya, the modern Oudh, a place of beauty and splendor:

"In bygone ages built and planned By sainted Manu's princely hand."

But the line of the prince is threatened with extinction. He decides to lay his plea before the gods by the sacrifice known as the Asva-Medha, in which the victim is a horse. After the offering has been made with extraordinary magnificence, the high priest in charge makes known to the king that he shall have four sons to uphold his royal prerogatives and maintain Dasharatha's line. One of these is Rama, whose wife Sita was a woman of extraordinary beauty:

"Rama's darling wife, Loved was as he loved his life; Whom happy marks combined to bless, A miracle of loveliness."

And Sita was deeply devoted to her lord. But the demon Ravana desires ardently to possess the fair queen. He hits upon a plan to gain access to her quarters. Assuming the form of a humble priest, an ascetic, he gains possession of her by craft; and, taking her in his chariot, he carries her away to Lanka, a "fair city built upon an island of the sea." Thus Rama, like Menelaus of the classic myth, has lost the woman of his love. Rama decides to make use of a large army of monkeys, with which he will march against the city of Lanka. But the wide waters stretch between him and the island where his fair Sita is in possession of the vile Ravana. Rama invokes the goddess of the sea, and she comes in radiant beauty, telling how a bridge may be built to cross the waters that lie between the royal lovers. The monkeys--as busy as the little imps that reared the temple of Solomon, according to the Mohammedan legend--build a bridge of stones and timbers. Lanka is reached, and Rama begins the fight for her possession. Indra looks down from heaven upon the holy contest and decides to send his own chariot down, that Rama may mount in it and ride to victory. In single combat, riding in Indra's chariot, Rama vanquishes Ravana, and Sita, his wife, is restored to his bosom.

As evidence of the exalted nature of the early ideals of womanhood and of man's faithfulness to the dictates of true love, we may turn to the words of Prince Nala, who even when about to ingloriously forsake his unprotected wife, sleeping in a dangerous wood, spoke thus:

"Ah, sweetheart, whom not sun nor wind before, Hath even rudely touched, thou to be couched In this poor hut, its floor thy bed, and I, Thy lord, deserting thee, stealing from thee Thy last robe, O my love with bright smile, My slender waisted queen. Will she not wake To madness? Yea, and when she wanders lone In the dark road, haunted with beasts and snakes, How will it fare with Bhima's tender child-- The bright and peerless? O my life, my wife, May the great sun, may the Eight Powers of air, Guard thee thou true and dear one on thy way."

Woman occupies an interesting place in many of the early fables of India. Sir Edwin Arnold has translated into English a number of the stories from the Hitopadesha, which has been called "the father of all fables," and may easily take rank with the illustrious 茝 op. Stories which present womanly traits, the tricks and wiles of love, are there, and are graphically told. Such are the fables of The Prince and the Wife of the Merchant's Son, which illustrate how the darts of love, even in ancient India, struck their mark without waiting upon reason or social standing, as the handsome prince, son of Virasena, cries concerning the beautiful Lavanyavati: "The god of the five shafts has hit me; only her presence can cure my wound."

An account of woman in Hindoo literature would be incomplete without some allusion to the drama. This was developed after the Alexandrian conquest and shows marks of Greek influence. In the drama we may discern woman of Brahmanic India from an interesting viewpoint. Of all the dramatic productions of the Hindoo poets, there is none so famous as that of Shakuntala, by Kalidasa, the great court poet of Vikramaditya. As is true of many of the earlier Hindoo masterpieces the exact date of its composition is not known. Some students place this work as early as the first, some as late as the fifth century of the Christian era. The drama of Shakuntala is of interest as illustrating the effect of caste. It is a drama in seven acts, and, because of its importance, its story may be recounted.

As King Dushyanta, King of India, is driving in his chariot through a forest, armed with his bows and arrows, in hot pursuit of a black antelope, a word forbids him to slay the innocent creature. It is the word of a hermit and the antelope belongs to the hermitage. The king is obedient to the request, and is conducted to the dwelling of the great saint Kanva, who is absent upon a distant pilgrimage, and has left his foster-daughter Shakuntala in charge of his companions. The king finds himself in the midst of a secret grove. He stops his chariot and alights. As he goes reverently through these holy woods "he feels a sudden throb in his arm. This argues happy love and soon he sees the maidens of the hermitage approaching to sprinkle the young shrubs with watering pots suited to their strength." Among these beautiful maidens, rare in form and grace, the king observes one especially; it is Shakuntala, foster-daughter of the hermit, half concealed by the trees, but standing "like a blooming bud enclosed within a sheath of yellow leaves." A beautiful girl is she, but the king stands puzzled. For if she be of purely Brahmanic birth, she is prohibited from marrying one of the warrior class, even though he be the king. As Shakuntala moves about watering the flowers of the wood, she starts a bee from one of the jasmine flowers. The bee pursues her, as if to do her harm with its sting, but Dushyanta comes to the rescue; and the fair girl of the hermitage feels some strange thrill as she sees the king, an unusual visitant in that hallowed neighborhood. Off she hurries with her two companions, but a series of happy accidents enables her to cast side glances at the king: a prickly Kusa-grass has stung her foot, she must wait a moment, a bush has caught her robe, she must stop to disentangle it. And love is born. In the second act, while Dushyanta is thinking of his love, two hermits arrive who tell him that demons have taken advantage of Kanva's absence from the sacred grove and are disturbing the sacrifices, and requests that he come and defend the grove from their intrusion. He consents with keen delight and he will not leave the grove, even though his mother requests his presence at a sacrifice offered in his own behalf. He sends his representative, but cautions him to say nothing concerning his love for the fair Shakuntala. In the third act, the king is discovered walking in the hermitage calling upon the god of love "whose shafts are flowers, though the flowers' darts are hard as steel." He tracks the object of his love by the broken stems of the flowers she had plucked in her rambles, and at length finds her in an arbor with her attendants. She reclines upon a stone bench strewn with flowers, she looks pale and wasted. Her maidens seek to know the cause of her sickness, and she tells her love in a poem, written on a lotus leaf. Just here the king rushes in and avows his passion. He tries to overcome her scruples against a marriage, so out of accord with the regulations of caste. He hears a voice of ill omen telling of the demons "swarming round the altar fires." He hastens to the rescue. In the fourth act, Shakuntala is seen wearing the signet ring of the king, which ring has the charm to restore the king's love, should it ever grow cold. Kanva returns from his pilgrimage in time to see the preparations being made for Shakuntala's departure. The old hermit submits resignedly to her going and gives his blessing to the departing one. The fifth act presents Dushyanta, like King Saul, overcome with a deep and stubborn melancholy. He is under a curse of Durvasas, and this induces complete forgetfulness of his wife Shakuntala. "Why has this strain," says the king, "thrown over me so deep a melancholy, as though I am separated from some loved one?" Here the hermit and Shakuntala, who is about to become a mother, are ushered into the presence of the king. He does not know her; denies he ever knew her. The Shakuntala is about to produce from her finger the ring which should be proof of the marriage. But, alas! she discovers it to be lost. "It must have slipped off, in the holy lake when thou wast offering sacrifices," said Gantami, who had accompanied her. The king laughs derisively. Despite her endeavors, the king fails to recollect the marriage. The sad Shakuntala buries her hands in her robes and sobs piteously. At length the ring is found by a fisherman, in the belly of a carp. It is brought to the king, who places it upon his finger, when he is overcome with a flood of recollections. But his wife and little son have been carried away to a secret grove far away from earth in the upper air. The king, conducted in the celestial car Indra, at length joins them. There the royal pair are reconciled and reunited, and the drama comes to a close with a prayer to Siva.

Many of the Hindoo lyrics breathe of love and woman's graces, showing now a high respect for womanly charms, now indulging in humor at her frailties. "The God of Love," says the poet Bhartrihari, "sits fishing on the ocean of the world, and on the end of his hook he has hung a woman. When the little human fishes come they are not on their guard, quickly he catches them and broils them in love's fire." Again, the poet sings: "She whom I love, loves another, while another is pleased with me." A song from the famous Kalidasa will illustrate the poet's attitude toward a woman of beauty.

"Thine eyes are blue like flowers; thy teeth White jessamine; thy face is very like a lotus flower, So thy body must be made of the leaves of Most delicate flowers; how comes it then That God hath given thee a heart of stone?"

It would be impracticable to trace the history of the chief women of the long line of kings in the several dynasties which successively ruled in India. In fact, it would not be possible to do so, even though there might be material important for our present purpose. It was probably in the days of the Mogul dynasty that emerged the most influential female characters in historic times. The brilliancy of the court of the Mogul kings and the prominence of some of the queens and princesses give to this period, the sixteenth and seventeenth centuries of our era, an especial fascination. Akbar, known as the Great, was a religious reformer, as well as a great sovereign. His favorite wife was a princess of a Rajput family, and to her was due no little of Akbar's success. It was through his influence that the earliest attempt was made to prohibit the suttee, or self-immolation of widows, a religious custom which had already begun to dot the hallowed places of the land with little white pillars that commemorated such sacrifices. One of Akbar's wives is said to have been a Christian woman. Akbar's son, Emperor Jahangir, was also wedded to a woman of great force, one who is said indeed to have been the power behind his throne. He called her Nur Mahal, or "Light of the Harem," for she was his favorite wife. It was during Jahangir's reign that the English first established themselves at Surat. Nur Mahal was a woman who knew how, like Jezebel and Lady Macbeth, to take into her own hands the reins of administration when a strong grasp became necessary. Many of the intrigues that characterized the emperor's reign are attributed to her. Coins of the realm were stamped in her name, and at last she was buried by the side of her husband at Lahore. During the period of the Mogul dynasty the queen lived in the midst of the greatest splendor, which, indeed, is generally more or less true of the wives of Indian kings. Jewels were theirs in extravagant abundance. Fountains played for their enjoyment. Marble baths were provided for their comfort, and numberless slaves waited on their bidding. The magnificence of the royal houses greatly impressed the Persians when they conquered the land, or they would not have said, as is illustrated by their inscription upon one of the palaces they had taken: "If there be a paradise on earth, it is this, it is this!" Among the best specimens of architectural magnificence was that erected by Shah Jehan, son of Jahangir. It was he who built the famous Taj Mahal at Agra, his favorite residence. He also erected the costly peacock throne at Delhi. The Taj Mahal was built as a mausoleum for the Empress Mumtazi Mahal, who died while giving birth to the Princess Jehanava. Isa Mohammed designed the building, and its erection was begun in the year 1630. After seventeen years, the employment of twenty thousand workmen, and the expenditure of millions of dollars, the Taj Mahal was finished. It is one of the most magnificent public buildings in India, and one of the most famous in the world. With its dome of two hundred and ten feet in height, its tropical garden, its mosaics and inscriptions, its marble of white, black, and yellow, its crystals, jaspers, garnets, amethysts, sapphires, and even diamonds, it is the richest and most notable tribute of marital love that has ever been erected.

Another monument built in honor of a woman is the famous tower Kootab Minar, the highest pillar in the world, being of red sandstone and two hundred and thirty-eight feet high. It is said to have been built that the king's daughter, from the vantage ground of its high turret, might look out upon the mosque which could be discerned in the distance.

Let us revert for a moment to the ancient Hindoo writings and their influence upon the history of Hindoo women. To the religious books of India woman has to-day no personal access. Her religious sacrifices and ceremonies before marriage are with reference to the procuring of a husband. After marriage she may approach the deity, but only in the name of her husband. Him she must revere almost as if he himself were a god. She hopes that in time she herself may be born a man. Anciently there were in India virgins dedicated to the service of the temple and pledged to a life of purity, like the vestal virgins of ancient Rome. In the course of the centuries the custom was degraded; and young women in large numbers became the dancing girls at the temples, and others openly dedicated themselves to a life of shame at the shrines. They are euphemistically termed "God's slaves," but might more properly be spoken of as slaves to the bestial passions of the profligate Brahmans of the temple to which they belong. Dedication of virginity to a popular deity, through his priest, became common. The young woman was said to have been married to the god, and was given over to a life of shame.

Brahmanism, which has been defined as "the religion which exalts the cow and degrades the woman," has been one of the most potent factors in shaping the life of woman in India. Among the Hindoos, woman has no independent spiritual life. Her hope is in being married to a man. Through him must her fortune be secured, and only in obedience to him can she hope for any ultimate happiness. Woman has been regarded by the sages of India as a snare to man's rectitude and an obstacle to his best interests. Buddha is said to have been seated one day in a grove near the banks of the Ganges, with many about him who had come to do him reverence. As he saw a woman, the lady Amra, circumspect and pious, approaching in the distance, Buddha said to those about him: "This woman is indeed exceedingly beautiful, able to fascinate the minds of the religious: now, then, keep your recollection straight. Let wisdom keep your mind in subjection. Better fall into the fierce tiger's mouth, or under the sharp knife of the executioner, than to dwell with a woman and excite in yourselves lustful thoughts. A woman is anxious to exhibit her form and shape, whether walking, standing, sitting, or sleeping. Even when represented as a picture, she desires most of all to set off the blandishments of her beauty, and thus to rob men of their steadfast heart. How, then, ought you to guard yourselves? By regarding her tears and her smiles as enemies, her stooping form, her hanging arms, and all her disentangled hair, as toils designed to trap man's heart."

Caste, in India, dominates everything from the cradle to the grave, and has greatly affected the life of woman. The lines of demarcation are deep-drawn and inexorable. The social gulfs are impassable. As one has remarked, the only tie between the castes is the cow, which is revered by all. There are four castes. To quote Manu, "The Brahmana, the Kshatriya, and the Vaishya castes are the twice born ones, but the fourth, the Shudra, has one birth only; there is no fifth caste." But there are the outcasts who, because of some violation of caste rule, have lost their social status and are despised by all, even the lowest. The highest caste, according to popular belief, descended from Brahma's mouth, this is the priestly class. The second came from Brahma's arms, this is the warrior class. The third from his thighs, this is the merchant class; least of all are the Shudras people, born of Brahma's feet. The highest caste influences, in a measure, the customs of the lower castes. The women of the low caste are burdened with many outside duties, caring for their children in the intervals. They therefore enjoy no little freedom. The women of the high caste, however, are shut up in the zenanas, and so know little of the outside world.

[Illustration 3: INTERIOR COURT OF A ZENANA From an Indo-Persian painting The zenanas are the apartments of the women, and are quite secluded, the windows invariably looking upon the inner quadrangle of the house. The wives are closely confined to the house. In order to enjoy a social visit, permission must be given by the husband, who is rarely willing to grant the coveted freedom. There is not much gayety about the zenanas, though sometimes there may be music, dancing, and mirth. Petty duties, trivial acts, and idleness make up "the life behind the curtain." The girls and boys are permitted to play together until the girl is about ten years old, then she must begin to keep purdah; that is, she must go behind the curtain.]

The zenanas are the apartments of the women, and are quite secluded, the windows invariably looking upon the inner quadrangle of the house. The wives are closely confined to the house. In order to enjoy a social visit, permission must be given by the husband, who is rarely willing to grant the coveted freedom. There is not much gayety about the zenanas, though sometimes there may be music, dancing, and mirth. Petty duties, trivial acts, and idleness make up "the life behind the curtain." The girls and boys are permitted to play together until the girl is about ten years old, then she must begin to keep purdah; that is, she must go behind the curtain. She must dwell in the seclusion of the women, not allowing a man, not even her own brothers, to look upon her. The Hindoos cannot believe that a woman may be good and free at the same time; she may be good, she may be free, but both, never. The Mohammedan Hindoo women are of course influenced by the teachings of the Koran, which regards the best women as those who never see any man but their husbands and sons, the next best those that have laid eyes only upon their relatives. Very meagre is a girl's educational training. Besides the domestic duties, in which she is instructed that she may be fitted for her married life, the girl is taught a few prayers which may be of service to her in winning the favor of the deities concerned with marital relations, and some popular songs by means of which she may while away the hours. The deference which members of the female sex are always expected to show to those of the male manifests itself somewhat differently in different sections of India. In the northern parts, where the women uniformly wear veils, they can more readily cover their faces at the unexpected appearance of a man, or they may run into another apartment. In southern India, where veils are not common, the women are not compelled to hide from the presence of men, but must always rise and remain standing out of deference to them. The Hindoo woman will not call her husband by name; she uses such terms as "Master, Chosen," and "Husband," and the husband, on the other hand, never alludes to his wife, nor does anyone inquire of him concerning her. The absorption of the wife's identity into that of the husband is complete. After marriage they become one and he is the one. There is little wonder at this when Manu says: "By a girl, by a woman, or even by an aged one nothing must be done." "In childhood, a female must be subject to the father, in youth to her husband, and when her lord is dead to her sons; a woman must never be independent." And the Vedas declare that he only is a perfect man who consists of three persons united, his wife, himself, and his offspring.

The expense of a marriage ceremony is very heavy in India. It is the most expensive of all the festivities of the Hindoos. Among the higher caste the outlay is usually above two hundred dollars. This, for a country where the people are so poor, is a large outlay. Since religion makes it necessary for the girls to marry, two daughters may bankrupt a family. When it is remembered that the father must not only support his wives and children, but also his aged parents, his indigent or idle brothers and their families, the nearest widowed relations, and numerous other dependants, it may be seen that a breadwinner's life in this land of recurring famines is not always a happy one. It is not an uncommon thing in India for four generations of family life to be crowded into one house. The occasion of a marriage is, of course, one of prime interest. It is the only incident in which a woman may become the centre of an event of great religious significance. Then Vedic prayers are offered up and festivities run high. Men dancers or Nautch girls may be seen singing the amours, the quarrels and reconciliations of Krishna and his wives or his mistresses. These are not a whit elevating. The truth is India is not lacking in obscenity, not even in the frescoes of its temples. Though little be given to the Hindoo girl, much is expected of her when she becomes a wife. For, says the laws of Manu, "She must always be cheerful, clever in the management of household affairs, careful in cleaning her utensils and economical in expenditure."

The necessity of bringing forth sons and being a good loyal wife generally may be discerned in the law of Manu, which says: "A barren wife may be superseded in the eighth year; she whose children all die, in the tenth; she who brings only daughters into the world, in the eleventh; but she who is quarrelsome, without delay."

Faithfulness of a wife to her husband and her husband's interests must be unquestioned. Thus alone may a woman find her higher blessedness. "A faithful wife," says Manu, "who desires to dwell after death with her husband must never do anything that might displease him who took her hand whether he be alive or dead. By violating her duty to her husband a wife is disgraced in this world, after death she enters the womb of a jackal and is tormented by diseases, the punishment of her sin."

One of the most remarkable customs of a remarkable people is that of child marriage. Since a woman attains her blessedness, if not her spiritual entity by union with a man, marriage should be early. It is regarded as a disgrace for a father to have an unmarried daughter upon his hands. In Oriental lands generally the marriageable age of girls is about twelve years, the period at which, in those countries, a young girl usually attains to physical womanhood. But in India even infant girls are married by their parents to other infants, or to older boys, or to men. A woman is not esteemed at all till she is married and becomes the mother of a son. Then she becomes at least worthy of a certain respect.

The history of the life of a Hindoo girl of high caste may be thus drawn. Word comes from the zenana that it is a girl. Instead of congratulations and joy at the little one's advent, the mother is reviled by an angry husband because she brings him a daughter instead of a son. In his reproaches all the household join. For has she not disgraced her husband? And is she not accursed rather than blessed of the gods? The little one is hid from the eyes of the father when he enters the zenana, lest his anger burst forth anew. Two years roll around, and the little girl hears sounds of rejoicing and of feasting in the house. A boy is born, and the father's attitude is changed toward the mother, and somewhat toward the daughter; but even yet she is a negligible quantity. The mother loves and sometimes caresses the girl. Occasionally the father, too, will notice her; and when the brother has become old enough, the two little ones may play together. In a short time, it may be between the ages of five and six, the little daughter is arrayed in silk and costly gems. The day of her wedding has come, though she herself knows little of what it all means, and timidly assents to what her father in his unquestioned authority has done. She is brought to the man whom the parent has chosen from his own caste. They look upon each other for the first time, and the little girl scarcely sees him now for her timidity. The ceremony is over, and the husband returns to his own home. For the child wife must be taught the duties of housewifery. Her mother is diligent in imparting the required knowledge. It consists of proficiency in the arts of cooking, spinning, weaving, and waiting upon her husband, more particularly when he is eating. The fundamental duty of marital obedience is instilled with supreme care. At about eleven years the girl wife is deemed ready to assume the serious duties of wedded life. The husband comes and takes her to his own home. If his circumstances permit he is royally seated, it may be, upon a gaudily bedecked elephant, and she is conveyed in a closely covered palanquin. The girl wife is now among strangers, she must make her way as best she can. Life is not always easy for her. The Hindoo mother-in-law at once becomes master of the new situation, and the daughter must be a willing slave. Her apartments are not over cheerful, and the other women of the zenana receive her with chilling indifference or with positive cruelty. At twelve years of age the young wife is in all probability a mother. If the child be a son, she is emancipated from her thraldom to the husband's mother. She is now worthy in the sight of her husband, and if all goes well, her life is lifted to a higher plane.

Since a woman is bound to her husband as long as she lives,--even though the husband himself be dead,--remarriage for her is out of the question. Social ostracism would surely follow the woman who would dare marry again. The man, however, may marry as often as he pleases and as many wives as may be to his liking and convenience. The English government attempted the impossible by the passage of a law--enacted in 1856--legalizing the remarriage of widows. Few, however, were able to face the social hardships and loss of property which remarriage involved. The widow who refuses to marry may often hold her property, even though she live a life of shame.

Financial conditions have much to do with the number of wives which each husband acquires. The Brahmanic caste may marry almost without limit. Indeed, it is permitted to them to make a business of marriage. Sometimes an illustrious Brahman may go up and down the land, marrying girls, always of course within his own caste, receiving presents from the parents of the bride,--who esteem it an honor for their daughter to be wed, especially to one so distinguished,--but passing on and never returning to claim his wife. But the father is satisfied with the bargain, for his daughter is at last free from the disgrace and ridicule of being unmarried; and being the wife of a Brahman of a high caste, the girl will be happy in the world to come.

Since the members of the kshatriyas, or warrior class, are not permitted to accept gifts as are the Brahmans, or priestly class, the former cannot enjoy the privilege of enrichment by the process of multi-marriage. They therefore have fewer wives, the number being regulated by their power to support them. The same is also true of the number of the daughters whom they are willing should survive, infanticide being commonest among the people of this caste.

It must not be thought that every utterance of the sacred books is on the side of the woman's inferiority. A single passage from Manu proclaims that "A daughter is the equal of a son," but the law proceeds to let it be known that it is only through the husband or the son that this equality is realized. This doctrine is true not of women only, for even a man is made perfect only through his possession of a son or sons. "Through a son he conquers the world, through a son's son he obtains immortality, but through his son's grandson he gains the world of the sun." Indeed, "there is no place in Heaven for a man," says Vasishtha, "who is destitute of offspring."

With the exception of child marriage, there is probably no fact concerning the Hindoo woman's life that has received so much attention as the customs which bear so hard upon widowhood. Beginning with the assumption that the death of the husband was sent as a punishment for the wickedness of the wife, in some previous state of existence it may be, it is easy to conclude that the widow's life should be made as miserable as possible. She is therefore maltreated, neglected, and at times almost starved. When death takes away him in whom alone she had any reason for being respected, her head must be shaved, all jewels and wearing apparel are taken away, and instead the coarse weeds of the widow are put on. One meal a day is permitted, and no more. Even the women themselves are most harsh in the treatment of their bereft sisters. For as soon as it is known that the husband is dead, the women rush immediately upon the bewildered, grief-stricken wife, tear her ornaments from her body, shave her hair from her head, and pronounce the severest curses upon her whose sins in a bygone state had killed her husband. They advise her to appease the wrath of the deity by throwing herself with the husband upon the funeral pyre and thus as far as possible wipe out the awful disgrace. Formerly, many yielded to self-immolation, and immediately put an end to a life that otherwise would be a prolonged misery, or at length, driven to frenzy by their thousand deaths of torture, in some way cut short their terrible agony.

There are about one hundred and forty million women in India. At the age of fifteen, more often several years earlier, they are either wives or widows.

Since child marriage is so common in India, there are many widows of very tender years. There are said to be twenty-three million widows in India; at least two million of these became widows in early childhood. Of these, eighty thousand are still under nine years of age, and six hundred thousand have not yet reached the age of twenty. The sorrows produced by religious belief concerning widowhood and by social customs cause many very young girls to end their lives by self-destruction. Pundita Ramabai, in her High-Caste Hindu Woman, says of the widow: "She must never take part in the family feasts; is known by the name of harlot; if she escapes from her home, no respectable person will take her in; suicide, or a life of infamy is inevitable."

Happily, the self-immolation of widows in India has now well-nigh passed away. The English government has done much to break this awful custom, which was thought to be the only means of destroying the force of a widow's eternal misery and of bringing to her any future blessedness. This horrible death, known as suttee, was made unlawful in 1830. But "cold suttee," as some have called the living death which widows suffer from social customs, is still maintained.

From all that has been said, it is not strange that fathers may sometimes be found who will be willing, for so many rupees, to sell their daughters to a course of infamy, or that men may sometimes lend their wives for a money consideration, or that the suicides of females have been so numerous in India.

There are above five million fewer women in India than men. This marked discrepancy may be accounted for by the infanticide which prevails in some parts and among some classes of the Hindoos, notwithstanding all that the government can do to prevent it. Female infants are sometimes strangled, sometimes exposed to wild beasts, or generally neglected. The dark, unsanitary conditions of the women's quarters, and the extraordinarily harsh and unintelligent treatment of women at the time of childbirth, also play their part in the death rate of females.

All this is in marked contrast to the position of women in Siam. Here the seclusion of the Turkish harem and the Hindoo zenana does not exist, and the women are probably the freest, most independent of the women of the East. They openly attend to their duties, bringing their food to market, buying, selling, aiding in the management of the house and field. A man does not spend his money without consultation with the wife, should he prize the family peace: the woman usually carries the purse. Inheritance of house and lands is through the mother rather than through the father--a survival of the ancient mother-right. Women even in this comparatively favored land, however, are seldom educated, except it be in schools established by Christian foreigners. If a woman wishes to learn at all, it must be through her husband or brother at home.

Woman in Burmah also is comparatively free, neither the zenana nor the veil prevailing there. She too holds the purse strings; but in all other respects she is distinctly inferior to her husband and must constantly acknowledge it. A good wife will never say "I" in talking to her husband concerning herself, but must speak of herself as "Your servant." In the eyes of the man, the woman here is not only inferior, but vile, even to the touch. Her garments are polluting to the passer-by; hence, she always draws them more closely about herself as she passes a man upon the streets.

In Assam also woman holds a far higher place than in other parts of India or in Burmah, even among the rude and warlike people. To the Nagas of the hill country of Assam a girl is most welcome at birth and by many preferred to a boy, for she is more docile, helpful, and obedient; she is less expensive to rear and more filial in her attitude to her aged parents. This last consideration is one that counts for very much in all Oriental lands. Instead of the early child marriages of India, here we find marriage at about thirteen, the bride not leaving the parental roof till three or four years after. The wife is respected and consulted, the husband often deferring to his wife. "I will come from the house and tell you," means "I will ask my wife."

At marriage an iron bracelet is placed on the wrist. This is sometimes worn with gold circlets to lessen the sense of subjection. But the iron bracelet does not thus lose its significance, for the woman has everything to remind her of her secondary place in society. Sir Monier Monier-Williams gives the following summary of woman's life in India: "In regard to women, the general feeling is that they are the necessary machines for producing children (Manu, lx: 96), and without children there could be no due performance of the funeral rites essential to the peace of a man's soul after death. This is secured by early marriage. If the law required the consent of boys and girls before the marriage ceremony they might decline to give it. Hence, girls are betrothed at three or four years of age and go through the marriage ceremony at seven to boys of whom they know nothing; and if these boy husbands die the girls remain widows all their lives."

Since the boys soon find out their superiority to their mothers, the latter have little part in shaping the characters of the children, and therefore comparatively small influence in moulding the destiny of the people. Wherever the cow is exalted and the woman degraded a nation can hope for little from its women. "We all believe," says a prominent Hindoo, "in the sanctity of the cow and in the depravity of woman." Unwelcomed at her arrival and often harassed and kept in subjection till her death, she can contribute little to the welfare of her people. It may be said, however, that the Hindoo woman is in the main satisfied with her lot, and is the mainstay of Hindooism.

VIII

BESIDE THE PERSIAN GULF

It is a familiar remark that the essential difference between the civilization of the East and that of the West is disclosed in the status of woman in each of these regions of the earth. Erman, in writing of the women of Egypt, broadly remarks that in the West woman is "the companion of man, while in the East she is his servant and toy. In the West at one time, the esteem in which woman was held rose to a cult, while in the East, the question has frequently been earnestly discussed whether woman really belonged to the human race." But he justly adds, this is not absolutely fair, either to the East or to the West. While in India woman has been denied a soul, and among the Teutonic tribes she was honored with a superstitious reverence, yet not all the veneration can be accounted upon the one side, nor all the degradation upon the other. Among the primitive Aryan peoples woman's place appears to have been no mean one. The early traditions of the women of Bactria, ancient Iran, and the region of the Oxus converge with those preserved in the Rigveda of the Hindoos to indicate a high degree of respect for woman, for marriage, and for the other domestic virtues.

The science of comparative philology has helped us to discover some of the primitive ideas attached to the names of the female members of the household. The root ma, matar, "mother," signifies the creatrix, "she who brings children into the world." The coming of a girl into the countries bordering on the Persian Gulf does not seem to have been the matter of regret that it was so frequently in the Orient; for the name "sister" appears to be connected with svasti, "good," or "good fortune"; while the daughter manifestly held the important place, in the pastoral life of the times, of milkmaid, from duhitar, "she who brings the milk from the cows."

Lenormant, writing of this ancient period, says: "Marriage was a consecrated and free act, preceded by betrothal and symbolized by the joining of hands. The husband, in the presence of the priest, both while the priestly office was invested in the head of the family, and also after the priesthood became separate, took the right hand of the bride, pronouncing certain sacred formul? the bride was then conducted on a wagon drawn by two white oxen. The father of the bride presented a cow to his son-in-law, this was intended originally for the wedding feast, but in later times it was taken to the house of the bridegroom; this was the dowry, an emblem of agricultural richness. The bride's hair was parted with a dart; she was conducted around the domestic hearth and was then received at the door of her new abode with a present of fire and water."

Many of these ancient customs which prevailed in the regions of Irania in the earliest times existed in the various branches of the Indo-European family in their scattered locations. There may be mentioned the fire ordeal, such a trial as that through which the virtuous Sita, heroine of the Ramayana, was compelled by her suspicious husband King Rama to pass in order to destroy his suspicions. There were two methods of testing a woman's virtue. By the first, she must pass unharmed through a trench filled with live coals. In the second, a succession of concentric circles, about ten inches apart, was marked out. A red-hot lance head, or another piece of similarly heated metal, must be carried by the accused woman without being burnt across the first eight circles and thrown into the ninth, and it must even then be sufficiently hot to scorch the grass within the last circle. If the hand that bore the red-hot metal was not burnt, the innocence of the accused was established.

In the legendary period of Persia's history woman performs an honorable and--it is needless to add--a romantic part. Indeed, there has been an interest of romance attached to Persia from the early days when Herodotus travelled and Xenophon gave the world his Cyropedia. Persia's great epic poets, notably Firdausi in Shahnamah, have preserved many of the early traditions of this land. More particularly do the deeds which gather about the name of Shah Jamshid, one of the earliest of Persian rulers, stand out in bold character. According to the ancient legend, it was he who not only introduced the handicrafts of weaving, of embroidering upon woollen, cotton, and silken stuffs, but also it was he who divided the people into the four social strata,-- priests, warriors, traders, and husbandmen. Both these contributions to Persia's early history may be said to be of prime importance in the development of the womanhood of the country. Of this king many interesting stories are related, episodes in which heroic womanhood conspicuously figures. War and love, deeds of daring and of chivalry hold a large place in the Persian legends.

The thrilling stories of King Jamshid's meeting with the irresistible daughter of Gureng, King of Zabulistan; of their love and marriage; the legend of the fair Tahmimah, daughter of the King of Semangan, and how she fascinated and led captive the love of the youthful warrior Rustam, whose fame had come to her ears; the unhappy trick by which she deceived her absent husband, saying that the infant born to them was a girl, so that the child might be left with her,--a deception which ended in the tragedy of young Suhrab's death at the hands of his own father; Rustam and Tahmimah's death from grief; the romantic finding of a queen for King Kai Kaus, a lady who was to become the mother of King Saiawush; the story of Byzun and the fair Princess Manijeh--all these, and more, render the Persian epic literature rich in tales of love and chivalry.

It is out of the long and bloody struggles between the Iranians and the Turanians, who for over ten centuries battled for supremacy, that the early epic stories have largely sprung. There was no prejudice in the ancient days of Persia against a strenuous as well as an amatory life for womankind.

In the chapter upon the women of the Assyro-Babylonian people, the story of Semiramis, the illustrious queen, has been told. So widespread was the legend, however, that it belongs to the Persians as well as to the inhabitants of the Tigris-Euphrates basin. The story was well known in the region of Armenia, and may have been introduced into Persian history because of its political value.

Among the early women of distinction must be named Homai, who has indeed been identified with "the Persian Semiramis." She was a princess of renown and daughter of Bahman, and to her has been given the credit of being the author of a collection of tales known as Hezar Afsane, which comprises about two hundred stories told upon a thousand nights. It is from this collection by the Princess Homai that many suppose the Arabian Nights was constructed. How much of the material from the former went to make up the latter is not capable of present proof, but that the general idea and plan and some of the names, and the groundwork of many of the tales, were borrowed from the work of the Persian princess seems quite certain. Homai is mentioned in the Avesta, the sacred book of the Persians; and the Persian poet Firdausi makes her the daughter as well as wife of Artaxerxes Longimanus. Her mother is said to have been a Jewess, Shahrazaad, among the captives brought from Jerusalem to Babylon by Nebuchadnezzar. She is reported as having delivered her nation from captivity, and has been identified with Esther of the Hebrew Scriptures, as well as with Shahrazaad the Jewess of the Arabian Nights. Professor Gottheil thinks that the case here is well made out by Kuenen and others. The period of Cyrus the Great brings us upon the borderland between legend and history. Very romantic is the story told by Herodotus concerning the mother of Cyrus. Astyages, the Medean king, had a daughter named Mandane. This young woman was given in marriage to Cambyses, son of Theispes. Shortly after this, King Astyages had a dream in which there appeared a vine springing from his daughter Mandane and spreading till it had overshadowed all Asia. Wishing to know the meaning of this unusual dream, Astyages received from the Magi the interpretation that a son of Mandane should some day reign in his place. Alarmed at this, the king called a trusted servant, Harpagus, and commanded that he make plans to put to death the infant to which Mandane was soon to give birth; and the wife of Cambyses was closely guarded. Harpagus, however, unwilling himself to be guilty of so bloody a crime, directed that a herdsman of the king expose the infant son on a desert mountain, where its death would be certain. The herdsman, however, instead of leaving the little one to perish, reared him himself instead of his own stillborn son. The child received the name of Agradates, but later that of Cyrus, who by his achievements won the cognomen "The Great." According to Ctesias, Cyrus, after defeating Astyages, married his daughter Amytis, who had been the wife of a Mede named Spitaces, whom Cyrus put to death. Herodotus, as we have seen, says that the mother of Cyrus was a daughter of Astyages. The two statements may be both correct, however, since an Oriental conqueror would not hesitate to marry his mother's sister if the procedure gave him greater power over a conquered territory.

It was a woman, according to Herodotus, who at length brought the great conqueror Cyrus to his end. Desiring to vanquish the Massaget? a warlike tribe inhabiting the steppes north of the river Jaxartes, he sent out his army, with the greater confidence of victory since this people was then governed by a woman. When the Queen of the Massaget? Tomyris, perceived the approach of the large army of Persians and the work of building bridges across the Jaxartes, she sent a herald to Cyrus, proposing a fair and open contest between the two forces, on whichever side of the river Cyrus might select. Cyrus chose the side of the river next the Massaget? but made use of a piece of strategy by which the Massaget?were defeated and the queen's son, who led in the battle, was captured. Queen Tomyris, on hearing of the disaster, wrote a bitter message to Cyrus, and threatened revenge that would be most direful if her son were not returned alive. Cyrus gave no heed to the threat. Thereupon, Tomyris mobilized all the forces of her kingdom against the Persian army. "Of all the combats in which the barbarians have ever engaged among themselves," says the ancient historian, "I reckon this to have been the fiercest." First, the armies stood apart and shot their deadly arrows. When the quivers were all emptied, the forces joined in hand-to-hand encounter with lances and daggers, neither yielding, till at length the army of the queen prevailed by the destruction of the larger part of the Persian army. Cyrus himself was slain; and as Tomyris passed his bloody corpse, she heaped insults upon it, saying: "I live, and have conquered thee in fight; and yet by thee I am ruined, for thou tookest my son with guile; but thus I make good my threat, and give thee thy fill of blood."

The story of Araspes and Panthea, related by Xenophon, is one of the earliest pieces of romantic fiction. It is told in the Cyropedia, and is intended to illustrate the steadfastness and virtue of the great Cyrus. Among the early gifts to the conqueror was a Susian lady, wife of Abradates, King of the Susians, and regarded as the most beautiful woman in Asia. Cyrus, never having yet seen her, committed her to the care of Araspes till he might call for her. But the guardian fell so in love with his fair ward that he feared the displeasure of Cyrus. The king, however, astutely seizing upon his supposed anger toward Araspes, decides to send him, as if a fugitive, to the enemy, that information might be received by Araspes and communicated to him. Moreover, Panthea now sends to Cyrus a message that her own husband Abradates would himself become a fast friend to her lord, should he be allowed the privilege of coming to him. Thus Cyrus, unlike many another king and warrior, by supreme self-control in the matter of his loves gained friends and subdued enemies.

The kings of Persia, while usually marrying but one legal wife, enjoyed the universal custom of supporting a vast harem, and of inviting into it daughters of neighboring kings. Usually the purposes were peaceful, but sometimes they were of a hostile character. This was the case when Cambyses, having resolved to carry out his father's plan of making a conquest of Egypt, demanded of Amasis, Egypt's king, his daughter in marriage, hoping thereby to pick a quarrel. Amasis replied by sending, not his own daughter, but another damsel of his realm, who, unable or unwilling to keep the secret, divulged to Cambyses the deception that had been practised upon him. The Persian king desired no better pretext for war, and the marriage trick was avenged by Egypt's fall.

The wives of the kings sometimes exerted much influence in the realm, either for good or bad. Amestris, the only lawful wife of Xerxes, is said to have been instrumental in the death of her husband by the hands of two of his chief men. Amestris was his own cousin. That she instigated this murder is not at all improbable, since there was ample ground for jealousy on her part because of the notorious gallantries of Xerxes. Indeed, the Hebrew Book of Esther draws a picture of the corruptions of his court which in general outline is certainly true to the facts.

Royal personages sometimes married their own sisters. This, however, was contrary to the ancient custom. Cambyses, who succeeded Cyrus upon the throne, fell in love with Meroe, his youngest sister, and wished to marry her. Not wishing to fly in the face of the custom of the Persians, he called together the judges of the empire and inquired of them whether there might not be a law which allowed the marriage of brother and sister. The judges informed him that there was no such law among the Persians, but that there was a law allowing the king to do whatever he pleased. Disgusted and enraged, the king ordered his sister to be put to death; so that if marriage with her was prohibited to him, it might not be possible to a lesser man. This was no surprise, however, to a people who had known of the cruelties of this tyrant, whose own brother Smerdis had been brutally executed at his command. Cambyses having died of a self-inflicted wound, his successor, known as the Pseudo-Smerdis, or Gomates, married all his predecessor's wives--a common custom among Oriental monarchs; for the harem might easily be regarded as a part of the spoils of conquest, or of the inheritance, as the case might be. Gomates kept his numerous wives confined in separate apartments, for the intrigues of the seraglio were the bane of the Persian as of the other Oriental dynasties.

When Darius I. came into possession of the Persian throne he proceeded to add dignity to his kingly claims by marrying Atossa, daughter of Cyrus, who had already been successively the wife of her brother Cambyses and of the false claimant Smerdis. Such political and incestuous marriages became quite common in Persia. One might marry not only a sister, but a daughter, and even a mother. At the instigation of Parysatis, Artaxerxes II., her son, married his own daughter.

Atossa figures in an interesting story, which may, however, lack historic truthfulness. Democedes, a physician of Crotona, had healed the injured foot of Darius, and was now called upon to visit Atossa in an illness. Democedes, anxious to return to his native land, sees his opportunity. Atossa, healed of her malady, is induced to appear before Darius and reproach him for idly sitting still and not extending the Persian dominion. "A man who is young," said she, "and lord of vast kingdoms should do some great thing, that the Persians may know it is a man who rules over them." Darius replied that he was even then preparing an expedition against the Scythians. "Nay," answered his wife, "do not fight against the Scythians, for I have heard of the beauty of the women of Hellas and desire to have Athenian and Spartan maidens among my slaves, and thou hast here one who above all men can show thee how thou mayest do this--I mean he who hath healed thy foot." Atossa prevailed. But the expedition was only a reconnoitring party sent out in ships to Greece and Italy. Democedes reached his home, and sent Darius word that he could not return, because he had married the daughter of Milon the wrestler; but the expedition met only with disaster.

That Persian women of royalty often took no inconsiderable part in political and military activity is illustrated by many examples from the days of Persia's strength. Xenophon has immortalized the zeal of Parysatis in her efforts at placing her son Cyrus, the younger, upon the throne, and her plottings in his behalf against his elder brother Artaxerxes. Parysatis failed, but won no small power even in her unsuccessful efforts.

Alexander the Great, on his Eastern campaign, seemed as willing to marry the daughters of conquered princes of the East as to be worshipped as a god by his obedient followers. Indeed, he would frequently give respite to a strenuous life of conquest by marrying an Oriental woman. While Alexander was engaged in his Phoenician campaign, Darius wrote Alexander a letter offering him not only all lands west of the Euphrates River, but also his own daughter, Statira, as the price of peace. It was on this occasion that the famous dialogue between Alexander and his general Parmenion occurred. The latter had advised that the offer of Darius be accepted and no further risk of battle be undertaken. "Were I Alexander," said Parmenion, "I should take these terms." "So should I, if I were Parmenion," said Alexander; "but as I am not Parmenion, but Alexander, I cannot." Accordingly, he wrote to Darius in reply to his offer: "You offer me a part of your possession, when I am lord of all; and if I choose to marry your daughter, I shall do so whether you give consent or not." Events justified Alexander's boast, for both the territory and the daughter fell into the hands of the Macedonian victor. It was not, however, till the conqueror reached the palace city of Susa, on his return from India, that he celebrated his marriage with Statira, a daughter of Darius and Parysatis, who herself was daughter of Ochus, predecessor of Darius. Alexander wished to encourage such unions with Persian women, and went so far as to offer to his soldiers a full payment of all debts to those who would take to themselves Persian wives--an argument which appealed powerfully to the extravagant spendthrifts, but was of little force with the sober and provident of his followers. Many of the former availed themselves of their general's offer and followed his illustrious example. Ten thousand soldiers received presents for marrying Eastern wives, and at least eighty of

Alexander's courtiers celebrated their marriage to Persian wives while at Susa.

The intermarriage of Greeks with Persian women was desired by Alexander as one means of welding together the Greeks and the Persians into one united empire. In the opinion of the Greeks, however, a union between the sons of Hellas and the daughters of the East could not be regarded as a regular marriage; and yet, Roxana, the Bactrian, was exalted to be Alexander's queen. The spirit of the East, however, conquered the conquerors, and polygamy was introduced among the Greek invaders, Alexander himself having married three wives of the East, Roxana, Statira, and Parysatis. The most noteworthy matrimonial coup of Alexander during his Eastern conquest was, of course, that with Roxana. Her son, born after Alexander's death, and called by the name of his father, laid claim to the title of "the great king"; but Alexander's Eastern plans, so far as they looked toward a universal empire, melted away in the early morning of their conception.

After the decline of the Greco-Persian power and the rise of Parthian supremacy, we enter a new epoch in Persian history. The Parthians had long been a rude, nomadic people. Their women were uncultured, and played little part, except in a physical way, in the new era that dawned upon the land of proud Persia. The Parthian women were, however, sturdy, self-sacrificing, and brave, adapted well to the dashing character of the Parthian warrior, whose tactics in battle struck terror to the stoutest hearts, even among the brave Greeks and the well-nigh invincible Romans.

Following the downfall of the Parthians comes, under Ardeshir, the rise of the Sassanian dynasty, which many suppose to be a revival of the once glorious line of Ach鎚enian kings. It was not long before woman began to figure prominently in the new history. Sapor I., son of Ardeshir, or the Sassanian Artaxerxes, as he is called, finding difficulty in bringing the province of Hatra under his sway, receives an overture from the daughter of Manizen, the ruler of Hatra, an ambitious young woman,--without moral scruples,--with intimation that if she were made Queen of Persia she would promise to betray her father's forces into Sapor's hands. The compact was faithfully carried out by the damsel; but Sapor, when he came into possession of Hatra, ordered the traitress to be put to death, instead of marrying her, for Sapor not unnaturally felt that he could not be safe on his throne with such a wife. It was during the reign of Sapor that a new element was injected into Persian social and religious life which was destined somewhat later to influence almost every home in Persia. This was the rise of Manicheism, named for its founder Manes.

This was a new form of Christianity--a syncretic faith into which entered a little of Zoroastrianism, somewhat of Judaism, a modicum of Buddhism, and some Christianity. Manes's teachings seemed so plausible that many were swept away by them; they appeared to be destined to shake the older faiths from their foundations, and they changed many of the customs as well as portions of the worship of the people. Manes was a zealous patron of the decorative arts. The art of weaving carpets of silk and of wool, which has given employment to so many female fingers from that day to this, and the fine embroideries which have made Persia famous are to be attributed in no small degree to the influence of Manes.

The lives of the women of the Sassanid?were not always to be envied. The story, though it may have changed form and color somewhat by transmission, is not an improbable one which tells of King Varahran's anger at his queen. One day, seated with her in an open pavilion overlooking the plain, he saw two wild asses approaching. With his bow the strong man, skilled in the chase, transfixed both of the animals with one well-aimed shot. Turning to his spouse to receive the applause he thought due him, the wife replied: "Practice makes perfect." Angered at the lightness with which his skilful feat was received, he ordered her to be executed, but quickly repented, and simply divorced her from the palace. In quiet moments, he repented of his haste. For years, he had no trace of the former queen, but when hunting one day he beheld a scene which quickly excited his curiosity and admiration. It was a woman carrying upon her shoulders a cow, with which, indeed, she easily walked up and down the stairs of the country house. On asking her concerning the remarkable feat, she replied, as she dropped her veil: "Practice makes perfect." The king recognized his wife, now no longer young, but still possessing physical charms, and invited her to take her place again in the palace. The woman had commenced to carry the cow when it was but a tiny calf, and had shrewdly planned the feat in the hope that some day she might win back her husband's respect. It has been suggested that cows are small in Persia, as is indeed the case, but more probably some small animal, such as a goat or a gazelle, first figured in the story.

Persian kings of the house of Sassan intermarried frequently with Turkish women, and one of the best known of this dynasty, Hormisda, had a Turkish mother. It was he who won the mortal enmity of one of Persia's greatest generals by sending to the veteran a distaff, together with a woman's costume, suggesting that he give up the art of war for that of spinning. The suggestion cost the king his sceptre. The soldiery, however, raised to the throne his son, the many-sided Chosroes Parveez, whose name stands out prominently not only as a foster-father of the arts among the people, but as pre 雖 inent in a long line of Persian kings because of his unswerving love for his wife Shirin all through his long and, in some respects, most honorable reign. His harem, however, was one of the most extensive in all Persian annals.

Modern Persia has, of course, lost much of the grandeur of the days of Mandane or of the mother of Xerxes. Persia, being an inland as well as a mountainous country, with scarcely any railway facilities in the entire country, and no navigable waterways, has been very little influenced by modern ideas or customs. As there are many tribes and nationalities in the land, and many different religions as well, many differences are found in manners, customs, and even in language. Each nationality and each sect continues distinct from the other. Broad differences have engendered social distinctions and sometimes enmity and strife.

No single statement as to the relation of the sexes in Persia will apply to all the peoples of the country. The large majority of the people being

Mohammedans, the customs are very similar to those of all other countries where Islam rules. Among the Nestorian Christians and the Catholic Christians women are unveiled and free to come and go. Among the so-called "Fire Worshippers" of the Monsul mountains, men and women associate in their great feasts, and the sexes dance and sing together. The laws of the people fix the number of wives at not more than six, and, of course, the girl may not choose her husband; but is sold by her parents, though she may remain single by paying through hard labor a sum to the father for the privilege of remaining under the parental roof. Among the Parsees, the modern followers of Zoroaster, who number about twenty-five thousand, woman is given a better opportunity for education than among the Mohammedans. Obedience to her husband is, of course, her first duty; and married life is looked upon as specially blessed, and rich Parsees are known to aid in a pecuniary way those who are marriageable, but lack the material means to make them happy. Polygamy is prohibited among the Parsees, except that after nine years of sterility, a wife may expect another woman to share the home of her husband. Divorces are forbidden, and wives have comparative freedom. The wealthier Persians, generally found in the towns, reside in large dwellings having several apartments. The masses of the people, however, live poorly in mud houses or huts from thirty to forty feet square, with one room and a single door.

Woman's work in Persia, as generally in the East, is multiform as well as menial. The women, of course, do the baking. They use yeast in the making of their bread. Having kneaded the dough, they set it aside to rise, after which they divide the mass into small parts, and with a rolling-pin they roll these pieces of dough very thin, and sometimes to the size of two feet in length by a foot in width, and then stick them to the side of the oven. The latter is a cylindrical hole in the ground, lined with clay and located near the centre of the house. It is about four feet deep, and approximately two and a half feet in diameter. The women make fire in this oven but once a day. The wife bakes once or twice a week, if the family be small, but if large, every day or every other day. This oven, whose top is even with the floor, is also the place around which in cool weather the family gather upon mats to keep themselves warm. The fuel is not wood, which is very scarce, but manure. At first both the smoke and the odor are very perceptible, but when once the fire is burning freely, the impurities of the fuel are drawn up through an opening in the roof, a window, just above the oven. Out of this window, which remains open day and night, the smoke is supposed to go, as indeed it will, if ample time be given. The Persian housewife is thus enabled to keep her house ventilated, but its walls and ceilings soon become very black with soot. In rainy weather the good housewife must place a pan or other receptacle immediately under the window--for this opening in the ceiling is both the avenue for light and for ventilation, hence must not be closed. If a woman wishes to know her neighbor's business, she will creep upon the top of her neighbor's roof--for houses are very often close together, and eavesdrop through the open window.

Weaving is done both by women and by men. The weaving and spinning apparatus, as well as the crude cotton-gins, are in the same room where the family eats, sleeps, cooks, and converses. As a rule, the men weave the light goods, such as cotton fabrics, while the women make the carpets, rugs, and the like. The women are the spinsters, and, with untiring energy, they rise early and spin all day. It is said that a woman of ordinary skill can spin a pound of cotton a day, provided she works very hard. For this she receives, if done for another, about twenty cents.

The women do the milking. In fact, it is regarded as beneath the dignity of a man to milk, if not as a positive disgrace. The women milk cows, buffaloes, sheep, and goats. Butter is made from buffalo milk, which is given by the animals in large quantities and is exceedingly white. Since clabber is more highly prized than fresh milk, the housewife, as soon as she has finished her morning's milking,--they milk twice a day,--heats the fresh milk almost to boiling, allows it to cool a little, and then adds a table-spoonful of sour milk. Speedily the whole begins to coagulate, and the next morning, with the addition of syrup, it forms the customary breakfast. The good housewife finds it indispensable to keep a little sour milk at hand in order to hasten the coagulation. Women residing in towns do their churning in earthen vessels or pitchers, called meta, always using sour milk. Among the nomadic people of the country sheepskins are used for this purpose. These sheepskin churns are filled, and suspended by means of cords from a wooden frame. The churn is thus shaken back and forth by the women till the butter comes. If butter in excess of the immediate need is produced,--and the poorer classes use it sparingly,--it is converted into oil, which keeps its quality for a year or two and is much used for cooking.

The women are also the millers, braying the corn in mortars in primitive fashion, or beating it to meal upon a flat stone with a stone hammer, or, in some advanced households, grinding it in hand mills. It requires two or three women to use a hand mill, which consists of two huge round stones, one revolving upon the other. Two or more women will take hold of a handle attached to the upper stone and turn, while another pours the grain, from an earthen jar, through a hole in the upper millstone. As only a little wheat can be ground at a time, it requires much patience, and the men generally give over the labor to the women.

Harvesting is also done by the women. The season between June and August of each year is therefore peculiarly severe upon them. Their domestic duties must be finished soon after sunrise; then, with their sickles, they start out from the villages to the harvest fields, a mile or two distant. One may often see the baby in its tiny cradle flung across the shoulder of the mother on her way to the day's labor. She puts the cradle down in the shade in view of the reapers, and performs her daily task in the broiling sun. While the women reap, the men gather the bundles and bind them for the threshing floor. At the close of the day, homeward they trudge, tired and soiled by the day's work; the mothers carrying their little ones back to their homes, where the domestic duties of evening are to be performed before comes the opportunity for rest. When grain harvest is over, the vineyards are to be gleaned, and the women are to do most of the work of picking the ripe, luscious branches of grapes, filling the huge baskets and carrying them to the place where the fruit is to be spread out to be dried. In fifteen or twenty days the grapes have become raisins, and they are again taken up and piled away, ready for the market. Wine and molasses are also made from grapes, the work being largely the task of the women.

Just as Persia has its Ruths gleaning in the fields, so also Rebekah with her water pot may be seen daily. In lieu of modern buckets, the Persians are content to have their women take large earthen jars, morning and night, to the public wells, springs, or streams outside the village. There the women fill their pots, lift them first to the hips, then to the back or shoulder, and trudge home with their burden, chatting happily as they go, and becoming straight and strong by the muscular exercise involved. Eight or ten trips may be necessary before each woman has filled all her jars, and so procured the necessary amount of water for the daily use.

There is a saying in Persia: "When cousins marry they are never happy." And yet, as a rule, marriages are within the religious sects. If a Christian--Christians in Persia are of the ancient Nestorian faith--should marry a Mohammedan woman, he would be compelled to renounce his religion for the Mohammedan, as the ruling class would not allow it to be otherwise. Christian parents, on the other hand, would not give their consent to the union of their daughter with a worshipper of Islam. Occasionally, however, attractive Nestorian girls are captured and carried off, and compelled to accept the Mohammedan religion, and married to a Persian or a Turk. Generally, girls marry within their own villages, since each neighborhood is, as a rule, a community uninfluenced and unvisited by people from other communities. Persia is no exception to the ordinary Oriental rule, that marriage contracts are made by the parents--the children accepting with unquestioning obedience the conditions that have been prepared for them.

A young man, being where isolation of the sexes does not prevail, may, however, and often does, show unmistakably his preference for the girl of his liking; and since the communities are often small, isolated marriages of those who have known and loved one another from infancy are not infrequent. The wise parent finds out if the two young people are really in love, though both will often vehemently deny what is plainly true, and tries to arrange matters in accordance with the eternal fitness of things. The girl in question, however, is never consulted in the matter. All girls are supposed to marry, and a youth who remains long single is considered of all creatures the most miserable. As is general throughout the East, Persian girls are ready for conjugal life at twelve years of age, certainly at the age of fifteen. Betrothal often takes place as early as infancy. Parents will sometimes undertake to cement, or at least to express, their strong friendship by engaging their infants, one to another. These two, growing up with the understanding that they are finally to be husband and wife, often become ardent lovers, and the match is a happy one.

When a young man has become of age, which in many cases is very early in life, especially among the rich classes, the parents will send two or three male friends to act as mediators, who will go to the house of the girl in question and ask her parents for her hand. After some deliberation, with apparently great reluctance, the request is granted. To seal the contract, one of the mediators rises and kisses the hand of the father. The contracting parties return to their homes and report their success to the parents of the young man. In accordance with the affirmative report, his parents, within a few days, meet the parents of the girl and conclude the arrangements for the wedding.

The first in the order of preparation is the buying of the wedding clothes for the bride; for these the father of the prospective bridegroom pays. The father must make presents to the members of the girl's family and to her friends. The chief officers of the town must also be remembered. After this the parties make ready for the marriage. While the bride is engaged in preparing for the wedding, there are feasts and revels at the houses of both the bride and the groom. Provision for these sumptuous feasts is made by the groom's father. This feasting lasts from three to six days. The predominating features in it are music and dancing, in a style peculiar to Persian life and custom. Mirthful song is provided by professional singers, to the great delight of those present. After two or three days of incessant preparation on the part of the girl, and of festivity on the part of the ever mirthful guests, the men and the boys, following a leader, go to bring the bride home. As soon as the gay company has arrived, a feast is in readiness for them. A dance in the house or in the yard follows. Meantime, the bride is being prepared to take her journey to her future home. At last it is announced that she is ready, and the musicians play a doleful tune, while the girl kisses her parents good-bye; and bidding adieu to all the friends of her childhood, she is soon mounted on the horse which is to carry her. At that moment the musicians change their mournful tune to one more lively, and off the whole company marches with the bride to her destination. At the arrival of the bride, which is reported by a young man, all the people of the community emerge from their huts and come out to witness the festive scene. After some ceremony, the bride dismounts before the house of the most prominent man in the town, into which she is escorted, and there she is received and entertained with honor.

That night again the town in general enjoys hilarious feasting and mirth, especially in the house of the groom. The next day the musicians go to the different parts of the town where the guests are being entertained, and summon them to the enjoyment of another feast. As soon as this is over, they accompany the groom, led by the music and dancers, to the place where the bride is being entertained; and thence, if they be Catholic Christians, they at once proceed to the church, where the priest performs the marriage rite. The husband and wife are now ready to be escorted to their future home, which is the birthplace of the groom. The rest of that day is spent in conversation and feasting. The female friends of the groom look, for the first time, upon the unveiled bride; and they examine the embroidered work, which the girl has made with her own hands, and which constitutes a part of the bridal equipment. The day being over, the friends depart and the bride and groom are launched on their new life.

The women of the Persian seraglio are more closely confined, if possible, than the women of the Hindoo or of the Turkish harems. In ancient days it was customary to put the women who entered the royal harem under a strict regimen or course of preparation. A glimpse of this purifying process is given in the Hebrew Book of Esther, the author of which shows minute acquaintance with Persian life and customs. "Now when every maid's turn was come, ... after that she had been twelve months, according to the manner of the women (for so were the days of their purification accomplished, to wit: six months with oil of myrrh, and six months with sweet odors, and with other things for the purifying of the women), then thus came every maiden unto the king; whatsoever she desired was given her to go with her out of the house of the women unto the king's house."

The custom of strict seclusion and oversight of the women, introduced by the ancient kings to guard better a pure lineage and to exhibit greater state, has had large influence in Persia, except among the nomadic peoples. The arrangements of the house for obtaining privacy for women are usually the same throughout the land. The first apartment of the house is for the use of men; the second or interior apartment, called the "anteroom," is for the women, and no men are allowed to intrude into the "harem" or "forbidden place"; else the voice of the eunuchs, or guardians, will be quickly heard crying out: "Women--away," and every face in the harem will be at once veiled from the sight of the intruder.

"I am a woman" is frequently given and regarded as an ample reason why a modern Persian girl need not learn to read. Every city or town has its school for boys, but there are no schools for girls (unless they be mission schools), since it is commonly believed that it is a prudent policy to keep the female sex satisfied with their present position in the economy of life. The wealthier parents may, however, sometimes employ private tutors for their girls. The deep-seated line that marks a woman as different from a man appears even in the method of capital punishment meted out to women. While a man who is to be executed will have his jugular vein cut, be nailed to a wall, or be blown from a cannon's mouth, a woman will be sentenced to have her head shaved, her face blackened, to take a bareback ride upon a donkey along the public highway, and finally to be beaten to death in a bag. Or she may be stripped of all clothing and placed in a bag full of cats, which will soon scratch or bite the unfortunate victim to death.

Domestic peace does not always hover like a white dove over Persian homes. Even among the Nestorians, the ancient Christian sect, it is very common for the husband to assert his lordship over his spouse by giving her an occasional flogging. The women expect this as one of the conditions of their position. The failure of this method of emphasizing the husband's authority, however, would appear from the testimony that "the number of women who revere their husbands is as small as the list of husbands who do not beat their wives."

In this land of the ancient Magi it is not strange that there should be many superstitions connected with marriages and engagements. Sometimes it is manifest that the husband does not love his wife. If this be the case, the wife or her mother may consult a magician. He will write for her a charm. This is to be sewed into some designated part of her daily apparel; a like charm is prepared for direct effect upon the husband, and this must be secretly sewed into his clothing. The hoped-for result of these charms is the renewal of conjugal affection. Another charm, which is highly regarded, directs the wife to cut off a few hairs from both her own and her husband's head, to burn them together and from their ashes make a potion which the husband is to be caused, clandestinely, to drink. Some magicians will direct that the love prescription be placed under the hinge of the door of the house, so that as the door is constantly opened and shut, the husband's love will as constantly grow toward his spouse. Sterility is uniformly regarded as a misfortune, if not a curse. Incantations and charms are frequently employed to induce fecundity. The Persian women and Orientals generally have innumerable superstitions. For example, when a hen is heard to crow, it is regarded either as a good or a bad omen. To ascertain exactly which it may be, the crowing hen is blindfolded and carried to the top of the flat roof. She is then dropped through the open window into the centre of the room below. If the hen turns toward the corner of the house, it is considered a good omen, and all is well. If on the other hand, she starts toward the door, it is regarded as portending evil, and the hen is killed at once. This odd custom suggests another, somewhat similar, once in vogue in Persia. Suppose a woman has lost a piece of money, and she suspects that some disloyal neighbor, she does not know whom, has taken it. To prevent a public trial and to spare the innocent the disgrace that may come upon those wrongly suspected, all the neighbors agree that at a certain time every man and woman of the vicinage shall go, one after the other, to the dwelling from which the money was stolen, and in passing, each person shall throw a handful of dirt into the window of the person whose money has been lost. One goes and returns to his own house, and then another, till all have thrown in a handful. When the last one has deposited the dirt he has brought, the owner goes in and finds in the midst of the total deposit the lost treasure; for the guilty party, fearing that he will at length be detected and suffer punishment, and knowing that he cannot be detected if he throws the money down into the house along with his handful of dirt, avails himself of this means of escape from the charge which he fears.

There are no women who have a harder, and apparently a happier, life than do the women of the Kurds. The men of the tribe deny that women are possessed of souls. A woman must not, therefore, be present where a man is at prayer. If she should touch him while performing this hallowed duty, it is thought that she might get the benefit of the prayer. Indeed, it is believed that if she touch him, she obtains his soul. Should a woman be seen approaching, the man at prayer may rise, go out from the prayer circle, take his gun and shoot the woman, and then piously return to his devotions.

The Kurdish women are very dark in complexion and picturesque in their apparel. They use paints and other cosmetics in abundance, to please the eye of their husbands. Their day of toil is a long one, for, after finishing their household duties, they are expected to hasten to the fields to tend the flocks, or to gather fuel for the winter. At night they return with large packs upon their shoulders, enough for two donkeys to carry. They may be seen spinning and singing on their way to and fro, as though their lot were the happiest in the world. Little thinking of the ordinary ailments of women, they trudge along over the fields or the mountain heights; and frequently a Kurdish woman may be seen returning home in the evening, happy, with her huge bundle of sticks for the fire, and with the infant to which she has given birth during the day! A Kurd usually thinks more of his steed than of his wife, who may sometimes be compelled to vacate her place in the dwelling to make room for the horse.

Any account of Persian women is incomplete without some reference to woman in the native poetry of the Persians. No poetry of the East has been so generally admired, translated, and read as the Persian. In it woman finds a large place. And yet, it cannot be said that she is presented always in the light of the brightest ideals of virtuous womanhood.

The Persian poet Hafiz is said once to have been asked by the philosopher Zenda what he was good for, and he replied: "Of what use is a flower?" "A flower is good to smell," said the philosopher. "And I am good to smell it," said the poet. Too often woman is shown as the plaything of man's passion and fancy. Yet the virtue of heroic womanhood in the early days is presented with great force and beauty.

The Persian poets, in the treatment of love, leave little place for reflection, still less for practical considerations. It is spontaneous love, "love at first sight," which they deem alone worthy of their song. "Love at first sight and of the most enthusiastic kind is the passion described in all Persian poems, as if a whole life of love were condensed into one moment. It is all wild and rapturous; it has nothing of the rational cast. A casual glance from an unknown beauty often affords the subject of a poem." These words well sum up the Persian poets' most common attitude toward love and the female graces. The following lines written concerning the beauty of the daughter of Gureng King of Zabulistan, are typical:

"So graceful in her movements and so sweet, Her very look plucked from the breast of age The root of sorrow;--her wine-sipping lips And mouth like sugar, cheeks all dimpled over With smiles and glowing as the summer rose-- Won every heart."

These words, too, were said of a damsel who had won fame as a warrior in her father's army, and her skill, valor, and judgment had made enemies fall at her feet. Indeed, one of the most romantic portions of the Shahnamah of Firdausi are the passages describing the meeting of the gallant King Jamshid with the beautiful daughter of Gureng, whose father had given her permission to marry, provided only it should be spontaneous love which should guide her in the choice:

"It must be love and love alone That binds thee to another's throne, In this thy father has no voice-- Thine the election, thine the choice."

One day, as by chance, the handsome young King Jamshid arrived at the city, a fatigued stranger, and was not permitted by the keepers to pass through King Gureng's rose garden. Weary, Jamshid sat down at the gate, under a shade tree. The damsel sees him, and at once falls in love with his manly form and demeanor. She brings him wine, by which he may be refreshed, and pours out her tender soul to him. Presently a dove and his cooing mate alight upon a bough above their heads. The damsel asks which of the birds her bow and arrow must bring to the ground. Jamshid replies: "Where a man is, a woman's aid is not required; give me the bow."

"However brave a woman may appear, Whatever strength of arms she may possess, She is but half a man."

Blushing, the girl gives over the weapon, and Jamshid says: "Now for the wager. If I hit the female, shall the lady whom I most admire in this company be mine?" The damsel, her heart bounding with throbs of love, assents. Jamshid drew the string and struck the female bird so skilfully that both wings were transfixed with the body. The male bird flew away, but presently returned and perched itself again upon the bough as if unwilling to leave its stricken mate. The damsel grasped the bow and arrow, and said: "The male bird has returned to his former place; if my aim be successful shall the man whom I choose in this company be my husband?"

Just then the aged nurse of the princess appears, and recognizes in King Jamshid him whom the oracles had predicted would be the young girl's spouse.

"... happy tidings, blissful to her heart, Increased the ardor of her love for him."

They are married. And the story of her father's displeasure and of his treachery toward Jamshid, the latter's betrayal and death, the young wife's inconsolable grief and sad self-slaughter move before the reader in a most thrilling fashion. This Persian poem, setting forth the romantic side of female character, is one of the greatest pieces of literature ever written.

The Persian romances delight in making the women do most of the loving and the courting. The heroines are the first to feel passion and the most rapturous in expressing it. They, however, like Saiawush in the Shahnamah, are fond of coyness until they have determined to yield to the force of love. But when the love of a Persian woman has once gone out, the Persian poets usually depict it as strong and steadfast to the end. It speaks like that of Manijeh, the unfortunate Byzun:

"Can I be faithless then to thee, The choice of this fond heart of mine, Why sought I bonds when I was free, But to be thine, forever thine?"

Even the best poets, such as Firdausi, who was called the "poet of Paradise," Persia's great national poet, often present woman's charms in lines highly overdrawn. Such these are concerning the Princess Rudabah:

"Screened from public view Her countenance is brilliant as the sun; From head to foot her lovely form is fair As polished ivory. Like the spring, her cheek Presents a radiant bloom--in stature tall, And o'er her silvery brightness, richly flow Dark musky ringlets clustering to her feet."

Khakani, considered the most learned of Persia's lyric poets, wrote some beautiful verses in which womanly charms find place. Such is his poem The Unknown Beauty, in which occur the lines:

"I saw thy form of waving grace! I heard thy soft and gentle sighs; I gazed on that enchanting face, And looked in thy narcissus eyes; Oh! by the hopes thy smiles allowed, Bright soul-inspirer, who art thou?"

The great price placed upon womanly beauty is clearly discerned in such writers as Sadi, who died about A. D. 1292. In his Gulistan, or "Rose Garden," he tells the story of a doctor of laws who had a daughter. She was so extremely ugly that she reached the age of womanhood long before anyone wished her in marriage, although her fortune and dowry were large--for "Damask or brocade but add to deformity, when put upon a bride void of symmetry," says Sadi. Finally, to avoid perpetual maidenhood, the girl was given in wedlock to a blind man. Very soon a physician who could restore sight to the blind happened to come that way. "Why do you not get him to prescribe for your son-in-law?" the father was asked. "Because," said he, "I am afraid he may recover his sight and repudiate my daughter--for the husband of an ugly woman ought to be blind."

Few poets have written more of love and womanly grace than did Hafiz, who died in A. D. 1388. In the Diwan, which has been compared to a story of pearls, Hafiz says:

"To me love's echo is the sweetest sound Of all that 'neath the circling round Hath staved."

A story is told of Hafiz and Tamerlane, which is doubtless apocryphal. Coming upon the poet one day, Tamerlane said: "Art thou not the insolent versemonger who didst offer my two great cities Samarkand and Bokhara for the black mole upon thy lady's cheek?" "It is true," replied Hafiz, with much calmness; "and indeed, my munificence has been so great throughout my life that it has left me destitute; so, hereafter I shall be dependent on thy generosity for a livelihood." This apt reply of Hafiz is said to have so pleased the conqueror that he sent the poet away with a present.

It may be said, as a rule, that the Persian poets emphasize almost exclusively woman's physical charms. "Women, wine, and song" are, in truth, the chief burden of the poems. The sensuous side of love is most frequently disclosed. There are, however, some exceptions to this general rule, as may be discovered in passages from the writings of Jami. While it is the beauty of the unmarried woman which most frequently and most naturally holds place in Persian song, yet the married life is not forgotten. Firdausi, in his account of the beautiful Rudabah, says of wedlock:

"For marriage is a contract sealed by Heaven-- How happy is the warrior's lot amidst His smiling children."

And Firdausi makes Kitabun say:

"A mother's counsel is a golden treasure."

Examples of the recognition of love that is deep and full of meaning are not wanting among the Persian poets.

Nizami, Persia's first great romantic poet, who lived in the twelfth century of our era, wrote nothing better than his romance of Bedouin love, the story of Laili and Majnun, which has been happily termed the Romeo and Juliet of the East. "France," says a recent writer, "has its Abelard and Eloise, Italy its Petrarch and Laura, Persia and Arabia have their pure pathetic romance." Many see in the story of Laili and Majnun an allegorical or spiritual interpretation. At least, it illustrates the stress which the Persian poets put upon a true, undying devotion, and the Orientals consider it the very personification of faithful love.

The higher ideals are often found in the dramatic literature. Many consider Jami's celebrated Yusuf and Zulaikha, a dramatic poem modelled after Firdausi, to be the finest poem in the Persian language. Sir William Jones pronounces it "the finest poem he ever read." It gives account of Yusuf--the Israelite Joseph--and Zulaikha, Potiphar's wife. In this is disclosed how the human soul attains the love for the highest beauty and goodness only when it has suffered and has been thoroughly regenerated, purified, as was the life of

Zulaikha. The poet, seeing the emptiness of mere beauty, reaches the inevitable conclusion that

"He who gives his heart to a lovely form May look for no rest--but a life of storm If the gold of union be still his quest, With fond vain dream, love deludes his breast."

The Dabistan was first brought to public notice by that enthusiastic Orientalist of more than a century ago--Sir William Jones. In it there is a dissertation on the "Hundred Gates of Paradise," in which occur directions for entering the place of blessedness. Sons and daughters are to be given in early marriage. Milk must be given to a child as soon as the mother gives it birth. Directions are given to women in sickness and in childbearing. Implicit obedience to husbands is strictly enjoined, and warning is carefully given against the woman of unchaste life.

The Zend-Avesta, as well as the great body of Persian poetry, has preserved much of the ancient life and flavor of Iran. There is scarcely any feature in the literature of the religion of Zoroaster, which holds a more emphatic place than that which enjoins purity of life. Domestic virtues are accorded high place in these teachings. Says the Zend-Avesta: "Purity is the best of all things; purity is the fairest of all things, even as thou hast said, O righteous Zarathushtra,--Purity is, next to life, the greatest good." Zoroaster inquires of Ormuzd which is the second best place, when earth feels most happy? To which Ormuzd makes reply: "It is the place whereon one of the faithful erects a house with a priest within, with cattle, with a wife and with children and good herds within, and wherein afterward the cattle continue to thrive, virtue to thrive, fodder to thrive, the dog to thrive, the wife to thrive, the child to thrive, the fire to thrive, and every blessing of life to thrive."

IX

THE WOMEN OF ARABIA

Woman's conservatism has already been referred to in these pages. There is probably no people in the world, certainly no branch of the widely scattered Semitic family, among whom ancient ideals and customs have been more persistent than among the Arabians. Indeed, Arabia occupies a unique position in the world's history. From her territory there probably went out the different branches of the Semitic people, a part of the human family which is second to none in its influence upon the course of history. For one of its branches, the Assyro-Babylonian, probably developed the earliest civilization which has come down to us; another was the most powerful of all ancient faiths, the Hebrew, while two other historic religions, the Christian and the Mohammedan, had their origin in Semitic soil.

Arabia is truly a land of mystery; but for this very reason the interest in her people is yet the keener. She has but few ancient monuments written upon tablets of stone and hardened clay--in palaces and ancient temples--as have Egypt and Assyria. Her records are in legend, story, tradition, and the persistent customs of her people. With the exception of the influence of the birth and the death of a culture which awakened the world and helped to scatter the Dark Ages, and of the rise of Mohammed, there have been few changes in this remarkable land.

Two forces stand out as most potential in the shaping of the Arab woman's character. These may be summed up in the words, the desert and the cult; the latter being in some sense the product of the former. To these may possibly be added a third. That is the war spirit, without which the lord as well as the lady of the Arabian peninsula would have written out for themselves a far different, and perhaps a far less romantic history. For there were those who, even like Khaled, spurn the love of a noble maiden from his "pride of the passion of war." Even love making, which holds an important place in Arabic literature, gives way to what was regarded as the noblest of all occupations, the making of war.

Womanhood, in the so-called "time of ignorance,"--the days before Islam wrought so marked a change in the life of Arabia,--enjoyed a freedom and strength which spoke of the open air and the far-stretching plains. As she followed the fortunes of her nomad chief, the woman was indelibly writing her history. It is in religious ideals too that woman must always find the key to her standing and influence among any people.

Among the early Arabs the female idea held no small place in their religious beliefs and practices, and this is true of the early Semites generally. This is specially noteworthy, however, as Robertson Smith has pointed out, in the olden Arabic cult. Gods and goddesses went in pairs, and the goddess was usually the more important divinity. The jinn, which held so conspicuous a place, were regarded as feminine. In the Mineon pantheon, Wadd and Nikrah, "Love" and "Hate," female divinities, played an important role in the religious life of this branch of the Arabic people. Wherever the female divinity is prominent, woman enjoys considerable privilege and influence in religion, and this was true in ancient Arabia.

The people believed in an inferior order of divine beings--emanations, secondary spirits--compared to angels by some Mussulman writers. These beings were of the female sex and known as Benat Allah (daughters of Allah). Mohammed in the Koran, however, strongly condemned this earlier belief as not consonant with the unity of God, which is a doctrine so emphatically preached in the religion of Islam. Each tribe not only had its Kahin, or "diviner" (Hebrew, Kohen, "priest"), but its Arrafa, or "sorceress."

Woman's sphere in the olden days of Arabia was no mean one. Arabic women have from time immemorial shown themselves, on occasion, to possess a courage and hardihood unsurpassed in history. Arabia has had her Amazons. In prehistoric times, armed heroines of invincible bravery have left their record in the myths of this ancient people. And in the days of authentic history, women have fought valiantly to advance the cause for which their husbands and brothers waged war so fiercely.

The high place held by women in the ancient wars of Araby still survives in the thrilling custom of having some courageous woman accompany an Arab force into the battle. The maiden is mounted upon the back of a blackened camel, and placed in the front of the line as it makes its onslaught upon the enemy. As the fighting men press forward to the battle she sings verses of encouragement to her compatriots, and insults are flung from her lips against the opposing force. It is around this young woman and her camel that the fiercest battle rages. Should she be so unfortunate as to be killed or captured, the calamity is unspeakable and the rout utter. But should her friends be victorious, it is she who heads the triumphal march.

As we might expect, the spirit of chivalry is not lacking in Arabic song and story. In the romance of Antar, the story of the hero's love for Ibla, "fair as the full moon," and the account of her rescue, breathe the spirit of genuine romance. Antar does not hesitate to strike down the man who has "failed in respect to Arab women." The Arabian Nights, though in less degree, has also preserved to us evidences of ancient chivalry and romance.

Hagar, of whose sad life the Hebrew narratives give us record, though herself called an Egyptian woman, became ancestress of an Arab clan and plays some part in Arabian tradition. She was the ancestress of the restless, roving Ishmaelites--a typical Arabian tribe. Mohammed, in explaining the preservation of an ancient idolatrous custom of visiting in religious pilgrimages the hills of Safa and Marwa, where once were worshipped two idols, one representing a man and the other a woman, says, in the Koran, that it was between these two eminences that Hagar wandered, distracted, running from one to the other, till the angel showed her the miraculous spring which saved her boy's life.

Indeed, the Arab legend says that when Hagar and Ishmael were driven from Abraham's tent at Sarah's behest, she was conducted far into the desert, at the place where Mecca now stands. When her provisions are exhausted, laying the boy down, she runs to and fro in despair. In his thirst and suffering, Ishmael strikes his head against the earth, and a spring of sparkling water gushes out. Some members of an Arab tribe, thirsty, and seeking their lost camels, come, guided by birds, to the spot, seeking to quench their thirst.

Never having known water to spring in that locality before, they received Hagar and Ishmael with especial reverence, and bade them take up their permanent abode with them, lest because of their departure the spring might dry up. To Ishmael was given in marriage one of their maidens, Amara, daughter of Sa. This is but one of the many instances of the overlapping of Hebraic and Arabic legends.

Many are the stories told by the Arabs concerning the famous Queen of Sheba, who herself was an Arabian woman. She belonged to that southern branch of the family known as the Sabeans. Her fame has gone into many legends, both Arabic and Hebrew. Her visit to King Solomon of Israel furnishes the basis of most of these. As a lover of wisdom, or the philosophy of practical life, she was drawn to the ruler of the Hebrews, whose reputation had extended far and wide. Solomon proved especially successful in answering her favorite riddles and in untying for her the most knotty questions. Among the many Talmudic legends is this interesting one. The queen took groups of small boys and girls, dressed them precisely alike, and demanded of Solomon that he distinguish the boys from the girls. The king commanded that they all wash their hands. The boys washed only to the wrists; the girls rolled up their sleeves and bathed to their elbows. Thus the secret was disclosed. The Mohammedan legends concerning this remarkable queen are full and minute. Having with her own hand slain the reigning king, she herself, being of royal lineage, was proclaimed queen, and "protectress of her sex." She reigned with great wisdom and prudence, and administered justice throughout her kingdom. According to these Arabian legends, the Queen of Sheba, who was called Balkis, became one of Solomon's wives, though he allowed her to continue her beneficent reign over her own people.

The women of old Arabia, the dames of the desert, were comparatively free, as their open-air life would naturally suggest. The Arabian poets, in drawing the ancient life, so portray it. In the romance of Antar, already mentioned, are found many delightful episodes, in which the woman appears as the loving friend, partner, and counsellor of her husband. These carry us back to the heroic age of Arabia. The custom which permitted infanticide in case of female children seems in marked contrast with the high place of woman in early Arabic literature. This cruel custom is the motive of one of the most attractive of the early romances, that of Khaled and Djaida. The latter, when a babe, that she might not be known as a girl, was called by her mother by the name Djonder, and given a prolonged feast such as is accorded only to boys at their birth. About the same time, the chief of the tribe--and uncle to Djonder--had born to him a son, who was called Khaled. The cousins grew up, both learned in the arts of war, and both made for themselves names for their high courage. Djonder was taught to ride and to fight, as though she were a man, and the very name of Djonder became a terror to his foes. Khaled heard of his cousin's exploits and rushed to see him, that he might witness his skill at arms. But his father, being at enmity with Zahir, his own brother and father of Djonder, would not permit Khaled to know Djonder. At length the desire of Khaled was realized. He was strangely enamored of his cousin, whom, however, he thought to be a young man like himself. Djonder, too, fell desperately in love with the valiant Khaled. The latter chooses the field and war instead of love, however, and leaves Djonder in tears. Later, by the fortunes of war, they meet on the field of battle in single combat. Djonder has so concealed her identity that Khaled does not know with whom he fights. After a long contest of marvellous prowess, neither is victor. Djonder reveals herself. The old love returns. It is Djonder now who resists the importunity of Khaled's love. After testing him by several difficult and dangerous exploits, she becomes his wife.

Of music and poetry the Arabs from the most ancient days have been passionately fond. The nomad life tends to develop both poetry and song. The most ancient bards in all lands were wanderers. David, "the sweet singer of Israel," was a shepherd lad. Hesiod heard the call of the Muses while leading his flock at Mount Helicon. Caedmon, England's earliest poet, was watching his herd when the call came to sing. The Arab bard sings freely of his camel, the antelope, the wild ass, the gazelle, of his sword, his bow and arrows, of wine, and, above all, of his ladylove.

In the famous literary collection known as the Muallakat, made by Hammad about A. D. 777, seven of the best poems of the early Arabs are brought together. Those that most fitly set forth the love of woman are the poems of Imr-al-kais and Antar. Sa'id ibn Judi, the true representative of Arabian knighthood, must not be forgotten as the poet most loved by the fair sex. The flavor of these lyrics may be discovered in the brief poem of Antar upon A Fair Lady, "whose glittering pearls and ruby lips enslaved the poet's heart:

"Such an odor from her breath Comes toward me, harbinger of her approach; Or like an untouched meadow, where the rain Hath fallen freshly on the fragrant herbs That carpet all its pure untrodden soil."

For variety of gifts and force of character there is no Arabian woman who is comparable in fame to Zenobia. By birth she was a Palmyrene, and without doubt, of Arab blood. The descriptions of her personal beauty tell of her black, flashing eyes, her pearly teeth, and the grace of her form and carriage. Her bodily strength and commanding manners gave her influence over all with whom she came in contact. As wife of Odenathus, King of Palmyra, she contributed much to her husband's success and power. She was a woman of rare native qualities as well as of extraordinary accomplishments. She was a linguist, being familiar with the Coptic, the Syriac, and the Latin languages. She was skilled in the arts of war, and gifted with remarkable political insight and sagacity. After her husband's death she ruled as Queen of Palmyra, and personally conducted successful conquests, causing the nations around to tremble before her; and even Rome itself found her no mean antagonist in arms. The high spirit of the queen would not permit her to account herself a vassal even to the imperial city on the Tiber. She had won Egypt, Syria, Mesopotamia, and parts of Asia Minor to her sovereignty, but in the contest with Rome she was defeated, though many Romans had joined her army. The battles of Antioch and Emesa were lost. Zenobia fled to the Persians, but was captured. Those near her were put to death, but Zenobia graced the triumph of Aurelian, the victorious general who led her into the Roman capital in A. D. 271. For years she resided there with gracious dignity and unconquered pride. She was essentially a woman of affairs and as queen was mistress of every situation, giving all to know, "I am queen, and while I live I will reign." As wife she is said to have declined to cohabit with her husband, except so far as was necessary to the raising up of an heir to the throne of Palmyra. The brilliancy of her court was scarcely ever surpassed by any queen, while her personal charms and almost marvellous achievements rendered her one of the most remarkable, if not the greatest woman of ancient times.

In the days of Mohammed a new influence is brought to bear upon Arab life, and therefore upon female character. Mohammed's relation to woman might be of itself lengthened into an interesting chapter. Abdullah, Mohammed's father, was married to a woman of noble parentage, named Aminah. She was a woman of sensitive, nervous temperament, and her son doubtless inherited from his mother qualities which made his subsequent religious ecstasies both physically and mentally possible. Aminah is reported to have been miraculously free from the pangs of childbirth when her son first saw the light. For several months she nursed the infant, but sorrow is said to have soon dried up the fountain of her breast, and Halimah, a woman of marked fidelity to her charge, became Mohammed's foster-mother. A kahin, or sorcerer, is said once to have met Halimah with the boy. "Kill this child," said he; "kill this child." But Halimah, snatching up the child, made away in haste. The sorcerer saw in the boy an enemy of the ancient idolatrous faith.

It was not till the rich widow of Mecca, Khadijah, came into Mohammed's life that he began to make himself felt in the world. Wishing someone to attend to some business affairs for her, Khadijah secured Mohammed's services. So well did he execute his task that the rich widow became enamored of the young man. She asked him for his hand. At twenty-five years of age, Mohammed married the woman who was destined to influence his life so powerfully, she being at least fifteen years his senior. It was not long before Mohammed turned his thoughts toward religion and set himself to the task of reforming the religious ideas and practices of his people. With what result the world knows.

It is Mohammed's attitude toward woman and his teachings concerning her that most concern us here. His love for Khadijah, his first wife, was pure and constant; and his mother he always honored with a most devoted spirit. It is with reference to Mohammed's personal bearing toward the female sex that he has received the most scathing criticisms. How many times he was married subsequently to his wedding with Khadijah is a matter of dispute; but there were probably no less than fourteen other wives, besides the widow of Mecca. Since Mohammed allowed his faithful followers but four wives, it was necessary to explain why he himself should have exceeded that meagre number. The prophet was ready with his reply, that while men generally were to have no more than four, a special revelation to himself had given him the right to go beyond that number.

Among those whom Mohammed espoused was his child wife Ayesha, who lived long after the death of the prophet and took an active part in shaping the political history of Islam immediately after Mohammed's demise. She fostered a burning dislike toward Ali, Mohammed's son-in-law, to whom the prophet had given his daughter Fatima. Because of Ayesha's intrigues Ali was unable to succeed Mohammed as kalif. Abubekr, Omar, and Othman in turn held sway. But at length Ali was victorious, taking Ayesha a prisoner and becoming the fourth of the line of the kalifate. Ayesha in personal daring belonged to the heroic type of Arabian womanhood. In the battle of the Camel, A. D. 656, she actually led the charge. Ali, like his distinguished father-in-law, considered himself an exception to the ordinary rule which accorded but four wives to the faithful, having married eight others besides his loved Fatima.

Among the kalifs there was none whose court was more magnificent than that of Haroun al Raschid. So greatly did he dazzle the eyes of his generation by his brilliancy, that his name became associated with many romances. The account of the wives and favorites of Haroun borrow a halo from their association with his illustrious name. The Thousand and One Nights are replete with the romantic adventures of the days of this brilliant kalif. But the actual life of the women of the Arabian peninsula cannot be accurately gauged by the appearance they made in the stories of romantic adventure.

Mohammed's attitude to woman has, of course, been the decisive religious influence in shaping the history of woman's life among the followers of Islam since his day. The Mohammedans have a legend that when Adam and Eve sinned, God commanded that their lives should be purified by both the culprits standing naked in the river Jordan for forty days. Adam obeyed, and so became comparatively pure again; but Eve refused to be thus washed, and, of course, her standing before God has been relatively lower ever since.

The Mohammedan woman does not worship upon an equality with the man. Not that the prophet positively forbade the female sex from public attendance upon worship at the mosque, but he counselled that they should make their prayers in private. In some parts of the wide territory under the prophet's power, neither women nor young boys are allowed to enter the mosque at the time of prayer. At other places women may come, but must place themselves apart from men, and always behind them. "The Moslems are of the opinion," says Sale, "that the presence of females inspired a different kind of devotion from that which is requisite in a place dedicated to the worship of God," and adds that very few women among the Arabs in Egypt even pray at home.

The Koran has much to say of woman. One lengthy sura is taken up almost entirely by this theme. The ancient doctrine of woman's creation from the man is accepted, and probably was derived from contact with the Jews, the influence of which contact is marked throughout Mohammed's teachings. Honor "for the woman who has borne you" is frequently taught; justice and kindness toward female orphans is repeatedly enjoined. Women should be given freely their just dowries, and should not be omitted from the rights of inheritance; but a son may receive as much as two daughters. The prohibited degrees for marriage are most carefully laid down. Accusing a chaste woman of adultery is regarded as one of the seven grievous sins. The prophet counsels that husband and wife adjust their disputes amicably between themselves, "for a reconciliation is better than a separation." Thus one after another, in a manner altogether lacking in order or in systematic treatment, Mohammed gives forth his commands concerning women. Matters of marriage, divorce, dower, chastity, and the like are frequently before the prophet's mind; but his precepts, while making concessions to human weakness, are far higher than his example. The teachings of Mohammed, even at their best, placed woman on a distinctly lower plane than man, rendered her a subservient tool on the earth and painted a heaven where man's sensuality was to be gratified to the limits of his capacity for enjoyment.

The Arabs, while sensual in their nature, have some strict laws concerning chastity. If a woman be guilty of lewdness, she is summarily put to death by her nearest relative. Unless this be done the family will lose all social recognition and civil rights. If it appears that she has been forced to the crime, the ravisher must flee or pay the penalty with his life, or if not, the life of those next of kin is in danger. If the malefactor be caught at once he is slain by the relatives of the woman. If not he may escape death through negotiations by which "the price of blood" is paid for the woman as if she had been killed. Sometimes arrangements of marriage are effected, but even then "the price of virginity" must be paid to the girl's parents.

The method by which a family purifies itself of the unchastity of a daughter is horrible enough. The family of the young woman assembles in some public place; the sheiks and leading men are present in considerable number. Some close relative stands with sword in hand, and says: "My honor and that of my family shall be purified this day by means of this sword which I hold in my hands." The guilty woman is then led out, laid upon the ground, and her head severed from her body at the hands of her father, brother, or some next of kin. The executioner then walks dignifiedly about the bleeding form three times, passing between the head and the trunk of the body, saying at each circuit: "Lo! thus our honor is left unstained." All dip their handkerchiefs in the blood of the culprit and take their leave, without any show of emotion. The body is left unburied, or is hacked to pieces by the woman's relatives and cast into a ditch.

Often, however, it is possible to save the young girl's life. Someone who is sufficiently kindly disposed toward her steps forward at the critical moment when she is being led forth to death and intercedes to save her life. This protector approaches the girl and says to her: "Wilt thou repent of thy fall? If so, I will defend thee." She replies affirmatively: "I will give thee the right to cut my throat if I commit this crime again." The man is then required to strip off his clothing in the presence of the multitude, declare that he has never seen this woman commit any crime, that it must therefore be the power of an evil spirit that took possession of her; "I therefore redeem her," says he. Then the whole scene changes from one of tragic solemnity to one of intense joy. The girl returns to the bosom of her family, reinstated; and no one thereafter has the right to cast any reflections upon her past life.

Pierrotti, in his Customs and Traditions of Palestine, tells of a scene witnessed by him when architect-engineer to Surraya Pasha, of Jerusalem. During a visit to Hebron in company with some Armenian gentlemen, he found the whole community stirred. A youth of eighteen had met in the fields a girl of fifteen, who was betrothed, and had tried to kiss her without her consent. She told her parents of the young man's misconduct. The families belonged to different clans or districts, and so were enemies. Efforts on the part of the boy's parents, through the sheiks of the two communities, were unavailing, though the father entreated earnestly for his son, and even promised to give up all he had as a ransom for his life. The girl's father demanded the boy's blood as propitiation for the wrong. And so, in the presence of an assembled crowd, the parent drew his sword and struck off his child's head, without a tear, saying: "Thus wipe I away every stain from my family." Overcome, he then instantly swooned away. His friends restored him to life, but his reason had fled. A clan war at once commenced, and those who had demanded the youth's destruction were slain in the strife.

Concerning the slaying of a woman, there are certain customs which sound strange to the Western ear, but are in keeping with the general law of "the price of blood" which prevailed among the ancient Hebrews, though in a somewhat modified form. If a man should be so unfortunate as to kill a woman, the members of the family that is wronged seek revenge, just as is the case should a man be slain, but "the price of blood" is never so high in case of the woman, it being about two thousand piastres, or about eighty dollars. This sum goes largely to the relatives of the woman. If the woman be married, the husband's damage is measured at eight hundred piastres and a silk dress. Should the murdered woman be pregnant, the slayer is amerced as if he had killed two. If the offspring would have been a boy, it is as though a woman and a man were slain, and "the price of blood" is so measured. If it would have been a daughter, the smaller price is charged, the father receiving the full price for the child and his eight hundred piastres for the murdered wife. Should it be a maiden, however, who has been slain, arrangement is often made whereby a sister of the slayer is given by her family to the brother of the slain as his wife; or if this arrangement is not feasible, the price of a woman is paid as first described.

A very curious custom exists among the Arabs in connection with the ancient "law of asylum." They recognize the right of sanctuary for those upon whom summary vengeance may be taken for some blood crime. But flight is often exceedingly dangerous because of the possibility of ambuscade along the way; and even when a village which owes protection to a fugitive undertakes to give him safe escort, the defenders may be overcome and the offender slain. Under such circumstances, it is customary to give him over to the escort of two women, who are his defenders. For it is a point of honor among Arabs not to attack or harm anybody or anything that has been placed under the protection of a woman.

That the modern Arab sometimes, however, has great confidence in the power of his wives, over others at least, may be illustrated by an amusing incident told by Loftus. During his researches his party was attacked by a company of Arabs, on account of which some of the assaulting party had been seized and lodged in prison. One of the chief sheiks of the country came to make friends with the explorer and to entreat for the release of the culprits. This was refused. Later a coup was conceived. Loftus looked out and saw the sheik's harem, in most radiant costumes, approaching the tent in single file, led by the sheik and a black eunuch. Thus the Arab hoped to appeal to Occidental chivalry through the prayers of the masked beauties who surrounded the tent, declaring they would not raise the siege till the occupant yielded to their entreaties.

The rich Mohammedan ladies are far less industrious than the poorer classes. Entering the harem at the tender age of twelve to fourteen years, the young woman is condemned to a life of sloth and sensuality. There is little opportunity for self-improvement or for enjoyments of a high order. They eat, drink, gossip, suckle their young, quarrel, plot, and eke out a miserable existence--always under the control of their masters.

The country women have greater freedom and far more influence with their husbands than do the women of the harem. Polygamy among the former class is rare, and hence the women are more highly regarded than those of the city. The peasant woman is industrious, engaged in some useful employment about the house or in the field. She buys and sells and gets gain for her husband and her home, and often is highly esteemed by him; but he will not let you know it, if he can avoid doing so. In public he always assumes the attitude of superiority. If but one can ride, it is the man and the children who sit upon the beast; the woman walks along at the side, carrying a bundle on her head or a baby at her breast--sometimes jogging along with both. If Arab and wife must both walk with burdens, the man carries the lighter load. And the woman must prepare the meal at the journey's end, while her lord reposes--and smokes. Excavators in the East have frequently found Arab girls who desired work, and with their baskets they would for hours carry out the earth with endurance apparently equal to that of the men.

The Arab girls, as a rule, grow up in ignorance. It is not thought worth while to educate the daughter; and, indeed, it is regarded by many as destructive of the best order of society to give woman any opportunity which may cause her to desire to usurp the power which heaven has placed in the hands of men. There is, accordingly, little enlightened housekeeping, little to stimulate a woman's mind, little opportunity here for "the hand that rocks the cradle" to move the world. Sons grow up with little respect for their mothers, for there is nothing to make it otherwise. The husband, should he wish to divorce himself from his wife, simply orders her to leave his house, and his will is law. Civil government takes no cognizance of matrimonial affairs, and religious authority allows the husband to do much as he may see fit in his own house.

[Illustration 4: AN ORIENTAL WOMAN'S PASTIME After the painting by Frederick A. Bridgman She is not a companion, but only a gilded toy, a decorative object.... Among the higher class she is still kept in strict seclusion, and her time is passed in luxurious idleness, save for the hours she employs at her embroidery or tapestry. The garden, with its heavily perfumed blossoms, pleases her; the ceaseless plash of the fountain falls musically on her ear; all her physical needs are ministered to. But everything conduces to the dreaminess of her nature, to slothful habits; her activities are fettered by the law of Mohammed. After all, her garden is but an exquisite prison.]

The women of the Arabs, like the men, are fond of tattooing their bodies, regarding the figures they stamp into their flesh as highly ornamental, though perhaps originally there was a religious significance in them. The figure to be imprinted is first drawn upon a block of wood and blackened with charcoal. This is then impressed upon some part of the body, and then the outlines are pricked with fine needles which have been dipped into an ink made of gunpowder and ox-gall. The whole is subsequently bathed with wine, and the figure is marked indelibly.

Even the poor are very fond of personal ornaments. Chains, rings, necklaces, gold thread, may be seen in abundance, if not in costliness. It is not unusual for an Arab woman, though clothed in tattered raiment, to wear several rings of silver. But if this metal be beyond her means, then of iron or copper and sometimes of glass. Ornaments of variously colored glass are very popular among Arab women; often they can afford no other. Even bracelets are made of this material, and are much worn. Some of the nomadic tribes still wear anklets.

The women of the desert are often seen with nose-drops, or rings in one or the other side of their nostrils, which in consequence tends to droop like the ear. This custom prevails in other parts of the East, more particularly among those whose occupation is thought to call for much ornamentation, such as the dancing girls and odalisques. The ancient Hebrews sometimes used to put rings in swines' snouts for practical reasons, as indeed the Arabs do to-day in the noses of horses, mules, and asses to aid in evaporating the moisture from the nostrils, but the beauty or the utility of a ring in an Arab woman's nose has never been satisfactorily determined.

The Arab women of good quality do not, as a rule, wear their hair very long. It usually reaches about to the neck, and is tied with a colored ribbon. Many of the poorer and less cleanly among them, however, wear their tresses long, ill-kempt, and filthy. The men often think more of their beards than do the women of their locks.

The favorite flower is that of the shrub called Al henna. It is the plant from which is obtained a dye much used by Oriental ladies upon their skin and nails as a cosmetic. The manner of preparation is thus described: "The young leaves of the shrub are boiled in water, then dried in the sun, and reduced to a powder which is of a dark orange color. After this has been mixed with warm water, it is applied to the skin." The use of henna is very old; and when the woman has finished the work of art--she herself being the subject--she looks, as one has said, like a vampire stained with the blood of its victim. The flower of Alhenna, however, is beautiful and strongly fragrant--reminding one in appearance of clusters of many-colored grapes. These blossoms are used as ornaments for the hair and as decorations for the houses, the fragrance often conquering the malodorous atmosphere of many ill-kept, uncleanly homes.

As is the custom with Oriental ladies generally, the women in riding place themselves astride the beast, like a man, and seldom present a graceful appearance to a Western eye. Loftus has thus described an Arab lady as she sits astride the patient mule: "Enveloped in the ample folds of a blue cotton cloak, her face (as required by the strict injunctions of the Koran) concealed under a black or white mask, her feet encased in wide yellow boots, and these in turn thrust into slippers of the same color, her knees nearly on the level with her chin, and her hands holding on to the scanty mane of the mule--an Eastern lady is the most uncouth and inelegant form imaginable."

Mohammedans are never seen walking with their wives in the street, and are seldom seen in company with them or any other woman in any public place. Should a man and his wife have occasion to go to any place at the same time, he goes in advance and she follows on behind him. Jessup, in The Women of the Arabs, gives the following explanation advanced by a Syrian of the aversion which the men feel with reference to walking in public with women:

"You Franks can walk with your wives in public, because their faces are unveiled, and it is known that they are your wives, but our women are so closely veiled that if I should walk with my wife in the street, no one would know whether I was walking with my own wife or another man's. You cannot expect a respectable man to put himself in such an embarrassing position."

If inquiries are made by one man of another concerning his family, the boys and the beasts are invariably mentioned first; the wife last of all. Among the ancient Arabs the birth of a female infant was looked upon as little short of a domestic calamity and sometimes the infant was not allowed to live. The horrible custom, wad-el-benat, of burying infant daughters alive grew out of an unwillingness of parents to share the scant support of the home with the newcomer, or, as has been suggested, from ferocious pride, or false sentiments of honor, fearing the shame that might come should the girl be carried off and dishonored by the enemies of their tribe. The birth of a son, however, was considered the occasion of great rejoicing. The daughters of the modern Arabs are usually well cared for, though apparently with little affection. They are useful in agricultural pursuits, and they are for sale as wives when they become of a marriageable age. Their marketable value is determined by their rank, their fortune, or their beauty. Among the Arabs marriage is seldom an affair of the heart, but is purely a commercial transaction. Three thousand piastres, or about one hundred and twenty dollars, is regarded as a good price to pay for a wife. The price is generally less. The father of the young man pays the bill; his wealth regulating somewhat the amount paid. The parents of the young couple make all the arrangements, though generally assisted by relatives and interested friends. Much bargaining and delay are often gone through with as a matter of course. If the whole sum finally agreed upon cannot be paid in a lump sum, the parties of the first and the second part fix upon the size and frequency of the instalments; the bride being claimed only when the last instalment has been paid.

The time for the wedding is next settled upon, whether it be days, weeks, months, or years in advance. When that event is at length celebrated, the Arab love of feasting has full opportunity to give itself rein. Days are spent in these rounds of pleasure before the young couple settle down to the stern facts of practical copartnership.

The Arab women have a number of folk songs which are sung by them at weddings and at the birth of children. Some of these may be here quoted as revealing the Arab woman's idea of physical grace and of womanly virtue, and of those qualities which are desirable in the wife and the mother. Here is a song to the bride:

"Go thou, where thy destiny leads thee, O fair bride! Tread delicately on the carpets. Should thy spouse speak to thee, what wilt thou answer? Tell him thou art his, thou lovest him and he is thy delight"

Again, they sing:

"Oh yes, she is welcome! Let us hail the arrival of her whose eyes shine with beauty; Whose form is graceful; tall as a young palm tree, Who can shut the window without a stool!"

The rejoicing in maternity, and especially in the birth of sons, is notable among the Arabs. The women sing:

"Behold the wife hath brought forth; She has risen from the bed whereon she reposed, whereon she slept! She hath brought into the world a child, the fairest of boys; He will learn to play with the sword."

"No sorrow or harm shall come to thee if thou hast sons. God will give them to thee. He will make thee glad, Esteemed and honored throughout the country; Thou who art in the race as a gazelle."

Between the verses of the songs, the women who are not singing will repeat the refrain:

"La, la, la, la," etc.,

to emphasize their sympathy with the sentiments just sung.

Because of a deep reverence for the mystery of life, the Arabs give to the woman a separate tent or hut during the period of childbirth, and there she must remain for a period. There is a strong superstition concerning the results that might come from seeing or touching her or her belongings during the time of this separation.

In the naming of children, family names are not given, but individual names, to which is often added the name of the father, and sometimes that of the mother. The latter is probably the older, and many ethnologists believe it to have once been the universal custom among the Arabs; pointing to a day when polyandry prevailed, when it was customary for women to have several husbands, if they were not indeed the common property of the tribe.

The influence of the nomadic life of the ancient Arabians still has its power over the modern Arab if he be true or a dweller in tents. These desert roamers despise those Arabs who are engaged in the arts of husbandry. Dr. A. H. Keane, quoting from Junker, gives the following evidence of this prejudice: "In the eyes of his fellow tribesmen, the humblest nomad would be degraded by marriage with the daughter of the wealthiest bourgeois." But, as he adds: "Necessity knows no law, hunger pinches, and so these proud and stubborn were fain ... to renounce the free and lawless life of the solitude and at least partly turn to agriculture for several months in the year."

The Arabs are proverbially a hospitable people. Let a stranger once eat with an Arab family and he is a friend; certainly so long as the food is thought to remain a part of his body. But since the patriarchal idea survives, man is absolutely lord of his own house. Hence, in the house, the inequality of the sexes is most noticeable. The Moslem wife never sits down to a meal with her husband if any male guest be present; and should the husband be very strict and formal in his habits, she is not permitted to eat with her lord, even when there is no guest. It is her pleasure to serve. When the master of the house has finished his repast, he allows what remains to go to the rest of the family. By this the husband does not mean to be selfish at all; but customs which have prevailed for time out of mind give to woman an inferior place as a matter of course. But the guest is never turned away empty. Even in the poorest houses, the Moslems will offer the visitor a cup of black coffee, and it may be cigarettes.

Polygamy was common in ancient Arabia. In earlier days every man might marry as many wives as he could take care of, and the length of the wifehood was solely in the husband's hand. The family possessions were his property, and should he die, his widow was looked upon as a part of the estate. Unions between mothers and step-sons were not infrequent. Mohammed numbered this, however, among the "shameful marriages."

Sir William Muir, in his Annals of the Early Caliphate, says: "Polygamy and secret concubinage are still the privilege, or the curse of Islam, the worm at its root, the secret of its fall. By these the unity of the household is fatally broken, and the purity and virtue weakened of the family tie; the vigor of the dominant classes is sapped; the body politic becomes weak and languid excepting for intrigue; and the throne itself liable to fall a prey to doubtful or contested successors." "Hardly less injurious," says he, "is the power of divorce, which can be exercised without the assignment of any reason whatever, at the mere word and will of the husband. It not only hangs over each individual household like the sword of Damocles, but affects the tone of society at large; for even if not put in force, it cannot fail as a potential influence, existing everywhere, to weaken the marriage bond, and detract from the dignity and self-respect of the sex at large."

Mohammed's complete misunderstanding of the true relation of the sexes has had much to do with the degraded position of woman in Moslem lands, and the complete failure of Islamic social life. It is woman that makes or unmakes society. She is the keystone of the arch, not the mudsill.

Mohammed's state of mind regarding woman is universal among his followers, whether in Algeria, Tunis, or Morocco, in the land of the Lotus, in the Ottoman Empire, or in the lesser Mohammedan dominions. The customs springing from this state are, of course, modified among the different peoples, as, for instance, among the Moors through the admixture of Spanish and Moorish blood, which resulted in a somewhat better appreciation of woman. Yet she is not a companion, but only a gilded toy, a decorative object, to be fitfully enjoyed or waywardly put aside. Among the higher class she is still kept in strict seclusion, and her time is passed in luxurious idleness, save for the hours she employs at her embroidery or tapestry. The garden, with its heavily perfumed blossoms, pleases her; the ceaseless plash of the fountain falls musically on her ear; all her physical needs are ministered to. But everything conduces to the dreaminess of her nature, to slothful habits; her activities are fettered by the law of Mohammed. After all, her garden is but an exquisite prison.

By placing women upon so far lower a plane of social and religious life than man, Mohammedanism has not only degraded the female sex, but has disrupted, if not destroyed, those healthy family relations which lie at the very foundation of all social progress and national greatness.

X

THE TURKISH WOMEN

Out of the ruins of the Seljuk domination arose the Turkish Empire, founded by Ottoman, or Osman I., a nomad chieftain of great prowess, after whom the Ottoman Empire derived its name. Among the very first events narrated concerning the life of this important Turk was one of romance, for Ottoman was not only a bold warrior, but a brave lover, and withal, like the young Hebrew Joseph, a dreamer. In the little village of Itburuni there lived a learned doctor of the law, a man of aristocratic blood, one Edebali, with whom it is said Ottoman loved to converse, not only because of the gentleman's fine personal qualities, but because Edebali had a daughter, whom many named Kamariya, or "Brightness of the Moon," because of her beauty; but most called her Mal Khatum, or "Lady Treasure," on account of her pleasing personality. But the learned sheik did not take kindly to Ottoman's advances, for he had not yet "won his spurs," and his authority was not recognized by neighboring princes. Fortunately, a timely dream--that potent argument which is so effectual among the people of the East--came to Ottoman's aid in the pursuit of his suit. The dream is thus recorded: "One night Ottoman, as he slumbered, thought he saw himself and his host stretched upon the ground, and from Edebali's breast there seemed to rise a moon which waxing to the full, approached the prostrate form of Ottoman and finally sank to rest on his bosom. Thereat from out his loins there sprang forth a tree, which grew taller and taller, raised its head and spread out its branches till the boughs overshadowed the earth and the seas. Under the canopy of leaves towered forth mighty mountains, Caucasus, Atlas, Taurus, and H 鎚 us, which held up the leafy vault like four great tent poles, and from their sides flowed royal rivers, Nile, Danube, Tigris, and Euphrates. Ships sailed upon the waters, harvests waved upon the fields, the rose, and the cypress, flowers and fruits delighted the eye, on the boughs birds sang their glad music. Cities raised domes and minarets toward the green canopy; temples and obelisks, towers and fortresses lifted their high heads, and on their pinnacles shone the golden crescent. And behold as he looked, a great wind arose and dashed the crescent against the crown of Constantine, that imperial city which stood at the meeting of the two seas and two continents, like a diamond between sapphires and emeralds, the centre jewel of the ring of the Empire. Ottoman was about to put the dazzling ring upon his finger when he awoke." The story of the wondrous dream was told to the father of the fair Mal Khatum. He was at once convinced that the Fates had marked Ottoman for future greatness and for wide dominion. The moon-faced damsel fell a prize to the inevitable conqueror, son of Ertoghrul. Another early incident in Ottoman's career may be of interest in this volume upon the women of Turkey. Ottoman understood that a number of his rivals at arms were to be present at a certain wedding to be celebrated at Bilejik, in the year 1299; and that the event was to be made the occasion of his being entrapped and slain. Learning of the conspiracy against him, he secured for forty women of the Ottoman clan admission to the festivities. When all present were engrossed in the ceremonies of the hour, these forty sturdy warriors cast aside their female attire and not only captured the entire garrison, but also the fair maiden whose nuptials were being celebrated. She was a young Greek lady named Nenuphar, or "the Lotus Blossom," who afterward became the mother of Murad I. Ottoman now descended like an avalanche upon his rivals and their territory, extending his dominion even to Mount Olympus.

It is to Arabia and to Persia that Turkey owes most of its civilization, its religion, its literature, its laws, its manners, and its customs. Beginning with a Tartar basis, Turkish life has been chiefly shaped under the influence of a religion and a literature. As for the first, the debt is chiefly to Arabia; for the second, Persia must have the larger share of credit. Since these two forces, religion and literature, are doubtless the most effective in shaping the ideals of womanhood, and so in developing the female character among any people, we are compelled to look to the ancient lands of Persia and Arabia for the springs of Turkish life.

Remembering the kinship of Turkish literature to the Arabic and Persian, it would not be difficult to surmise that woman would hold no insignificant place in the literature of Turkey. While there are as many as twenty-five different written languages used in the Empire, the literary language is a product of the original Tartaric tongue and strong Persian and Arabic elements. Very much of the romantic material that goes to make up the Turkish literature is drawn from such early stories as the great Persian epic Shahnamah.

The romance of Laili and Majnun has made a deep impression in Turkish literature. Fuzuli of Bagdad, one of the greatest of Turkish poets, has reproduced the strong love of these characters of old Persian legend, besides giving to the nation's literature many ghazels in which fondness for the virtue of woman is presented with characteristic Eastern passion.

The Persian lady also figures in the work of Kemal Bey, who was regarded in his lifetime as "a shining star in the Turkish literary world," and one who did much to arouse the Turks to enthusiasm for their native country. He was the author of a trivial novel Tzesmi, of high repute in Turkish literary circles, in which a Turkish warrior of poetic talent and a Persian princess figure.

There are numerous love ballads of Moorish origin that are highly prized and have greatly influenced Turkish literature, such as Fatima's Love, Zaida's Love, Zaida's Inconstancy, Zaida's Lament, Guhala's Love, and the like; also much Moorish romance, as The Zefri's Bride. So we find Turkish poems breathing of love and womanly charms. Among such productions is that of Ghalib, whose Husn-u-Ashk, or Beauty and Love, is regarded as one of the finest productions of Turkish genius.

It must be remembered, however, in reading Turkish poetry of love that there is often, if not indeed generally, beneath what seems to be a sensuous and even voluptuous song or romance an allegorical or mystical significance. God is the Fair One whose presence the heart craves, and whose veil the suitor would see cast aside that his perfect beauty may be revealed to the worshipper. Man, therefore, is the lover; the tresses are the mystery of the divine character; the ruby lip is the sought-for Word of God; wine is the divine love; the zephyr is the breathing of His spirit; and so on. And yet, that many

Turkish, as is true of many Arab and Persian, poems are upon a low moral level of human passion, and are revolting to the ethical sense of the more sensitive natures, is not to be disputed.

Fame in poetry has not been unknown to Turkish women. Notable among these literary women of Turkey is Fatima Alie, daughter of the former state historiographer Dzevdet Pacha, whose history of the Ottoman Empire takes high rank. In Fatima Alie, Turkish womanhood finds one of its staunchest champions.

Zeyneb Effendi was a royal poetess in the days of Mohammed the Conqueror. She recounted in glowing lines her hero's achievements. So also Mirhi Hanum was a poetess of talent. She was born of a wealthy father, a grand vizir. She was so unfortunate as to have had as a lover one who did not reciprocate her passion. She, therefore, sung her young life out in avowed virginity, wearing an amber necklace, symbolizing her eternal choice of celibacy. Among other poetesses of note may be mentioned Sidi, who died in the year 1707, the authoress of Pleasures of Sight and The Divan. Mirhi, who has been styled "the Ottoman Sappho," was a poetess of Amasiya, full of the passion of love. She sang boldly concerning the object of her devotion, but her virtue was never questioned, nor her talent deprecated.

But the women of Turkey have been affected less by the literary influence of Persia than by the religious inheritance from the Arabs. Before Mohammed polygamy flourished among the various Arabian tribes. The prophet brought some order out of the chaos, and the harem became a more or less well-defined system, with its definite laws and regulations. Therein woman was somewhat advanced from the state in which she earlier found herself. And yet, Mohammed manifestly wavered in his treatment of women and in the ideals which underlay it. A certain equality between man and woman is at one time taught in the Koran, as when it said: "The women ought to behave to their husbands in like manner as their husbands should behave towards them, according to what is just." And again the prophet said: "Ye men have right over your wives and your wives have right over you." This truly is reciprocity. And yet he asserted that "woman is a field--a sort of property which her husband may use or abuse as he thinks fit;" and again, that "a woman's happiness in Paradise is beneath the sole of her husband's feet." Commercially, the girl was of more value than the boy, because she could be sold and made a wife, and perhaps she might be converted to the Mohammedan faith.

It is, in truth, the Turkish slave woman's physical beauty, as she was captured and came into the possession of Arab sheiks, which first brought the Turkish woman into notice. But these superbly attractive, dark-eyed slaves at length captured their captors, and the Turk became master of the Arab and the most virile exponent of the Arabian faith and civilization.

Concerning his ideals as to woman, the Turk imbibed much from the Arab, who valued woman mainly for her points of physical excellence--these were tabulated in a standard of eight "fours" as follows: "A woman should have four things black; namely, hair, eyebrows, eyelashes, and the dark part of the eyes. Four things white; namely, the skin, the white of the eyes, the teeth, and the legs. Four red; namely, the tongue, the lips, the middle of the cheek, and the gums. Four round; namely, the head, the neck, the forearm, and the ankle. Four long: the back, the fingers, the arms, and the legs. Four wide: the forehead, the eyes, the bosom, and the hips. Four thick: the lower part of the back, the thighs, the calves, and the knees. Four small: the ears, the breast, the hands, and the feet."

Since Mohammed allowed four wives to all Mussulmans, the sultan as a faithful follower of the prophet may have four official wives; and after these he may take as many non-official wives as his fancy may desire. The four favored ones are known as the kadins. First stands the Bach Kadin, who is the "first lady of the land." Next her is the Skindij Kadin, or "second lady." Then come the "middle lady" or Artani?Kadin, and last of all the Kutchuk Kadin, or the "little lady." When a kadin becomes the mother of a male child she is then entitled to be called Khasseki-Sultan, or "royal princess." When a daughter is born to one of them she is known as Khasseki-Kadin, or "royal lady."

The mother of the reigning sultan always holds high place at court, yet not because she is mother of the ruler, but because it is thought that each of the four legitimate wives of the sultan must in every detail of court life enjoy perfect equality with the others, from the services of "the mistress of the robes down to the lowest scullion." Thus, the mother, called the Valideh-Sultan, holds the rank that usually belongs to the wife of a monogamous ruler. Should the sultan's mother be deceased, his foster-mother holds this position of influence. The present sultan's foster-mother has conducted herself with much conservatism in her exalted position and, it is said, with strict attention to the dignity and economy of the harem. The Valideh is sometimes poetically known as Tatch-ul-Mestourat, that is, "the crown of the veiled heads." This means that the Valideh is regarded as queen of all the Mohammedan women, who are uniformly veiled, according to the teaching of the prophet. The Valideh is in her dignity most august. No woman, not even the Khasseki-Sultan, may dare come before her unless sent for. All women when they appear in her presence must be clothed in full court dress, and, whatever the weather may be, without mantles. When she goes out she is entitled to a military escort similar to that of the sultan. An ancient custom still prevails which demands that the Valideh, once a year, on the night of Kurban Bairam, present a slave girl of twelve years of age to the sultan. The slave damsel at once becomes a member of the harem, and it is possible for her to rise to the highest position a woman may attain at the Turkish court. It is now customary, however, for the young girl to be sent as a pupil in the institution at Scutari, which has been established by the sultan for the higher education of Mohammedan women. She is now more frequently married, with a dowry, to some officer of the court or member of the sultan's household.

The sultan is granted privileges not generally accorded others as to marriage. He may marry a Christian or a Jewess, if he should see fit so to do. As a rule, the women who thus marry are expected to become Moslem in faith, though there have been notable exceptions. Theodora, wife of Orkhan, was a Greek Christian woman, and with marked persistence held on to her ancestral religion. But Orkhan was unlike Mohammed II. in character; for the story is told of the latter's strong passion for the beautiful Irene, who, however, refused to abjure her faith. The priests of Islam reviled their ruler for loving one who would not accept the religion of the prophet. This was too much for Mohammed. One day the priests were assembled in one of the halls of the palace. Here, too, was Irene, covered with a veil of dazzling whiteness. With great solemnity the sultan lifted Irene's veil with one hand and revealed the young woman's great beauty to all who were present. "You see," said the Sultan, "she is more beautiful than any other woman you have ever beheld; fairer than the houris of your dreams! I love her as I do my life; but my life is nothing beside my love for Islam." With this, he seized the long, golden tresses of the unfortunate woman, entwined them in his fingers, and with one stroke of his sharp scimiter severed her head from her body.

A lady of imperial blood has the right to add "Sultan" to her own name. This is her privilege, even though she should marry a subject, which is sometimes the case. Her superior descent, however, is always recognized; for her husband may not sit down before her, unless she should so permit.

Turkish rulers have taken a different view of the value of foreign marriages from that which has usually prevailed in the East. Political ties have been made and strengthened by royal marriages. In Turkey, however, a custom, amounting to law, prevents the sultan from marrying a free woman, one taken from the high families of his own people, or princesses of foreign courts, that no tie of politics or affinity of blood should alter the superior impartiality of the supreme master. Thus, while he is above all his subjects so far as rank is concerned, he is inferior, on his mother's side at least, in the matter of birth, Hence, the meanest subject of the Empire of the Ottomans may here feel himself on an equality with the sultan, since he is "the son of a slave woman."

It is not customary for a ceremony to be performed when the sultan marries. Only three Turkish sultans are said to have undergone a ceremony on the occasion of taking to themselves wives. When the Greek Princess Theodora was wedded to Orkhan; when Roxelana became the wife of Sultan Suleyman;

and when Besma, an adopted daughter of a princess of Egypt, was married to Abd-ul-Medjid, the marriage ceremony was performed.

As a mark of certain inferiority, the bride is expected to enter the nuptial bed from the back, lifting the covering with much ceremony. It is never good form for a gentleman to inquire concerning the health of another's wife.

Mothers of the harem are often compelled to live in mortal fear for their infant sons, lest they be foully dealt with. For if a child have any prospect of some day being the Turkish ruler, his life is never regarded as altogether safe. The baby prince is brought up in the harem, with his mother and nurse; but since brothers and even uncles come before sons, the question of succession to the sultanate has often caused great disorder and bloodshed.

On the death of Mohammed, the great Arab leader, there was no mention of a law of succession. This was partly due, doubtless, to the fact that he left no son who might assume leadership of the hosts of Islam. At length, the Seljuk Turks attained to power, after which the empire fell into minor sovereignties, which were brought together at last into the Ottoman Empire. And while of late the stability of the reigning dynasty has been the most noteworthy of the East, yet the fact that there was not early established the ordinary custom of transmitting the sovereignty from father to son has been the cause of much intrigue, crime, and uncertainty in the dominion of the Turk. Cases have not been unknown in Turkish history where several hundred women of the seraglio were drowned in the Bosphorus because of plottings to depose the sultan. They were tied in the traditional sack and dropped into the sea. It was Ibrahim I., known as the Madman, one of the very worst of Turkish rulers, who first conceived the idea of thus disposing of the old women of the seraglio. Surprised and seized in the night, the unfortunate victims of the sultan's madness were tied in sacks and then sunk to the bottom of the sea. Only one of the large company of the unfortunates escaped, by the loosing of the sack, and was picked up by a passing ship and conveyed to Paris to tell the story of the cruel death of her companions. Among the many notable instances of the tragic end to which the plottings of the harem have come may be mentioned that of Tarkhann, mother of Mohammed IV. So desirous was she that her son should reign, that she slew all the other possible male heirs to the throne. She met her nemesis, however, by strangulation. It is upon her life and that of her rival that Racine has constructed his Bajazet.

Connected with the sultan's harem there are estimated to be about fifteen hundred persons. The harem consists of a number of little courts, or dairas; and the central figure of each of these courts is a lady of the female hierarchy.

In the royal household there are three classes of women. The kadins, of whom we have spoken, who may be termed the legitimate wives of the sultan, though they are never formally married. Next are the ikbals, or "favorite women." From this class the kadins are usually chosen. Then come the gediklis, "those pleasant to look upon." The ikbals may come from the number of these. The women of the third class are usually of slave origin, purchased or stolen perhaps from Georgian or Circassian parents. Those who are stolen are usually taken so early from their homes, and so clandestinely, that their origin is seldom known to them. If, however, the lady comes of high station her identity usually becomes known, and she not unfrequently succeeds in elevating her family to a position of power and emolument, either by direct influence or by intrigue. In addition to these three classes of women there are ustas, or "mistresses," who are maids in the service of the sultan's mother; shagirds, or "novices," who are children in training for the higher positions in the harem; and jariyas, or "damsels," who do the more menial work of the establishments.

Captured slave girls have sometimes had a most interesting career. They are brought in an almost continuous stream, but privately. In the earliest days of their presence in the harem they are called alaiki, and are placed under the care of elderly women, or kalfas, who bring them up to suit the tastes of an Oriental court. They are instructed in manners, in music, in drawing, and in embroidery. When later they reach the proper age, they become attendants upon the kadins and the princesses of the imperial household. There is no bar to their reaching at length the highest station that it is possible for a woman to attain, the favorite wife of the sultan.

The female department of the Turkish household is called the Hareemlick, the male apartments being named the Islamlick. The women's apartments are, of course, secluded. A male physician may see only the hand and tongue of the sick lady. A black curtain is stretched to separate her from his inspection. A eunuch conducts the physician to a point where the sick woman may thrust out her hand through a hole in the curtain so that the doctor may diagnose her disease.

Faithfulness in women is held in high esteem, restraint of the harem being intended to insure it. In former days it was not a thing unknown for unfaithful women to be drowned; but the custom has fallen into disuse. Ladies of the harem, however, have a fair amount of liberty. On certain occasions they go out driving and visiting; they frequent the bazaars and the public promenades, always in vehicles, never afoot. They enjoy entertainments among themselves. Theatricals are frequently witnessed by them in the garden of the palace. Operas are also often rendered for their enjoyment. When Turkish ladies visit one another in the harem,--which they may do without permission or restraint from their husbands,--it is customary to place their shoes outside the harem door that their husbands may know guests are being entertained.

The harem of one ruler is generally regarded as the property of his successor. The women thus inherited, however, are not always sure of favor. Sultan Mohammed II. killed, by drowning, all the women of his brother's harem. Indeed, women of the harems generally cannot be said to have ample protection; for no officer may enter any harem to inspect the conduct there, or for any purpose whatever, unless the law of the house admits him. The women, whether they be wives or slaves, are practically at the mercy of their masters. Some women of the sultan's harem have risen to positions of much influence and genuine power, though they have generally been of foreign birth. The mother of the noted reforming sultan, Mahmud II., who began to reign in 1808 when a mere child, was a French woman. His stout resistance of the allied powers won for him a certain admiration for doggedness, even if success did not crown his efforts to keep Greece in subjection. It was into this struggle that Lord Byron threw himself on behalf of Greece. Mahmud, it may be to some extent through the influence of his French mother, introduced French tactics into his army, but to no avail, and at length Grecian freedom was assured.

The wife of Mahmud, Besma, taken as a little girl from the life of a peasant, rose to a position of supreme dignity and great influence. Her beauty easily won the passion of Mahmud. She never lost sight of her humble origin and was much beloved by the masses of the people, even those of the most lowly classes. She was the mother of Abd-ul-Aziz, and it was she who unsuspectingly gave to the sultan, her son, the scissors with which he killed himself. At any rate, the unfortunate monarch was found dead in his apartments. The mother pined away in seclusion, and was seen only in her deeds of charity. It was Besma who built the mosque Yeni Kalideh at Ak Serai, and it is here she rests in the midst of a beautiful garden of flowers, of which, during her lifetime, she was so fond. On her death, about fifteen years ago, she was accorded a funeral of great magnificence, and she was generally mourned throughout the empire. It is said that when Besma was building the mosque, her money fell short of her purpose, so that she could build but one minaret instead of two, as custom entitled. Her son, however, came forward, offering the necessary funds, which she declined with the remark: "No, one minaret is sufficient to call the people to prayers; another would only glorify me; the poor need a fountain." So she built a fountain for the people, and it is one of the most beautiful in Constantinople.

One of the most celebrated--even if she be not one of the best--women of Turkey history was Khurrem, the "Joyous," whom Europeans generally knew as Roxelana. She was wife of the greatest figure in Turkish annals, Suleyman the Magnificent, who reigned about the middle of the sixteenth century. Roxelana, though her origin has not been clearly traced, was probably of Russian descent. From the first this strong-minded woman exerted great influence over Suleyman. In the first place, she forced him to marry her publicly and with much ceremony, a proceeding which was then without precedent. Usually to have it announced that a woman had become mother of a male heir to the throne was regarded as sufficient announcement of marriage with the sultan. But this woman, who had now risen from the position of a slave woman to that of the highest dignity possible for a woman in the empire, determined that her marriage with the great monarch should be full of publicity and pomp. There was feasting and, apparently, great rejoicing, though the people were surprised and hardly understood what it all might mean. Roxelana was, however, equal to the emergency, and with the sagacity and determination which were native to her sent many slaves among the people as they feasted, distributing presents of money and pieces of silk to the masses. From this time, she not only held absolute sway over the sultan, but evinced great skill in buying the friendship of the people by gifts and acts of charity. Diplomacy was characteristic of her, and from cruelty she would not shrink if it were necessary to carry out her purposes, for she induced Suleyman, generally so just and prudent, to destroy the oldest and most promising of his sons, since the young man, Mustafa by name, stood in the way of her own son Selim as heir to the throne. She succeeded in her designs, but placed on the throne one of the weakest and most worthless of Turkish rulers, "Selim, the Sot." Roxelana's beauty is described as that which "attests that mixture of the Asiatic and Tartar blood, wherever the dark eyes, the silken lashes, the creamy paleness of the tint, the languor of the attitude habitual to the Persian beauties, contrast with the rounded outline of the face, with the shortness of the nose, the thickness of the lips, and the warm coloring of the skin, traits peculiar to the daughters of the Caucasus." At fifteen, she is said to have been the marvel and even the mystery of the harem. Her memory knew only the rearing of the seraglio; but her remarkable alertness and force of mind as well as beauty of person made her from the first one of a thousand. Taught in the arts of music and dancing, versed in foreign languages, and the study of history and poetry, Roxelana added to her exuberance of youth a power of mind which marked her for preeminence.

Rebia, wife of Mohammed IV., is another example of womanly power over the head and heart of the supreme ruler of Turkey. Rebia was a Greek girl from the island of Crete. Lamartine says of her: "The delicacy of her lineaments, the brilliancy of her complexion, the ocean azure of her eyes, the golden auburn of her hair, the caressing tone of her voice, and the witchery of her wit made her to be dreaded still as the prison companion of a fallen monarch, of whom she might amuse the languor and reestablish the intrigue from the depth of his captivity." Even in Mohammed's dethronement, Rebia clung to the fortunes of her lord, over whom, during his power, she had always exerted decisive influence.

Italian women have also risen to a place of prominence in the royal harem. This was notably true in the case of the beautiful Safia, a Venetian captive girl, who had been brought into the seraglio of Sultan Murad III., who succeeded Selim his father in the year 1574. Murad was not strong, and was easily deceived by sycophants and ruled by women. Among the latter was Safia, sometimes known as Baffo, belonging to the family of Baffo of Venice. Baffo proceeded to rule her royal lord in the interests of her native land. Venice, after Suleyman's death, had become restless of Turkish rule, and proceeded successfully to throw it off. Baffo never forgot her origin, and ruled with a high hand, not only as Khasseki-Sultan, but also as Valideh. She set her son Mohammed III. on the throne as successor to her husband, even though the consummation could be reached only by the slaying of nineteen of the one hundred and two sons of Murad. Foreign women will probably never again play so large a role in Turkish affairs. The present sultan is said, however, to be fond of the social attractions of European women. He is probably the first Turkish sultan who has invited a European lady to dine with him.

The Turkish sultans have long lived in much magnificence. The old seraglio, or imperial residence (from the word seray, a palace), was beautifully situated "among the groves of plane and cypress that clothe the apex of the triangle upon which the ancient city of Constantinople is built." Now, however, the sultans have left these precincts around which clustered so many memories of the horrible tragedies enacted there, memories which even the magnificence of the place could not destroy, and established their present residence, equal in natural beauty to the old, but removed from the dirt and the memories, which had at length gathered about the old seraglio.

The women's quarters are situated in the innermost portion of the seraglio. Here are from three to twelve hundred women; at times there are even more. These women are all foreigners. Indeed, all the guards and attendants of the palace are of foreign blood. The sultan and his children are the only Turks dwelling in the inner departments of the royal palaces; and both he and they are born of foreign mothers. The women's departments are carefully guarded. There were specially appointed officers in the old seraglio as guards of the queens and their children. These were the Baltajis, or "halberdiers," who were four hundred in number. They, however, really attended the royal women only when the sultan took with him some members of his harem to bear him company on a journey or a campaign.

The Baltajis, on such occasions, walked by the side of the carriages of the imperial ladies and guarded their camp at night. Ordinarily, the sultan's harem was under the care of the black eunuchs, or about two hundred Africans, who were specially entrusted with the imperial ladies. Their chief was known as the Kislar Aghasi, or "master of the girls," and was regarded as one of the chief men of the empire.

The trade in captive boys and girls stolen from Europe, Asia, and Africa was once very large; the pick of them being brought by purchase into the sultan's palace, for one purpose or another. It was thought that his imperial majesty's life was safer in the hands of foreigners brought up almost from infancy in the palace, and knowing no other allegiance than that to the will of the sultan.

Times have changed, however, and it is not possible for the ruler of the Turks to regard the best of the children of white and black parentage as born to replenish his harem. Much of the old time medi 鑑 al splendor has been swept away, not only through the reforms of Sultan Mahmud II., but by modern conditions which make the old seraglio an impossibility.

In the olden days the young princes were closely confined in a part of the seraglio known as the Chimshirlick, or "boxwood shrubbery." It contained twelve pavilions each surrounded by high walls which enclosed a little garden. These were the residences of the sons of the sultan. Each young prince was kept guarded in his pavilion enclosure, from which he dared not emerge without his royal father's special permission. Thus a prince's minority was spent in the kafe, or "cage." Each youth had as attendants ten or twelve fair girls, besides a number of pages. These and black eunuchs, who were his teachers, were his sole companions. As a rule, the tongues of male attendants and of women unable to bear children were slit. At the tenth year a young prince leaves his mother and the harem for the guardianship of a lalo, or "male attendant," who is his companion day and night; next a mullah, or "priest," takes the youth in hand and gives him his schooling, which consists chiefly in instruction in the teachings of the Koran.

[Illustration 5: THE MUTES After the painting by P. L. Bouchard The women's quarters are situated in the innermost portion of the seraglio. Here are from three to twelve hundred women; at times there are even more. These women are all foreigners. Indeed, all the guards and attendants of the palace are of foreign blood..... The women's departments are carefully guarded.

Women who bear no children and the subaltern eunuchs have their tongues slit. Whan an order of death is issued, these mutes, with the fatal cords, enter and noiselessly fulfil their commands.]

Among the female officials of the seraglio is the Hasnada Ousta, or "grand mistress of the robes." She is usually an elderly woman of respectability and of dignity. This lady acts as vice-Valideh, caring for matters in the establishment to which it may not be possible for the Valideh Sultan to give her own personal attention. She holds a place of much honor, and women holding this position have been known to become Valideh. There is also the Kyahya Kadin, or "lady comptroller," who is generally selected by the sultan from among the oldest and most trusted of the Gediklis.

The dress of the ladies of the royal harem was formerly altogether Oriental; so also were the furnishings of the women's apartments. These last still consist largely of low divans, costly embroidery, couches, and the like; but European customs have now made themselves felt, not only in the furnishings of the rooms, but more particularly in the matter of feminine attire. Costly robes from Paris and Vienna have invaded the precincts of the harem; and these, added to the wealth of jewelry of which Oriental ladies are so fond, make it possible for the women of the rich Turkish households to be quite cosmopolitan in their modes of dressing.

Many of the lower ranks wear upon their head a sort of hood of black silk, the Egyptian chaf-chaf. To this is attached a piece of black netting, which can be dropped over the face of the wearer when she so pleases. The women of Constantinople, however, are not so careful in the matter of the veil as are the ladies living in cities under less cosmopolitan influence.

European ideas and habits have greatly modified Turkish customs. The yashmac is the face veil which the Turkish girl receives when she attains to the marriageable age. The word is derived from a verb which means, when fully interpreted, "May long life be granted you." The material is thin, fine lawn or similar stuff. The older and less attractive women, or ladies who do not wish to be recognized in a public concourse, as when shopping, wear a veil of thicker material.

The cloak used is the feridj? It is usually of black material, and its shape is intended to conceal the outlines of the figure. The feridj?is now much modified, however, by European tastes, and is not greatly different from the opera cloak worn by the ladies of Paris.

The once fashionable footgear, the yellow Turkish slipper, has given place generally to the slipper of patent leather worn by European ladies. Much of the beauty of color and picturesqueness of costume has therefore passed away, as may be seen from the following description of the Turkish woman's appearance at the middle of the sixteenth century: When they (the women of Turkey) go abroad, the ladies wear the yashmac made of gold stuff, heavily fringed, and confined to the head by a crown blazing with jewels. The figure is concealed by a cloak of richest brocade or velvet. Sometimes you may have the charm of seeing as many as one hundred arabas, or carts, very splendid and richly gilded, drawn by gaily decorated bullocks, each containing a number of these great ladies with their children and slaves.

"The procession is a most gorgeous sight. Each cart has as many as four mounted eunuchs to protect it from the curiosity of the public, who have their faces almost to the earth, or avert them entirely, as the caravan passes." So, also, Lady Mary Wortley Montagu has left, in a letter to the Duchess of Marlborough, written in 1717, a very graphic account of the costume of the sultana.

Lady Mary describes the dolma, or "vest of long sleeves," the diamond-bedecked girdle, the long and costly chain about the neck, reaching even to the knees, the earrings of diamonds shaped like pears, the talpoche, the headdress covered with bodkins of emeralds and diamonds, the diamond bracelets, the five rings upon her fingers, the largest ring Lady Mary ever saw except that worn by Mr. Pitt. There was also a pelisse of rich brocade brought to the royal Turkish lady when she walked out into her garden. Fifty different kinds of meat were served at her dinner, but one at a time; her golden knives were set with diamonds in the hafts; gorgeously embroidered napkins were in abundance, etc. Much of this magnificence and display has now passed away, but, as Stanley Lane-Poole says in his The History of Turkey: "While the house of the Ottoman monarch of to-day, if more in keeping with the spirit of the time, is very commonplace beside that of last century ... nevertheless, the modern seraglio is hardly an anchorite's cell."

Cosmetics were once used in profusion. The painting of the eyebrows and the dyeing of the finger tips with henna were considered marks of beauty. The custom is dying out entirely in Constantinople, though in the remoter regions of the empire the habit is still in vogue. The attempts at beautifying the face are often referred to by the poets as marks of beauty, as when Fuzuli dilates upon the

"Eyes with antimony darkened, hands with henna crimson dyed. Among these beauties vain and wanton, like to thee was ne'er a bride. Bows of painted green thy eyebrows; thy glances shafts provide."

Mohammedan countries of any culture have long held the bath in great esteem. Turkish ladies of high rank once frequented the public baths with regularity, but the modern improvements in the private houses have made this custom far less general.

The women of the Turkish empire present an almost infinite variety. Under the dominion of the sultan the nationalities are many and heterogeneous. So also it would be impossible to make any general statement of the treatment of women among the Turks. In many parts of Turkey there is but one wife in the household, and she is well treated and highly respected; affection prevails in the harems of not a few; while in others concubinage, neglect, harshness, ignorance, vice are present with their deadly effect.

Divorce may be readily obtained in Turkey; but parental influence often protects the woman who otherwise might fare unjustly. Mohammed also gave some protection to wives, since he considered a wife to have rights in her own fortune even while married, and held that if divorced, restitution of this fortune was to be made.

Turkish women, except those of the richer families, generally nurse their own children. Many children die in infancy through the ignorance of mothers of the lower classes. Some mothers still swaddle their little ones. In the event of illness, instead of a trained physician, many mothers send for a "wise woman" or a wizard. In the harems, it is suspected that many infants are actually killed. The Mohammedan population increases more slowly, notwithstanding the practice of polygamy, than the Christian population of the Turkish Empire.

It is the custom among families of the better class to give the boys over from infancy to the care of a dadi, or slave girl, whose business it is to care for him during his youth, and it is not infrequent that evil springs from this intimacy. Both boys and girls are under the care of a lalo, or male slave, when the children are out of the precincts of the harem. The influence of the slaves and menials, with whom so many Turkish children are thrown, is, as a rule, far from elevating.

Submission is a lesson that is very early taught to Turkish children. This insures an obedient, tractable spirit, and is the cause of all that is best in the Turkish character.

There are almost thirty million Turkish women, the masses of whom move upon a very low level of culture. This cannot, however, be said of all, for many of the upper classes and of the court are well educated, though the branches or subjects they are taught are not varied. Foreign governesses are often employed to teach the girls French, German, and English, which they can, in many cases, speak fluently. Language and literature furnish a large part of their education. A change is gradually coming over the Turkish people in this matter of the development of its women, and this, notwithstanding, the fear in many minds that a better educated woman will be a less manageable woman; a creature dissatisfied with her lot. A recent writer of acute observation of Turkish affairs has said of efforts on the part of American philanthropists to instil the spirit of the American public school into the minds of the Turks: "The general opinion seemed to be that the female sex had no intellectual capacity. The first efforts of the Americans to make the women sharers in intellectual progress and refinement were met with opposition, and often with derisive laughter. They created a new public sentiment in favor of the education of women. This is shown by the interest taken in the schools established by Americans for the education of girls. Pashas, civil and military officers of high rank, the ecclesiastics and wealthy men of all the different nationalities attend the examinations, and express their hearty approval of the efforts made by the Americans for improving the conditions of the women of Turkey."

The tendency of these influences is to win for women a greater respect from fathers, husbands, brothers; greater freedom in choice of their life partners; to defer the marriageable age from twelve years to fifteen or twenty; to secure for mothers greater respect from their children; and to elevate womanhood in every relation of life.

Turkish women who are still living under the patriarchal system--and in no small part of the empire does this ancient system prevail--develop under a different environment from that prevailing in the other parts of the realm. Under a patriarchate the mother yields to the grandmother and the great-grandmother. The wife holds not only a subservient place in the family, which often contains as many as forty persons, but she is often, literally, a slave to the mother-in-law, and her children are trained by almost everybody else but herself. The patriarchal system is gradually yielding, however; and more and more, even in the conservative regions of the world, newly married people are forsaking father and mother and cleaving to one another, setting up their own homes and developing the parental character, and training their young in their own sweet way.

Under strict Moslem influence, motherhood has a place of honor; at least in theory. For Mohammedanism gives to the woman who bears children and trains them faithfully a rank in heaven with the martyrs. Unfortunately, however, the light esteem in which women are held in Moslem lands makes against woman's power, even in her noblest opportunity,--that of moulding the children into character that is noblest and best. Much work has been done by foreign philanthropists in an effort to raise the standard of home training among the Turks. Stanley Lane-Poole, in his Studies in a Mosque, a book not written from the viewpoint of the modern missionary, but that of a candid and diligent student of historic conditions, says: "It is quite certain that there is no hope for the Turks, so long as Turkish women remain what they are, and home training is the imitation of vice." This is surely a dark picture. But the time may yet come when the Turkish woman will assume a position more like that of her Western sisters and become an elevating influence in the land whose present territory includes much of the most renowned soil the sun ever shone upon, not only that which saw the birth of the religion of the Jew, the Christian, and the Mohammedan, but also much that is rich in classic and medi 鑾 al memories--the country of which Byron wrote:

"The land of the cedar and pine, Where the flowers ever blossom, the beams ever shine; Where the light wings of Zephyr, oppressed with perfume, Wax faint in the gardens of Gul in her bloom. .... Where the virgins are soft as the roses they twine, And all save the spirit of man is divine."

Yes, even the land of the Turk may see such ideals of womanhood realized as those which made the women of the ancient Hebrews and the early Christians--who lived upon what is now Turkish soil--to be honored throughout the ages.

XI

THE MOORISH WOMEN

We are now to turn our attention to one of the most fascinating of all the women of the world--the Moorish woman. Her fascination does not lie altogether in her intrinsic charm, but in the atmosphere that romance has cast about her. And while there is, of course, a very close kinship between the Moorish women of Spain and Morocco and the women of the Orient, especially the Mohammedan women, yet, the lady of Moorish ancestry has a history and a life of her own which are well worthy of consideration.

The Moors brought culture to Spain, and it was not long after their expulsion that learning began to decline, and with it Spain. It was during the period of the Western movement of Mohammedanism that Islam made its contribution to the world's progress. In its very work of devastation, Arabian civilization was destined to render mankind great service. Conquering the north of Africa and then coming across the narrow Straits of Gibraltar, the Moors were destined to write out a wonderful history in their European home. So deeply did the Moors impress their life upon the Spaniards, that long after their expulsion they continued to influence Spain by the power of their thought and the impress of their customs. Even to-day, after the lapse of more than four centuries, Moorish footprints are traceable in Spanish soil. While the Moors brought culture into Spain, it cannot be said that they made any direct attempt to educate or to elevate their women. But among a people whose learning was relatively so high for its age, it was impossible to prevent the women from receiving a certain refinement and at times an elevation of mind which made them worthy of the respect and admiration of not only the prouder sex, but of the world. The capacity for true poetry and the gift of music were not uncommon accomplishments of these women. There was ample leisure for these arts to be cultivated by them. Charm of presence seemed to belong by nature and habit to the Moorish woman, as

"Some grace propitious on her steps attends, Adjusts her charms by stealth and recommends."

The Moorish women were pretty, as indeed their descendants are, especially when young. Like the ancient Egyptians, they blackened their eyelashes and eyebrows and used henna stains upon their finger tips. Beauty was at a high premium, not because there was so little of it in Moorish Spain, but because it was highly prized. Some of this peculiar type of beauty persists even to-day in parts of the peninsula. As Aranzadi (quoted by Ripley) says: "The very prevalent honey-brown eyes of the southwest quarter of Spain, near Granada, is probably due to strong Moorish influence."

The respect for women among the Moors of Spain was higher than it would be natural to expect in a land where Mohammed's influence was paramount. It is a tradition that the Prophet once declared: "I stood at the gate of Paradise and lo! most of its inmates were poor; and I stood at the gate of Hell and lo! most of its inmates were women." The Arabian nature was intuitive, ardent, impulsive. So the beauty of a beautiful woman awakened the feeling of love and chivalry. On the other hand, the women were warm-hearted, though custom required them to be dignified and self-contained. Among a people where generosity, courage, hospitality, and veneration for old age were conspicuous virtues, it is not strange that women should have received more than ordinary respect. And yet these very qualities, when abused, often degenerated into idleness, pride, ignorance, bigotry, and even the grossest sensuality.

Chivalry, however, had its better side, for "Here gallants held it little thing for ladies' sake to die," as the old Spanish ballad tells us. The Cid stories of valor--like that of Antar in Arabian literature, Orlando in Italian, and Arthur in early English legend--brought this powerful influence upon the imaginations and conduct of both men and women:

"For here did valor flourish and deeds of warlike might Ennobled lordly palaces in which was our delight."

Spain was for centuries known for its gallantry. Indeed, "the Spaniards bore away the palm of gallantry from the French," and have in some respects perpetuated the influence stamped upon them by the Moorish women, even to this day. As Thomas Bourke says, in his Moors in Spain: "Much of the chivalrous manner of the Granadians is no doubt to be attributed to their women, who were exactly qualified to create and keep alive this spirit of gallantry among their countrymen and to occasion those excesses of love, of which so many examples, equally extraordinary as pleasing, occur both in Spanish and in Arabian history."

What is the secret of the alluring and overpowering charms with which the Moorish women have fascinated the historian, enkindled the novelist and poet, set the musician's heart to vibrating and stirred the imagination of the world? A description of them which goes back to the old Arabian days is of interest in finding the secret of their power over the senses and the imaginations of men. "They are uncommonly beautiful; their charms which very rarely fail to impress, even at first sight, are further set off by a lightness and grace which gives them an influence quite irresistible. They are rather below the middle stature; their hair, which is of a beautiful black, descends almost to their ankles. No vermilion can vie with their lips, which are continually sending forth the most bewitching smiles, as if expressly to display teeth as white as alabaster. They are profuse in the use of perfumes and washes which, being exquisite in their kinds, give a freshness and lustre to the skin rarely to be equalled by the women of other countries. Their steps, their dances, all their movements display a graceful softness, an easy negligence, that enhances their other charms, and not only renders them irresistible, but exalts them beyond all power of praise. Their conversation is lively and poignant; their wit refined and penetrating, equally adapted to grave and abstruse discussions as to the pleasantest and most lively sallies."

The dresses of the Granadian women, not unlike those of the modern Turks and Russians, consisted chiefly of a long tunic, which was held in by a girdle. There was also an upper garment with straight sleeves. This was called a dolyman. Large drawers upon the legs and Morocco slippers upon the feet finished the costume, with the exception of their small bonnets, to which were attached costly veils, richly embroidered and descending to their knees, altogether presenting a picture which, at its best, made the Moorish woman one of the most graceful and picturesque of her day. The stuffs which went into a Moorish woman's dress were usually of extraordinary fineness, and the trimmings were costly, gold and silver edging being used without stint.

Hairdressing was not an unimportant part of her toilette. The black hair, befitting her complexion, was allowed to fall down in braids upon the shoulders, but in front there was a fringe. Strings of coral beads were often intertwined with the side locks; and the ornaments of the hair, often costly pearls, were allowed to hang down, giving a delicate tinkle as the woman moved her head. There were some little superstitions about the hair. It was thought that a direful curse fell upon those who joined another's hair to their own. To send a person a bit of hair, or even, by metonymy, the silken string which bound it, was a token of submission. Jewelry was used by the Moorish women in great profusion. They are still passionately fond of ornaments.

Even the poorest are well supplied, and the shapely brown arms of the little girls are encircled at the wrist and above the elbow with bands of brass or copper. As the women walk they "make a tinkling with their feet, because of all the rings and anklets and bangles which they wear with so much delight." This jewelry is the woman's personal property, and in case her husband should see fit to divorce her, it still remains her own.

One of the most important parts of a Moorish lady's daily life was the bath, a pastime which was both pleasurable and imperative, especially in the homes of the wealthier classes. Copp 閑, in his Conquest of Spain, has thus described the bathing equipment of a Moorish home: "Passing from the centre of a luxurious court through a double archway into another patio, similar in proportions and surroundings, and usually lying at right angles to the first, in the centre is a great estangue, or oblong basin, seventy-five feet long by thirty in width, and six feet in depth in its deepest part, supplied with limpid waters, raised to a pleasant temperature by heated metallic pipes. Here the indolent, the warm, the weary, may bathe in luxurious languor. Here the women disport themselves, while the entrances are guarded by eunuchs against intrusion. The contented bather may then leave the court by a postern in the gallery, which opens into a beautiful garden, with mazy walks and blooming parterres, redolent with roses and violets. Water is everywhere; one garden house is ingeniously walled in with fountain columns, meant to bid defiance to the fiercest heats and droughts of summer."

From these ample and often luxurious arrangements, it might be surmised that by the Moor water was regarded not as a luxury, but as an absolute necessity to a happy life. All classes shared more or less in the habits of cleanliness; for it is said that many of the poor would have spent "their last dirhem for soap, preferring rather to be dinnerless than dirty," while the Moors of the higher order were so scrupulously cleanly that they are said to have spent a very large part of their lives in the bath.

Strangely enough, the Catholics of Spain, determining to get as far away as possible from the customs of their Mohammedan captors, eschewed the bath because the Moors made so much of it; and men and women among them were known to be strangers to the touch of water. So far from cleanliness being regarded as next to godliness, dirt became the very emblem of Christian society, "monks and nuns boasted of their filthiness," and there is on record a female saint who boasted at the age of sixty that no drop of water had ever touched her body, except that the tips of her fingers had been dipped into the holy water at the mass!

Nine hundred well-equipped baths in the rich city of Cordova, and thousands throughout Spain, were destroyed by Philip II., the husband of Queen Mary of England, on the ground that they were but relics of Spain's occupancy by the infidel.

While Mohammed refused to Mohammedan women the right to marry any but a Mohammedan, yet he granted to his male followers the right to marry Christians or Jewesses if they saw fit. This privilege led to a considerable admixture of blood in Moorish Spain. Spanish pride did not suffice to prevent these intermarriages of Arab and Spaniard. Polygamy also being in vogue,--for their religion allowed the Moors four wives,--a blending of races went on rapidly, and the Moorish type of beauty may be discovered to-day in any part of southern Spain. The Christian influence in Spain tended to soften the almost necessary asperities of a life where plural marriages are sanctioned. The degradation incident to Mohammedan ideals concerning women was much checked by a counter current of Christian feeling, by which the Moors could not but be influenced. So, also, did poets and lovers in Moorish Spain show a respect for womanly worth and grace, if not womanly virtue, which marks an advance from the Mohammedan or even the earlier Arabian days.

As might be inferred from their Oriental antecedents, the Spanish Arabs gave much time to eating and drinking. The chief meal followed the evening prayer. The men ate alone, the women and children followed when their lord had finished his repast. The tray containing the food was placed upon an embroidered rug. Silver and fine earthenware were not wanting. Bread and limes were expected with every meal. A dish made of the flesh of a sheep or fowls stewed with vegetables was a common dish, as, indeed, it is a favorite among the Moorish people to-day. "The diner sat on a low cushion, with legs crossed. A servant poured water on his hands before eating, from a basin and ewer, which formed a necessary part of the table furniture. The meal then began with the Bismillah--'In the name of the most merciful God'--for grace. The right hand only was used in eating; and with it the host, if he had guests, transferred choice pieces from his own plate to theirs, and sometimes, as a mark of greater favor, to their very mouths. Ordinarily there were soups, boiled meats, stuffed lambs, and all meats not forbidden. Very little water was taken during the meal; in its place, and especially after the meal, sherbets were drunk, those flavored with violet and made very sweet being preferred."

The contact between the Mohammedans and the Christians in Moorish Spain inevitably brought conflict. Christians often unnecessarily threw away their lives in courted martyrdom. Many were the staunch women who thus willingly laid down their lives. The story of Flora, the beautiful daughter of a Moorish father and a Christian mother, has in it elements of the deepest pathos. The offspring of mixed marriages among the Moors was universally regarded by them as of necessity Mohammedan in faith. Flora's mother, however, had secretly instilled into her the beliefs of the Christian religion, though outwardly she was a good follower of the Prophet. At length, however, stirred by the sacrifices she saw the Christian martyrs making for their cause, her father being now dead, she fled from her home and took refuge among the Christians. Her Mohammedan brother searched for her, but in vain. Priests were charged with her abduction and were punished with imprisonment. Unwilling that they should be thus punished on her account, Flora returned and gave herself up, confessing that she was no longer a Moslem, but a Christian. All efforts to make her recant proved fruitless. There remained nothing except to bring her before the Mohammedan judge and try her for the capital offence of apostasy. The judge, however, willing to show mercy, sentenced Flora not to death as the law prescribed, but to a severe flogging. Her brother was enjoined to take the girl home and instruct her in the faith of Mohammed. It was not long, however, before she again made good her escape and joined some Christian friends, among whom a new experience awaited her. Here, Saint Eulogius, an enthusiast among the Christians, met Flora and conceived for her a love that was pure and tender, so admirable did he adjudge her steadfastness to the faith. It was a day when martyrs willingly laid down their lives, accounting it a proud distinction to die at the hands of the infidel. They courted death. So with Flora. Appearing before the judge one day with a Christian maiden who also sought a martyr's death, this girl of half Moorish blood, but with staunch Christian faith, reviled that officer and cursed his religion and the Prophet. The Mohammedan judge pitied the young girls, but had them thrown into prison. Here they might have weakened had not Eulogius urged them to stand fast in their holy faith. The sentence of death was passed upon them; and the girls were led away to execution. Eulogius, who loved Flora above all else on earth, and hence desired her to win what he considered the most glorious of all crowns, that of martyrdom, looked on in the hour of her death, and wrote: "She seemed to me an angel. A celestial illumination surrounded her; her face lightened with happiness; she seemed already to be tasting the joys of the heavenly home.... When I heard the words of her sweet mouth, I sought to establish her in her resolve, by showing her the crown that awaited her. I worshipped her, I fell down before this angel, and besought her to remember me in her prayers; and strengthened by her speech, I returned less sad to my sombre cell." Thus did Moorish blood and Christian faith unite to make a life of wonderful daring and fortitude.

To-day in Moorish states the strictest seclusion prevails for the women. The love of idleness, ignorance, and sensuality are their dominating traits. They are veiled when in public, and in the north of Africa wear a striped white shawl, called a haik, of coarser or finer material, according to the wealth or position of the wearer. This piece of apparel is thrown over the head and conceals the person down to the feet, the face being hidden by a white linen handkerchief, called the adjar, tied tightly across the nose just under the eyes. Says Sequin, in Walks about Algiers, in describing the Moorish women of that region: "In the street they present the appearance of animated clothes-bags, and walk with a curious shuffling gait, very far removed from the unfettered dignity of their lords and masters. They are not 'emancipated'; and though in the houses of the richer Moors the slavery of their women may be gilded, it is but slavery after all. The Mohammedan invariably buys his wife--that is to say, he pays a price for her to her family, large or small, according to her reputed beauty, or accomplishments as a housewife; and though when a girl is born to him, an Arab laments, a man with many daughters, if he knows how to dispose of them well, in time becomes rich. Arab women, unlike the men, are small in stature, and the wearing of the adjar has flattened their noses and made their faces colorless. It is a curious fact that this disguise was unknown among Arab women until the time of Mahommed's marriage with his young and beautiful wife Ayesha, as to whose conduct, indeed, it became needful for the angel Gabriel to make a special communication, before the Prophet's uneasiness could be removed. The jealousy of one man has been powerful enough to cover the faces of all Moslem wives and daughters for twelve hundred years."

The Moorish women of the better class are rarely seen upon the streets or in public places. Indeed, they are not expected to cross their threshold for at least twelve months after their marriage; and when that time has elapsed, it is seldom they are seen abroad. They go to the baths, and sometimes on Fridays they visit the cemeteries. Other recreations or amusements are not open to them, except that in the marriage ceremonies women have peculiar privileges, since these ceremonies are held in the women's apartments. "Marriage festivities last a week, during which time the chief amusement is the eating of sweetmeats and the dressing, bejewelling, dyeing, painting, and generally adorning of the bride, who is, as a rule, a girl of some thirteen or fourteen years old, and who is compelled to sit idle and immovable the whole time without showing the slightest interest in anything. She has probably never seen and has certainly never been seen by the bridegroom. At the conclusion of the ceremonies the bridegroom is introduced to the women's apartments, and permitted to raise his bride's veil, but etiquette obliges the lady to keep her eyes tightly closed on the occasion, and in some cases the unfortunate young woman's eyelashes are gummed down to her cheeks, to save the possibility of an indiscreet glance. If the face of the bride is displeasing to the bridegroom, he is at liberty after this one glance to reject her. If, on the contrary, he is satisfied, he drinks a few drops of scented water from the bride's hand, offers her the same from his, and the marriage is concluded."

In contrast with their once great enemies, the Spaniards, the Moors have no kind of public spectacle. For the Moors of Africa, story-telling, in which the Arabs have time out of mind delighted, the recitation of poems, to which is usually added a dance of almehs, generally negresses, expert in their art of pleasing the native assemblies. These entertainments are held in the open courtyard of some quaint old Moorish house; the centre of the court being reserved for the dancers and the musicians. The men fill the space around, beneath the arches, while in the galleries are the ghostly forms of veiled women.

It cannot be said that the Moorish women of to-day still retain that grace of form and charm of manner which the Moorish lady of five centuries ago possessed. A prominent woman, who has travelled widely in Moslem countries, has given this rather repellent description of the women of the Moors of to-day. "They are huge puncheons of greasy flesh, daubed with white and scarlet, strung with a barbaric wealth of jewels and scented beads. They eat and sleep, and then for variety's sake they sleep and eat. They gossip, scold, and intrigue; and are valued according to their weight. They blacklead their eyes, and paint their cheeks like Jezebel; beat their slaves, drink tea and chat and quarrel." Not a very attractive picture is this,--and perhaps a little gloomy,--but it is given as presenting a marked and altogether truthful contrast between the Moorish women of the days when chivalry flourished in southern Spain, and the women of the Morocco of to-day in their poverty and degradation. Once the women exerted a strong influence over the men; the truth is that frequently the "power behind the throne" was to be located within the harem. This was probably true during the reign of Hakam II., who was so fond of books that war and the practical concerns of government had little charm for him. He was the son of the great Kalif of Cordova, Abd-er-Rahman III. The latter had built a city to please his Ez-Zahra, and called it "City of the Fairest," but he did not turn over the government to his spouse. His son Hakam, however, allowed the influence of the women of the court to become dominant, and on his death the Sultana Aurora, mother of the young Kalif Hisham, became the most important personage in the state. It was she who was chiefly instrumental in introducing into power the young Almanzor. Gifted in the fine art of flattery and being brilliant withal, the princesses, and more particularly Aurora herself, fell in love with the talented young man, and turned all the currents of influence and power toward him. Thus did the women of the court succeed in developing one of the most successful and unscrupulous of Moorish leaders. He made all Spain tremble by his victories, and Christians sighed with relief when death at last conquered the conqueror.

The power of the wife of the Spanish Moor was by no means small. A fine example of her influence at times may be illustrated by the history of Muley Abul Hassan, the royal Moorish ruler of the Alhambra, who came to the throne in A.D. 1465. "Though cruel by nature," says Washington Irving, "he was prone to be ruled by his wives." He had married early in life a young kinswoman, the daughter of the Sultan Mohammed VII., his great-uncle. This Ayxa--or Ayesha, as she has been called--was, says the historian, of almost masculine spirit and energy, and of such immaculate and inaccessible virtue that she was generally called La Horra--"the Chaste." To her there was born a son, who received the name of Abu Abdallah; or as he is commonly known, by the abbreviation Boabdil. The astrologers were called upon to cast the horoscope of the infant, as was usual; and, to their great trepidation, it was found that it was "written in the book of fate that this child will one day sit upon the throne, but the downfall of the kingdom will be accomplished during his reign." At once the young prince and heir began to be looked upon with suspicion and even aversion by his father, who proceeded to persecute the child over whom such a prediction hung. He was accordingly nicknamed El Zogoybi--"the Unfortunate." It was a valiant and fond-hearted mother whose constant care and protection enabled him to grow up to young manhood; for she was a woman of strong character and of dominating will. But, alas! growing somewhat old, and losing some of her personal charm and influence, Ayesha must face a rival in the harem. Among the captives taken by the Moors at this time, says Irving, was one Isabella, the daughter of a Christian cavalier, Sancho Ximenes de Solis. Her Moorish captors gave her the name of Fatima; but as she grew up, her surpassing beauty gained her the surname of Zoraya, or "the Morning Star," by which she has become known to history. Her charms at length attracted the notice of Muley Abul Hassan, and, after being educated in the Moslem faith, she became his wife.

Zoraya soon acquired complete ascendency over the mind of Muley Abul Hassan. "She was as ambitious as she was beautiful, and, having become the mother of two sons, looked forward to the possibility of one of them sitting on the throne of Granada." Zoraya succeeded in gathering about her a faction, who were drawn to her by her foreign and Christian descent. These were anxious to assist her in her ambition and that of her sons, as they arrayed themselves against Boabdil and his mother. The latter, however, were not without their ardent supporters. There were engendered jealousies that were inveterate and hatreds that were deep. Intriguing was the order of the day. Fearing that a plot would succeed in deposing Muley Abul Hassan and in putting Boabdil upon the throne of his father, the prince, together with his mother, was thrown into prison and confined in the tower of Cimares. Hassan resolved not only to set the stars at defiance and to prove the lying fallacy of the horoscope, but to silence at once and for all, by the executioner's sword, the ambitions of his son Boabdil. But here the versatility of Ayesha again asserted itself. She at once began to make a way for Boabdil's escape. "At the dead of night she gained access to his prison, and, tying together the shawls and scarfs of herself and her female attendants, lowered him down from a balcony of the Alhambra to the steep, rocky hillside which sweeps down to the Darro. Here some of her devoted adherents were waiting to receive him, who, mounting him upon a swift horse, spirited him away." The young man, acting under the advice of ambitious friends and relatives, began to make preparations for war; and his own mother encouraged his heart and equipped him for the field, giving him her fond benediction as she lovingly girded his scimiter to his side. But his young bride wept, as she tried to fancy the ills that might befall him in so uneven a conquest. "Why dost thou weep, daughter of Ali Altar?" asked the invincible Ayesha; "these tears become not the daughter of a warrior, nor the wife of a king. Believe me, there lurks more danger for a monarch within the strong walls of a palace than within the frail curtains of a tent. It is by perils in the field that thy husband must purchase security on his throne." But Morayma, daughter of Ali Altar, found it hard to be comforted; and as her husband, the prince, departed from the Alhambra, she took her place at her mirador, and then, overlooking the Vega, she watched the departing loved one, whom she thought never to see again, as his forces vanished from her sight, and "every burst of warlike melody that came swelling on the breeze was answered by a gush of sorrow."

This succession of fateful incidents connected with the career of one who was destined to be the last to sit upon a Moorish throne in Spain is here recounted because the events give at once an insight into the strength and the weakness of the Moorish womanly character, with all its ardent love and spiteful hate, with its loyalty and its trickery, its hopes and its fears.

It was Ferdinand, with his wife Isabella, who was destined to return to the Spaniards the possession of their land, so long held by the Moors. The story of the overthrow of Boabdil is a narrative of chivalry and real pathos. Boabdil, standing on a spur of the Alpuxarras, with his mother Ayesha by his side, looked back upon the glory of his lost dominion. The towers of the Alhambra loomed up before him, and the rich and fertile Vega stretched out before his eyes for the last time. "Allahu Akbar," said he, sorrowfully, "God is most great," and burst into tears. "Well may you weep like a woman," said Ayesha, "for that which you were unable to defend like a man." This final standing place of the last of the Moorish rulers in Spain is still known as El Ultimo Sospiro del Moro--"the last sigh of the Moor." The standard of Castile and Aragon by the side of the Cross has supplanted the crescent of Islam; and Ferdinand, with Isabella, knelt in the Alhambra and gave thanks to God, while the Spanish army knelt behind them, and the royal choir chanted a Te Deum. Had Isabella been more gracious and kept faith with the infidel, the lot of the vanquished had been less sorrowful.

When the Moors were driven out from the home that had been theirs for more than seven eventful centuries, none suffered more than did the proud Moorish ladies. It is creditable, however, to their Spanish victors that they preserved as a part of their own national literature many of the ballads of the vanquished Moors. Lines from the Moorish Lament for the Slain Celin are expressive of the wail of maid and mother at the loss of their former glory and their expulsion from the place they had so long held:

"The Mooress at the lattice stands--the Moor stands at the door One maid is wringing of her hands and one is weeping sore. Down to the dust men bore their heads, and ashes black they strew Upon their broidered garments of crimson, green and blue."

The aged women also had their hopes stricken low by the downfall of their people:

"An old, old woman cometh forth, when she hears the people cry, Her hair is white as silver, like horn her glazed eye."

The fall of Granada brought bitterness to many a heart. The words of the ballad, Woe is Me! translated from the Spanish by Lord Byron, might well depict the feeling of the hour:

"Sires have lost their children--wives, Their lords,--and valiant men, their lives."

The aged Moor, pacing to and fro before the king, pours out his plaint:

"I lost a damsel in that hour, Of all the land the loveliest flower; Doubloons a hundred would I pay, And think her ransom cheap that day. Woe is me, Alhambra."

As one has written: "Beautiful Granada, how is thy glory faded! The flower of thy chivalry lies low in the land of the stranger; no longer does the

Bivarambla echo to the tramp of steed and the sound of trumpet; no longer is it crowded with thy youthful nobles, gloriously arrayed for the tilt and tourney. Beautiful Granada! The soft note of the lute no longer floats through thy moonlit streets; the serenade is no more heard beneath thy balconies; the lively castanet is silent upon thy hills; the graceful dance of the Zambra is no more seen beneath thy bowers. Beautiful Granada! why is the Alhambra so forlorn and desolate? The orange and the myrtle still breathe their perfumes into its silken chambers; the nightingale still sings within its groves; its marble halls are still refreshed with the plash of fountains and the gush of the limpid rills! Alas! the countenance of the king no longer shines within those halls. The light of the Alhambra is set for ever!"

"Farewell, farewell, Granada! thou city without peer! Woe, woe, thou pride of heathendom! seven hundred years and more Have gone since first the faithful thy royal sceptre bore! Thou wert the happy mother of a high-renowned race; Within thee dwelt a haughty line that now go from their place; .... Here gallants held it little thing for ladies' sake to die, Or for the Prophet's honor and the pride of Soldanry; For here did valor flourish and deeds of warlike might Ennobled lordly palaces in which was our delight. The gardens of thy Vega, its fields and blooming bowers, Woe, woe! I see their beauty gone, and scattered all their flowers!"

XII

WOMEN OF CHINA AND COREA

China, once the country of perpetual calm, has in recent years become the land of magnificent disturbances. Not an unimportant factor in the changes that have lately taken place in the Flowery Kingdom has been woman. The influence of the women of the nations is generally centripetal. Of the peoples of the earth the Chinese would doubtless be named as altogether the most conservative, and in this conservatism the Chinese women play a most important part.

Ancestry worship has marked this people from time immemorial, and if there be one characteristic of Chinese life stronger than all the rest, it is that of filial piety. This regard is not taught to end with childhood, but is to be lasting even in mature manhood. From the lowliest subject to the emperor himself the rule is imperative. The latter is father of the people of the realm, and as such is to be reverenced; he in turn is the son of Heaven. Confucius was careful to instil into his pupils filial regard--a virtue which the sages before him had urged upon the people. To such teachings is to be attributed much that is best in Chinese life.

Thus the Chinese system is a gigantic patriarchal system with its base resting on the earth, its head penetrating heaven. Mencius spoke often and in no uncertain words upon this theme. "Of all that a filial son can attain to, there is nothing greater than his honoring his parents. Of what can be attained to in honoring his parents, there is nothing greater than nourishing them with the whole Empire. To be the father of the son of Heaven is the highest nourishment." In this may be verified the sentence in the Book of Poetry:

"Ever thinking how to be filial, His filial mind was the model which he supplied."

Every department of life is reached by this trait. Someone once asked Mencius how it was that Shun, an exemplary character of more ancient days, had married without consulting his parents. For "if the rule be thus (i.e., to inform the parents), no one ought to have illustrated it so well as Shun." To which Mencius replied: "If he had informed them he would not have been able to marry. That male and female should dwell together is the greatest of human relations. If Shun had informed his parents, he would have made void this greatest of human relations, and incurred thereby their resentment. It was for this reason that he did not inform them." Thus only did Mencius save the filial character of the great and good Shun.

Since social and religious ideals are the most potent in shaping woman's life among any people, filial piety has naturally held a notable place in the making of Chinese womanhood, from the earliest period of Chinese history. Respect for age is, therefore, one of the most eminent of Chinese virtues. This is shown in innumerable habits of everyday life. Let a company be walking out together, the eldest will lead the way, while the others follow on, paired according to their respective ages.

The teachings of Confucius have without doubt influenced the thinking and the conduct of Chinese men in their relations with the female sex; even though he said little directly about women or their conduct. His loose ideas as to marriage and the admission of concubinage are among the blots upon his social teachings. The body of early Chinese literature gives a most suggestive insight into the ancient ideals concerning woman; and because of the dreary conservatism of the people these ideals are still potential.

The Li Ki, or "Book of Ceremonies," has many bits of counsel which are intended to regulate the everyday life of the people. Of course, there is much there concerning the life of woman, of wives, of concubines, of mothers; concerning betrothal, marriage, domestic and filial duties.

The Chinese are not usually regarded as a people overflowing with sentiment; and yet many of their ancient poems are not lacking in romantic interest. From such effusions as that which exclaims:

"O sweet maiden, so fair and retiring, At the corner, I'm waiting for you,"--

to deeper meditations upon feminine worth and character, the early poetry sweeps over quite a wide range of sentimental reflection.

The Shi King, a collection of Chinese poetry gathered by Confucius, an anthology of more than three hundred poems, contains some glowing epithalamia setting forth at length the unmistakable virtues of the bride. Others of them present the industry of a queen, the charming and virtuous manners of an admired maiden, or the affection of a spouse. While still others set forth the feelings of a wife who bewails the absence of her husband, away in the performance of duty; or, it may be, of a rejected wife giving forth her bitter plaint. A husband's cruelty is bemoaned; a woman scorns the praises of an artless lover; or a wife is consoled by her husband's home-coming.

These songs, born in the early days of feudalism, when the dukes or governors of the states would come together to consult with the king concerning public matters, breathe of a period long past. Among the officers in attendance on these occasions were the music masters. "Let me write the songs of the people," one has said, "I care not who makes their laws." To the music masters was assigned the duty of supervising the songs in use among the subjects of the realm. The songs approved by the king's music master were preserved as classics. It was from these that Confucius selected; and he preserved many in which the Chinese woman is the motive and inspiration. The ode celebrating the virtue of King Wan's bride is but one of many such poems giving a good insight into the ancient attitude of mind toward feminine beauty and virtue, as well as preserving some of the older customs attending the festal wedding day:

"The maiden modest, virtuous, coy, is found; Strike every lute, and joyous welcome sound. Ours now the duckweed from the stream we bear And cook to use the other viands rare. He has the maiden, honest, virtuous bright, Let drums and bells proclaim our great delight."

The Chinese drama, a much more modern art--though nothing seems modern in China--often depicts woman in her best as well as in her less favorable light. There is present here the true spirit of romance. In the Sorrows of Han, a historical tragedy setting forth conditions in the days of effeminacy:

"When love was all an easy monarch's care, Seldom at council--never in a war,"

Lady Chaoukeun, a farmer's daughter, who has been raised to be Princess of

Han, has never yet seen the king's face. She was eighteen years of age when brought into the royal palace, but by the intrigue of the prime minister she had been ignored and neglected. Her picture has been mutilated by the official, not only that he might destroy her prospects in the royal eye, but also that he might extort money in selecting other beauties for the palace. Her father, being poor, was unable to pay the amount exacted. But by chance the king comes upon her as she plays the lute in the darkness. He, enraptured by the music, asks to see her. Her beauty at once charms him. He hears the story of her sadness, and the plot of the minister is made known. The latter is at once condemned to lose his head. Making his escape, however, he reaches the camp of the Tartars, who are at this very juncture threatening the land, and gives himself over to their assistance. Being shown a true picture of Lady Chaoukeun in all her beauty, the prince of the Tartars falls desperately in love, and is willing even to offer peace to the king if he will but give up the beautiful princess. The king, sorrowful, but unable otherwise to save his land from devastation, delivers over his wife to the enemy, she herself consenting to be sacrificed that the kingdom and her husband's dynasty may be preserved. But, faithful in her love, she is not long in the hand of the Tartar prince. She seizes her opportunity, and throws herself into the surging river, along which the Tartar army was camped, and is drowned. When Khan, the Tartar prince, saw his prize had escaped his grasp, he decides to give back the traitor minister to King Han for punishment. That very night Han sees his martyr wife in his dreams. He arises to embrace her, but she is gone again. The play closes with the order for the beheading of him who has brought upon the royal house such sorrow.

Most of the romance in a Chinese woman's life, however, is found in the books, which tell of the earlier days. The first event in the life of most women in China, though she does not at the time realize it, is a sad one. There is usually scant welcome for the girl. Certainly, amidst the masses of the people, she enters upon a rough and weary way. She is reared in seclusion and ignorance. Her little brothers, even, are not her companions. If she should have any association with them, she is little better than their servant. Her name does not appear upon the family register, since she is expected to belong to another family when she is old enough to wed.

Does one ask of courtship in China? There is no such thing there, unless bartering by go-betweens could be called by that name. Girls spend their last days of maidenhood in loud wailing, and their girl friends come to weep with them. Well may they do this. After marriage, which is itself a bitter rather than a happy experience for the bride, they continue a life of worse slavery-- slavery abject and heartless--to women who have been slaves to other women. The mother-in-law in China rules her daughter-in-law with an iron hand, and the wife's future depends much more upon the character of the husband's mother than upon the husband himself. That the coming of girls into the home is not so welcome an event as that of boys is quite natural, for it is expected that at about sixteen years of age the girl will become a member of another family, returning but occasionally to the house of her birth. So that while a mother's hope of prestige lies in her sons, the ministering cares which she might expect in duty from her daughter must be tendered her by the wife of her son rather than by the sympathetic hands of her daughter, whose attentions must be unremitting to the mother of her own husband.

Betrothals are sometimes made in infancy. But since such contracts are regarded as being quite as binding as a marriage, wisdom usually dictates a postponement. Girls are therefore usually betrothed a year or two before marriage, which in most cases occurs at about fifteen years of age. Among the poorer classes, in order to avoid the expense ordinarily involved in betrothal, a mother will sometimes buy, or receive as a gift, an infant girl, who is reared as a wife for her son.

Marriage, however, in China as elsewhere, is always regarded as a matter of deep concern in a woman's career. But in China she has little share in the events which lead up to the wedding day. Proposals of marriage and the acceptances are often made without either party to the life union knowing about the transactions. Nor are the experiences of the nuptial day always joyous to the timid young bride. Up to the time of her marriage, the girl has spent her days in comparative seclusion. Thrust now suddenly among strangers, she naturally shrinks with a feeling almost akin to terror. This ordeal she must face with apparently little sympathy. Audible comments are made concerning her when she is at length in the home of her new-found parents, as they give their vivid impressions of the newcomer. In parts of China at least, it is customary for the unmarried girls along the route to throw at the passing bride handfuls, not of rice, but of hayseed or chaff, which, striking upon her well-oiled black hair, adheres readily and conspicuously. Not only must the girl be given in marriage by the parents, but the man must let his parents know of his desire to marry, and get counsel at their hands. In the sacred Book of Poetry it is expressly written:

"How do we proceed in taking a wife? Announcement must be first made to our parents."

Married women seldom have names of their own. A wife may have two surnames, that of her husband and that of her mother's family. If she have a son, she may be called "Mother of So-and-So." Nor is she expected to speak to others of her husband directly as her husband. She must use some circumlocution which does not directly state her relation to him.

Chinese economists might possibly defend polygamy and concubinage on the ground that these tend to produce a sturdier race than would be otherwise possible; for the concubines of the wealthier classes are usually taken from among the stronger working people, whose superior physical vigor is constantly adding fresh blood to the more delicate classes. But the moral evils of the system undoubtedly more than counterbalance any physical advantage that may accrue to society through its existence.

The birth of an infant works a marked transformation in a Chinese woman's life. So long as she is childless, she is expected to serve. When she becomes a mother, she at once takes up the sceptre. Wives, therefore, pray to their deities for the coming of a son; and when the object of their hearts' desire is realized, the delighted parents pay their devotions to the god who has sent the new joy into their lives. The sway of the woman over all the household, with the exception of her liege lord and her sons, is complete. The Shi King puts this in poetic form in describing the bride's entrance upon her new estate:

"Graceful and young the peach-tree stands, Its foliage clustering green and full, This bride to her new home repairs, Her household will attend her rule."

But remember that first she must become a mother. The brightest feature in the life of Chinese women, the one thing that brings them most comfort, is their boys. It is these which most surely lift women into a position of respect. And this is true, even though, according to the teaching of China's sages, the mother must be subject to her son as well as to her husband. "The one bright spot in the lives of Chinese women," an educated Chinaman has recently said, "is their resignation, their willingness to endure, to make the best of their circumstances." Indeed, of the Chinese as a race, this is true, though it is more emphatically true of the women. Certainly their lot is far harder than that of the men. From the cradle to the grave, in the view of one from the Occident, the Chinese woman's way is a dark and cheerless one. Few of the outer rays of the world's joy penetrate the seclusion of their lives. And while Chinese girls and women are amply capable of being made the intellectual and social equals of the opposite sex, the fact is they are not in any true sense companions of their brothers and husbands.

It is the lack of training that makes the Chinese woman, as a rule, uncompanionable. There are exceptions, to be sure. In their present lack of real preparation for the wider sphere of womanly usefulness, it is doubtless well that the women have no larger freedom. Wherever the Western school has gone, however, there has been given to the girls of China an opportunity for a broader outlook upon life through education and training.

"Of all others," says Confucius, in the Analects, "women servants and men servants are the most difficult people to have the care of. Approach them in a familiar manner, and they take liberties; keep them at a distance, and they grumble." These words throw some light, by way of illustration at least, upon woman's place in China as respects freedom to mingle with the outside world. The sex probably enjoys as much liberty as conditions justify. And yet keeping them from the world without does not tend to develop the most genial temperament; their faces do not evince cheerfulness or hope.

What is the attitude of a Chinese husband toward his wife? Of course, she is regarded as his inferior; and, as a rule, she actually is. Because of the limitations which from infancy have everywhere been thrown about her life, it could not be otherwise. When the girls must be married off to get rid of the craving of another mouth; and when wives are largely looked upon as but a means of rearing children, that these may do the pious duties in behalf of the ancestral dead, it could not be expected that the idea of the equality of the sexes should ever be conceived.

In China, as elsewhere in the broad world, wives are often neglected. From early Chinese literature, as well as from modern life, expressions of the wife's sad lament are heard. As one of the poets puts it in the mouth of a neglected spouse, whose husband comes not to her comfort:

"Cloudy the sky and dark--the thunders roll; Such outward signs well mark my troubled soul. I wake, and sleep no more comes to my rest, His cause I sad deplore, in anguished breast."

Second marriages, though often made are not highly regarded in China. Naturally love is less likely to spring up as in the earlier affiliation. The yengo, a species of wild goose is, among the Chinese, the emblem of love between the sexes. This bird especially stands for strong and undying attachment. For it is said that when once its mate is dead, it never pairs again. For this reason an image of it is worshipped by the newly married couples of China. There is a popular saying among the Chinese that a second husband to a second wife are husband and wife so long as the poor supply holds out. When this fails the partners fly apart, and self is the care of each. While it would be entirely unjust not to recognize the presence of genuine love on the part of many a husband, yet a wife may be handled severely by her spouse if for any reason he may think her deserving of such treatment. This is more true of concubines, whose lot is indeed a hard one. Whenever there is in the household more than one wife, jealousy, bickering, strife, and plotting are almost certain. The Shi King sets these forth in a little poem on the jealousy of a wife:

"When the upper robe is green, With a yellow lining seen, There we have a certain token Right is wronged and order broken."

The Chinese have a saying that it is impossible to be more jealous than a woman; and in the word for "jealous" there is an intended suggestion of another word of the same sound, but of different intonation, meaning "poisonous;" which play upon the word reminds one of the remark of the Hebrew sage that "jealousy is cruel as the grave."

The wife is not seen upon the streets with her husband. Nor does she, as a rule, eat with him. After the men of the family have finished their meals, the women take their turn at the board. Too little is the sympathy they get in their ailments; for generally scant is the attention paid to their suffering, and poverty often prevents a physician's care. Much, too, that goes for healing is hideously cruel and permeated with the wildest superstition.

It must seem the grimmest irony in one of Goldsmith's Chinese letters from his Citizen of the World, when he makes Lien Chi Altangi, while writing of his purpose to open a school for young women, say: "In this I intended to instruct the ladies in all the conjugal mysteries; wives should be taught the art of managing their husbands, and maids the skill of properly choosing them; I would teach a wife how far she might venture to be sick without giving disgust; she should be acquainted with the great benefits of cholic in the stomach, and all the thoroughbred insolence of fashion; maids should learn the secret of nicely distinguishing every competitor; they should be able to know the difference between a pedlar and a scholar, a citizen and a prig, a squire and his horse, a beau and his monkey; but chiefly they should be taught the art of managing their smiles, from the contemptuous simper to the long laborous laugh."

One of the cornerstones of Confucius's teaching was "reciprocity." But this doctrine he does not seem to apply to the practical relations of married life, about which he had little or nothing to say. Suicides of young wives would be far less frequent in China were this doctrine of the great lawgiver applied to marital life. A cruel husband may, almost with perfect impunity, greatly injure his wife, or even kill her, especially if he can make good a claim before the authorities that she had been unfilial to his parents.

The Chinese wife is, of course, not free from the evils of divorce. If she be guilty of such faults as scolding, disobedience, lasciviousness, or theft, which is next to murder in its heinousness, or if she be the victim of such misfortune as leprosy or barrenness, she may be sent back to her parents, if they be still alive. Among the causes for which divorce is possible, the failure to bear sons is the first. Widows sometimes remarry. In some parts of China the suttee, or "self-immolation," of widows is not unknown, the unfortunate woman being compelled to strangle herself, after which her body is burned.

The maternal instincts are seldom stronger than in the attitude toward the helplessness of infancy; yet, in China infanticide is of extraordinary prevalence. The greatest danger that besets a Chinese woman is at her birth. In an already overpopulated country, it is not strange that the custom of killing the female infant, for whom it is difficult to provide sustenance, should have gained ground. Besides, while the congested condition of the population is somewhat relieved by emigration of the men to other lands, the women do not leave; hence, there is a tendency toward a surplus of women. It frequently happens that if a Chinese mother has not yet been blessed with the birth of a boy, she will destroy her female offspring, with the thought that in this way she may hope the sooner to bear a son. If, on the other hand, she has one or more sons, she may allow two or three daughters to live. After this, many mothers will not hesitate to smother the girls at their birth. "By the accident of sex," says a recent writer, "the infant is a family divinity; by the accident of sex, she is a dreaded burden, liable to be destroyed, and certain to be despised." The Chinese officials have tried earnestly to break up this frightful custom of infanticide. Books have been written and circulated condemning the practice. Foundling hospitals have also been established, in order that this kind of murder might be checked and the rejected little ones cared for. Stone tablets have been erected on river banks, by pools, and in places at which the killing of girls might probably occur, or where their dead bodies are likely to be deposited. During a period of rebellion, and of dire poverty, so many desperate mothers throw their babes by the roadside for the dogs and birds of prey to devour, that "baby towers" were constructed at certain points, where the tiny dead bodies might be thrown, to avoid the dangerous offensiveness to the population.

But if in infancy the girl is not killed, she is allowed to live. Should pinching poverty come, she may be sold or given away. In some districts baby merchants are not unknown. When the little girls grow up they become serviceable in numerous ways in the domestic life; but many of them are sold to a life of shame.

A wise Chinese writer, Hwei Kwo, in discussing infanticide among his people, says: "Before you drown the infants you ought to think, 'I thus harshly violate propriety. But there are gods above; how can I deceive them? My ancestors are beside me; how can I present myself before them?' Before long the babe will call kwa, kwa, and want some nourishment; before many months she will call ya yah, and begin to talk, first calling year-niang (father, mother), and walk carefully about your knees. Before many years she will be helping you in all your hard work, and when she is married and bears a son, how very pleased you will be. If you get a good son-in-law, and their children are well to do, how much admiration and glory. 'If I endure present trouble, I may by and by eat my daughter's rice.'" But even these low and selfish motives are not sufficient to destroy the prevalence of infanticide, which is more particularly practised in southern China. It is almost, if not quite, unknown in the north.

Woman's standing before the law in China would not be regarded as high in a country where woman's rights have been agitated. Her property rights are practically nil, except as she enjoys them through male relatives. And yet, with all her limitations, the woman of China is in some respects in advance of her sisters of many other Oriental lands. She is not shut up in a harem, as she is in Turkey; she is not bound down by the harsh caste system, as in India; she is not looked upon as devoid of spiritual existence, as in Burmah; she is not degraded by the curse of polyandry, as in Thibet. In no Eastern land, with the exception of Japan, has woman a better opportunity to exert power and develop character than in China.

The dress of Chinese women might be thought by women of some other lands to be lacking in beauty and grace; and yet, it is in many respects highly sensible, being at least modest, healthful, and economical. It hides the contour of the person effectually, and this, among the Chinese, is its chief design. Being loose, it gives full play to the vital parts, as well as to the limbs, and the same thickness of materials prevails over the whole body. There is no waste in the cutting, and no unnecessary ornaments or appendages, eight yards of yard-wide goods being sufficient for a complete set of winter garments. The mental worry that comes to the woman of the West in selecting patterns, in cutting, and in fitting, is all done away with in China, since the Chinese lady always selects the same pattern,--or has had it selected for her by her great-grandmother,--and there is little need for fitting. Figures that would look unattractive in Western attire can wear the Chinese dress without disadvantage. Some have attributed the great age to which Chinese women so frequently attain--notwithstanding the often unsanitary condition of their homes, often floorless and windowless--to the hygienic character of their clothing. The winter clothes in the more northerly sections are padded garments that appear, to be sure, rather clumsy and uncomfortable. The use of woolen underclothing does not prevail. These padded garments hang about the body like bags; and sometimes when children fall down they are utterly unable to rise without assistance. It is needless to say that woman's winter attire is by no means graceful or convenient. If even the men do not use pockets,--which conveniences seem to a Westerner so indispensable,--it may be surmised that the women have no such contrivances in their dress. The ordinary costume of a woman consists of two garments. The upper one appears very much like an American lady's dressing-sack, only somewhat longer, with flowing sleeves, and is quite loose fitting, the fastenings being along a curve from the neck to beneath the right arm, and then in a straight line down that side. The lower garment is a pair of loose trousers. There is little or no difference in the style of the outer and inner garments, more or fewer being worn according to the state of the weather. A skirt is seldom worn in the Canton section, except by a bride at the time of her marriage. This custom, however, varies in different sections of China. In Shanghai, women are seldom seen without skirts. Notwithstanding the sameness and similarity of cut in Chinese costume, the quality of beauty is not entirely forgotten. A Chinese gentleman, when asked what things the Chinese women most delight in, replied: "First, beautiful clothes and ornaments with which to make themselves attractive. Secondly, to live in idleness. Thirdly, to have servants to wait upon them." The remark would suggest moral weakness which is, alas! far too common. Tsq-hia once asked Confucius what inference might be drawn from the often quoted lines:

"Dimples playing in witching smile, Beautiful eyes, so dark, so bright. O, and her face may be thought the while, Colored by art, red rose on white."

To which the teacher replied: "Coloring requires a pure and clear background." This was the great master's way of emphasizing character as a necessary accompaniment of true beauty. But this ideal is largely forgotten.

The custom of binding the feet is not so common as is often supposed. There are many localities in which the habit is almost universal; while in many sections, especially in the agricultural districts, the feet of the women are of normal growth. In the sections and among the classes in which this fashion prevails, the early suffering, as well as the later inconvenience, is intense. The Chinese woman, however, does not emphasize the importance of convenience as would her practical sister of the West; the suffering they bear with much resignation. Various explanations are given of the origin of foot binding. Some accounts state that it arose from a desire thereby to remove the reproach of the club feet of a popular empress; others hold that it sprang from a great admiration for delicate feet and an attempt to imitate them; others claim that it was imposed by husbands to keep their wives from gadding. Still other accounts say that the Emperor Hau Chu, of the Chan dynasty, in A.D. 583, ordered his concubines to bind their feet small enough to cover a golden lily at each step. He had golden lilies made and scattered about for them to walk upon when they were playing before him. The admirers of the ruler imitated the practice, and so it spread. This seems to be the most probable explanation, as the expression kam-lin, literally "golden lilies," meaning "ladies' small feet," and lin-po, literally "a lily step," meaning "a lady's gait," are in common use to-day. In the beginning, the feet were not bound so early nor so tightly as to-day, and the custom now varies greatly in different parts of the empire. The present, the Manchu government, has made efforts to prevent the practice of foot binding among the people, but with little or no success. The Manchus do not practise it themselves, and they are powerless to prevent it. As the Chinese sometimes say: "Fashion is stronger than the emperor."

The Chinese find it difficult to understand the freedom of intercourse which characterizes the sexes in the West. They regard such social freedom as being difficult to harmonize with modesty and morality. As a rule, Chinese women are modest and chaste. But it is thought that these are best assured by restricting their social freedom. On the streets the women, with the exception of the lewd, appear with becoming modesty and decorum. Notwithstanding the advantage that must come from the limiting of woman's sphere of influence, examples are not wanting in which Chinese women have exerted their native powers to a conspicuous degree in moulding the history of their times.

Through the isolation of the women, they become naturally more superstitious than the men; and, as might be surmised, the former are the stronghold of the ancient religious faiths of the Chinese. And yet none of the ancient religions nor the philosophies of the country have done much to elevate the feminine half of the nation. The best the Buddhist priest can hold out to the pious woman is the hope that in the next transmigration her soul may be born a man's.

Some women of the Celestial Empire have held commanding positions of political influence. Whether a woman might occupy an influential place in the management of Chinese public affairs has depended somewhat upon the character of the ruling dynasty. And while queens are not possible in China, because sons alone may hold the sceptre, women have been known to exert such influence in the matter of government as to be practically supreme. There have been a number of cases of empresses regent. There were two such instances during the Ming dynasty which were quoted as justifying a more recent regency that has been one of the most remarkable on record in any land. When the Emperor Hien-fung died on August 22, 1861, his son Chiseang, then but six years of age, was proclaimed emperor in his stead, under a regency composed of eight men. By a bold coup d'閨 at, Prince Kung, brother of Hien-fung, succeeded, by the aid of the army, in driving this regency from power and in proclaiming a new one composed of two empresses: Tsi An, the principal wife of the late Hien-fung, and Tszu-Hszi, the mother of the young emperor. Neither of these royal women knew the Manchu language, and Prince Kung was the power behind them, and was rewarded with the post of prime minister under the two empresses. It was not long, however, before an edict was issued degrading the prince, whose growing power and arrogance the empresses feared. And just here emerges the evidence that the prince was dealing with one of the most astute and aggressive women of the world, Tszu-Hszi, a woman who has compelled the world to reckon with her presence for half a century.

It is true that when the young emperor had reached the age of sixteen, and had been married about four months, the empresses, no longer able to present excuses for not doing so, issued a decree bestowing upon Chiseang, now called Tungche, the right to assume the management of the affairs of state. But his reign was brief, for after about three years, as it is said, he "ascended upon the Dragon to be a guest on high." Many suspected foul play, but certain it is that the outcome inured to the advantage of the two empresses. That which was more ugly still was the treatment of the young Empress Ahluta, wife of the late ruler. On the death of her husband she was about to give birth to a child. The empresses, however, saw their opportunity as well as their danger. For if Ahluta's child should be a son, not only would he be the legal ruler, but the mother herself would at once assume a prominent place in the government. Ahluta must be set aside. Soon she sickened--some said because of her grief for her husband, while others knew of the determination of the empresses to retain power at all hazards. Who then should be chosen heir to the throne? The empresses selected Tsai Tien, a son of Prince Chun, brother of the powerful Kung. The latter was again in complete control, by the grace of the two astute and ambitious women whose minds were firmly set upon retaining rule at whatever cost. The fortunate, or unfortunate, young man who had been made nominal emperor, not by inheritance, but by selection, was given the style of Kwang-su, or "Illustrious Succession." The way in which Tszu-Hszi, empress dowager, has been able to be the controlling factor in Chinese national life, crushing rivals, winning the support of politicians, and carrying out policies, is one of the wonders of modern political history. This seems the more remarkable in a country where women are generally forced to the background, and in an age in which tumultuous scenes and grave upheavals have been many.

The head of the army of the United States was not far from the truth when he pronounced the Empress-dowager of China, not even excepting the great and good Victoria, as altogether the ablest woman of the century.

Contiguous in territory and closely related in manners and customs to the Chinese are the Coreans. The Corean ruler, though in his own country an absolute monarch, was for several centuries a vassal of the Chinese Empire, and the educated class continue to employ the Chinese language in literary and social intercourse. In 1894, Corea having repudiated the suzerainty of China, war ensued between Japan and China, and as a result Corea has since been largely under Japanese influence.

The native Coreans fondly call their country "the Land of the Morning Calm." Its people are of the Mongolian type, and are therefore closely allied in sympathy to the Chinese and Japanese, with whom they have had social and political kinship and contact from time out of mind. The moral status of the women may be surmised when it is remembered that woman is regarded as without moral existence. It is not to be understood, however, that she has no name. When a very little girl, she receives a temporary surname by which she is known to her relatives and intimate friends. When she reaches the age of puberty, this appellation is no longer used by her friends. When she marries, her parents cease to call her by her childhood's name. She is now known to them by the name of the district into which she has married. Her husband's parents, however, speak of her as the woman of the place from which she came.

In Corea there is no family life in our true sense of that term, for the men and the women live in separate apartments. The husband is seldom seen in conversation with his wife, whom he looks upon as absolutely beneath him. The male and the female children are separated. When they reach the age of nine or ten years the girls are sent to the women's apartments; the boys take refuge with the men. The boys must not set foot upon the territory assigned to the women, and the girls learn that it is disgraceful to be looked upon by members of the opposite sex; so they hide at the approach of a boy or a man.

The Corean women have little or no legal standing. They are absolutely in the power of their husbands, who may not sell them, however, nor should their lords be too brutal. Percival Lowell, in his Land of the Morning Calm, puts it strongly when he says: "Mentally, morally, and socially, she (the Corean woman) is a cipher." But there are exceptions. In fact, we are not to infer that throughout the entire Orient the subjection of women is universally so complete as it is sometimes pictured by writers upon the social life of the East. Campbell, in his Journey through Corea, gives the following incident, showing how women may be very influential at times: "To make matters worse, the head man upon whom I had relied for assistance in hiring the men I wanted was absent, but his wife proved a capable substitute and seemed to fill her husband's place with unquestioned authority. Between bullying and coaxing, she rapidly pressed twenty reluctant men into service. The subjection of women, which is probably the covenant of accepted theories in the East, receives a fresh blow in my mind. Women in these parts of the world, if the truth were known, fill a higher place and wield a greater influence than they are credited with." Nor is it to be supposed that there is no respect shown to the women of Corea. The men give them at least an outward show of deference. They will step aside to allow a woman to pass in the street, regardless of her social position, and the ladies are often addressed in phrases of a most polite character. Children are taught respect for their mother, though they are enjoined to give more to the father. When a mother dies, her children are expected to mourn at least two years; for the father the period is longer. Someone has said that "there are three classes of Corean women; first, there are the invisible,--those who are always in their apartments, or, when out of them, ride in a closed palanquin. Second, are the visible invisible, who, possessing less wealth, must walk when they go out upon the streets, and yet are seen only as a mass of clothing moving before the eye. Third, there are the invisible visible class, the poor, who are seen, to be sure, but not noticed,--working women, whom etiquette prevents one from seeing."

The women's apartments do not greatly differ from the zenanas of India. In the interior of their apartments, screened as far as possible from publicity, the unmarried women may receive their parents and friends, with whom they chat and gossip upon matters of common interest, or while away the hours with games. After marriage, the confinement becomes still more secure, and the woman is inaccessible. "So strict is the rule," says Griffis, "that fathers have on occasions killed their daughters, husbands, their wives, and wives have committed suicide, when strangers have touched them even with their fingers." Woe unto the Corean wife who is not above suspicion in the eyes of her husband.

In the "Hermit Nation" one is accounted a boy until he is married, no matter what his age may be; but public sentiment prevents a young man from remaining long without a spouse to enrich, or at least to share, his life. The woman is a child till she is married, and sometimes long afterward.

The women of Corea usually marry outside of the village in which they are brought up. They have nothing whatever to do with the match that is to be made. Negotiations are carried on by the parents and a middle man. The bride, indeed, must be silent all through the nuptial ceremony. The marriage festival and the funeral are the two great events in Corean social life. When the festivities of the wedding are at an end the bride is conducted to her husband's home--in a palanquin, if the parties be well to do; on horseback, if they be poor.

There is but one true, or legal wife, but often many concubines, the number being determined largely by the wealth of the husband. Children of the true wife are the legitimate heirs. The other children, though not disgraced by their position, have no legal standing as regards the matter of inheritance. Children of concubines, however, may be legitimized, in case there are no lawful descendants.

The following interesting story, taken from Ballet's History of the Church in Corea, will not only illustrate certain customs in Corea, but show upon what a low plane the marriage relation moves in the Hermit Nation: "A noble wished to marry his own daughter and that of his deceased brother to eligible young men. Both maidens were of the same age. He wished to wed both well, but especially his own child. With this idea in view he had already refused some good offers; finally he made a proposal to a family noted alike for pedigree and riches. After hesitating for some time which of the maidens he would dispose of first, he finally decided in favor of his own child. Three days before the ceremony he learned from the diviner that the young man chosen was silly, exceedingly ugly and very ignorant. What should he do? He could not retreat. He had given his word. In such a case the law is inexorable. On the day of the marriage he appeared in the woman's apartments and gave orders in the most imperative manner, that his niece and not his daughter should don the marriage coiffure and the wedding dress and mount the nuptial platform. His stupefied daughter could not but acquiesce. The two cousins being about the same height, the substitution was easy, and the ceremony proceeded according to the usual forms. The new bridegroom passed the afternoon in the men's apartments, where he met his supposed father-in-law. What was the amazement of the old noble to find that far from being stupid and ugly, as depicted by the diviner, that the young man was good-looking, well formed, intelligent, highly connected, and amiable in manners. Bitterly regretting the loss of so accomplished a son-in-law, he determined to replace the girl. He secretly ordered that instead of his niece, his daughter should be introduced as the bride. He knew well that the young man would suspect nothing, for during the salutations the brides are always so muffled up with dresses and loaded with ornaments that it is impossible to distinguish their countenance. All happened as the old man desired. During the two or three days which he passed with the new family, he congratulated himself upon having so excellent a son-in-law. The latter, on his part, showed himself more and more charming, and so gained the heart of his supposed father-in-law, that in a burst of confidence, the latter revealed to him all that had happened. He told of the diviner's report concerning him, and the successive substitutions of niece for daughter and daughter for niece. The young man was at first speechless, then recovering his composure said: 'All right! and that is a very smart trick on your part. But it is clear that both of the young persons belong to me, and I claim them. Your niece is my lawful wife, since she has made to me the legal salute, and your daughter, introduced by yourself into my marriage, has become of right and law my concubine.' The crafty old man caught in his own net had nothing to answer. The two young women were conducted to the house of the new husband and master, and the old noble was jeered by both parties for his folly and his bad faith."

As in other parts of the Far East, the life of widows is exceedingly harsh. They may not marry again. Indeed, second marriages are never looked upon with favor, except among people of the lower classes who generally disregard the etiquette and ideas which prevail among the nobles and the rich who imitate them. A widow of high standing is expected to show grief for her husband not only by weeping over his death, but by wearing mourning as long as she lives; and children of widows born after widowhood are looked upon as illegitimate. Often, however, being debarred from lawful marriage, widows become victims of lust and violence. If, however, they are determined upon preserving chastity, they will frequently resort to suicide if their virtue be threatened. The method of self-slaughter among women is cutting their throat, or piercing the heart.

Like most women of the world, dress plays no unimportant part in the Corean woman's life. There is probably no part of her toilet upon which she bestows more zealous regard than upon her hair. Generally the natural growth is insufficient to suit her ideals of beauty, and so false hair is used in profusion. Corean women do not attend the banquets. These are for men alone.

XIII

UNDER THE CHERRY BLOSSOMS

THE WOMEN OF JAPAN

No woman of the Orient has in recent years enlisted so much of the world's attention as the woman of Japan. This interest has bordered upon real fascination. If the comparative alertness of mind has caused the Japanese men to be called the "Oriental Yankees," the attractiveness of the women might give them the right to be compared to the "Southern Beauties." They have been much written about and the world has read of them with keen appreciation.

Japanese civilization is comparatively modern. The islands owe much to Corea and China for the development of their letters and the refinement of their social life. Their alertness of mind and receptivity of character mark them among all the peoples of the Mongolian stock. This flexibility of temperament is no less true of the women than of the men, and it is partly these mental traits which give to the Japanese their attractiveness.

The women of the several strata of society present marked differences in Japan, as in other countries. This was more true in the days of feudalism, when the lines were more rigidly defined than now; though the influences of the feudal system are still perceptible and will long endure. But the women of court and castle, the women of the military class, and the women of the shop and of the soil, with all that was nationally common, lived a very different order of life. These differences are inevitable and, of course, abiding.

The chief glory of every Japanese woman is in becoming the mother of sons. And while daughters are not unwelcome, as is the case among some Oriental people, yet their birth is never so much the cause of rejoicing as is the coming of boys into the world. On the occasion of such an advent, messengers fly, notes are sent by friends, and all friends and relatives must visit the new arrival in the home. The visitor who brings his congratulations, must add to them toys, articles of dress, and the like--besides the dried fish or the eggs for good luck. The poor mother must well-nigh tax her already weakened strength to the very limit of physical endurance in receiving visitors and their congratulations. It is the father, or some chosen friend, who selects the newcomer's name, and if it be a girl, that of some attractive object in nature is usually chosen, it not being regarded as specially appropriate or as involving any compliment to name a child for a friend or loved one. This duty of naming the child occurs on the seventh day, and on the thirteenth, it is carried to the temple and placed under the special guardianship of some deity. After this the little one becomes accustomed to the ordinary routine of eating, sleeping, and crying. Very soon it may be seen on the streets and in public places strapped to the back of an older sister, or it may be a brother; and it is not long before the babies themselves are interested in the play of the older children, to whose backs they are securely fastened.

As our little girl emerges from babyhood she finds the life opening before her a bright and happy one, but one hedged about by proprieties, and one in which from babyhood to old age, she must expect to be always under the control of one of the stronger sex. Her position will be an honored and respected one only as she learns in her youth the lesson of cheerful obedience, of pleasing manners, and of personal cleanliness and neatness. Her duties must always be either within the house, or, if she belongs to the peasant class, on the farm. There is no career or vocation open to her: she must be always dependent upon either father, husband, or son, and her greatest happiness is to be gained not by the cultivation of the intellect, but by the early acquisition of the self-control which is expected of all Japanese women to even a greater degree than of the men. This self-control must consist not simply in the concealment of all outward signs of any disagreeable emotion,--whether of grief, anger, or pain,--but in the assumption of a cheerful smile and an agreeable manner under even the most distressing circumstance. The duty of self-restraint is taught to the little girls of the family from the tenderest years; it is their great moral lesson and is expatiated upon at all times by their elders. The little girl must sink herself entirely, must give up always to others, must never show emotions except such as will be pleasing to others about her; this is the secret of true politeness and must be mastered if the woman wishes to be well thought of and to lead a happy life. The effect of this teaching is seen in the attractive, but dignified manners of the Japanese women,--even of the very little girls. They are not forward or pushing, neither are they awkwardly bashful; there is no self-consciousness, neither is there any lack of savoir faire; a childlike simplicity is united with a womanly consideration for the comfort of those around them. A Japanese child seems to come into the world with little savagery and barbarian bad manners, and the first ten or fifteen years of its life do not seem to be passed in one long struggle to acquire a coating of good manners that will help to render it less obnoxious in polite society. How much of the politeness of the Japanese is inherited from generations of civilized ancestors, it is difficult to tell; but my impression is that babies are born into the world with a good start in the matter of manners, and that the uniformly gentle and courteous treatment they receive from those about them, together with the continual verbal teaching of the principle of self-restraint and thoughtfulness of others, produce with very little difficulty the irresistibly attractive manners of the people.

One curious thing in a Japanese household is to see the formalities that pass between brothers and sisters, and the respect paid to age by every member of the family. The grandmother and grandfather come first of all in everything--no one at table must be helped before them in any case; after them come father and mother; and lastly, the children according to their ages. A young sister must always wait for the elder and pay her due respect, even in the matter of walking into the room before her. The wishes and convenience of the elder, rather than of the younger, are to be consulted in everything, and this lesson must be learned early by children. The difference in years may be slight, but the elder born has the first right in all cases. Etiquette, procedure, and self-control among the Japanese girls are the most important of the influences shaping a Japanese woman's life.

Considerable respect is shown to the girl of the family by her brothers. The native and conventional politeness of the Japanese shows itself even in the names by which the children address one another. The parents may leave off the appellatives of respect, but brothers, sisters, and servants must treat the young lady with dignity, especially if she be the eldest daughter.

What preparation does the Japanese girl have for her position in the social fabric of her people? Fortunately for her, there is some effort made to fit her for her future duties. Quite early the daughter of a household begins to feel the responsibilities of home cares. Even those families which are able to provide ample domestic service will give to the daughter of the household the duty of making the tea and of serving it to the guests with her own hands. This is regarded as of greater honor to the visitor than if a servant had performed the task. The eldest girl of the family must learn to act in the place of the parents, should a visitor appear in their absence, or when the younger children need the care and oversight of an elder. In such matters as sweeping the rooms, preparing the meals, washing the dishes, purchasing viands, and sewing, the Japanese girl finds ample scope for a practical education to make her ready for the exactions of the life of a housekeeper when she herself shall become a wife and mother.

Besides these practical duties in which the girl is early trained, there is education in simpler mathematics and, to a degree, in literature and the art of poetry. She is expected to be familiar with the classical poetry of her country, more particularly the choice short poems, which are well known to both young and old Japanese. Education, in the stricter sense of the term, is on the increase among the girls of Japan, as well as among the boys and young men. Besides native schools, schools for the education of Japanese girls have been established by missionaries from Christian countries. And even higher education is making rapid strides, as is seen in the Kobe College for Women. But the advance of the state or public education during the past decade or more renders the foreign schools less necessary; and the private teacher, to whom the girls of the better families were formerly invariably sent, is gradually yielding to the larger school. And it may be said that to-day the girls are provided for, educationally, equally with the boys. Japan has made wonderful strides in educational matters, being receptive of new ideas concerning the common schools; but there are adjustments that must be made to the social ideals and customs of the people, because of the rise of the new education. Among these there is probably none more difficult and perplexing than that which grows out of the need of adapting the old ideas of early marriage for the daughter of a family to the growing demands and the enlarged opportunities for female education.

The Japanese girl has better opportunity to experience the pleasurable side of life than have girls of most Oriental lands. Her recreations are more numerous and varied. Among them are the annual festivals, such as the Japanese New Year, the several flower f⊠es, and, above all, the Feast of Dolls, which has been thus interestingly described: "The feast most loved in all the year is the Feast of Dolls, when on the third day of the third month the great fireproof storehouse gives forth its treasures of dolls--in an old family, many of them hundreds of years old--and for three days, with all their belongings of tiny furnishings in silver lacquer and porcelain, they reign supreme, arranged on red-covered shelves in the finest room in the house. Most prominent among the dolls are the effigies of the Emperor and Empress in antique court costume, seated in dignified calm, each on a lacquered dais.

Near them are the figures of the five court musicians, in their robes of office, each with his instrument. Besides these dolls, which are always present and form the central figures of the feast, numerous others more plebeian, but more lovable, find places on the lower shelves, and the array of dolls' furnishings which is brought out on these occasions is something marvellous. Before Emperor and Empress is set an elegant lacquered service, tray, bowls, cups, sak?pots, rice buckets, etc., all complete, and in each utensil is placed the appropriate variety of food. Fine silver and brass hibachi, or fire-boxes, are there with their accompanying tongs and charcoal baskets--whole kitchens, with everything required for cooking the finest of Japanese feasts, as finely made as if for actual use; all the necessary toilet apparatus--combs, mirrors, utensils for blackening the teeth, for shaving the eyebrows, for reddening the lips and whitening the face--all these are there to delight the souls of all the little girls who may have the opportunity to behold them. For three days the imperial effigies are served sumptuously at each meal, and the little girls of the family take pleasure in serving the imperial majesties; but when the feast ends, the dolls and their belongings are packed away in their boxes, and lodged in the fireproof warehouse for another year."

Besides the special festivals and holidays, there is opportunity all the year round for the little girls to play their merry games of ball and battledoor and shuttlecock, which they do with keen delight and with much grace of movement. The tales of wonder which are told them are a perpetual source of pleasure; for they have their Jack, the Giant Killer, in Momotaro, the Peach Boy, with his wondrous conquests, and many other tales to kindle their youthful imaginations. Among these are the early ancestral exploits, which tend to keep alive love of country. The Japanese girl may be seen occasionally in the theatre, seated on the floor with her mother and sisters, taking into her memory impressions of heroism and self-sacrifice, through the historical dramas which present the early experiences of patriotism and passion which characterized the fathers of old. Thus, the Japanese girl grows up to womanhood and is a finished product five or six years earlier than is an English or American girl. At sixteen or eighteen she is regarded as quite ready herself to take up the active duties of life.

The preparation given to the girls of Japan has been justly criticised in that, while furnishing the future woman with remarkable powers of observation and of memory, with much tactfulness and aesthetic taste, with deftness and agility of the fingers, there is little to strengthen the powers of reason and to cultivate the religious and spiritual side of the nature. Music is almost the sole possession of women, and many of them play the koto (a stringed instrument with horizontal sounding boards, not unlike the piano in principle) and the samisen, or "Japanese guitar," with great grace of touch and manner, but with little music, as adjudged by the Occidental ear;--however, standards differ. So, too, the artistic arrangement of flowers is an art much loved by the women of Japan. Their education and their daily occupation tend to cultivate the emotional at the expense of the intellectual side of life. Hence, much refinement but less strength, and the best and cleverest women of Japan, therefore, are attractive rather than admirable.

The diminutive size of the Japanese women, their pretty hands and feet, their taste in ornamenting shapely bodies, give them a personal attractiveness rarely surpassed. To what an extent the lowness of stature among the Japanese is to be attributed to their habits cannot be determined. It is the shortness of the lower limbs that is chiefly at fault; and the habit, early contracted, of sitting upon the legs bent horizontally at the knee, instead of vertically, inevitably arrests the development of the lower limbs.

The Japanese women have luxuriant, straight, black hair. The wavy hair which Western women prize so highly is not beautiful in the eyes of the ladies of Japan. Curly hair is to them positively ugly. They spend much care upon the arrangement of their tresses, and their mode of hairdressing is elaborate. Even the women of the poorer classes will visit the hairdressers. The locks are first treated with a preparation of oil, and then done up in the conventional style so familiar to all from pictures of Japanese women. This is expected with many to remain intact for six or eight days.

At present the modes of dressing the hair of female children and growing girls, as well as of married women, vary according to taste and circumstances. In ancient days, however,--and the custom still prevails in some of the more conservative regions,--the hair of the female children was cut short at the neck and allowed to hang down loosely till the girl reached the age of eight years. At about twelve or thirteen, the hair was usually bound up, although frequently this was delayed till the girl became a wife. In the romantic poem of Mushimaro, The Maiden of Unahi, we find this custom referred to, as well as the custom of secluding the young girl from the eyes of her would-be suitors:

"For they locked her up as a child of eight, When her hair hung loosely still; And now her tresses were gathered up, To float no more at will."

As a rule, the women wear no head covering whatever, except that which their luxuriant hair furnishes. In the coldest weather, however, they wrap the head gracefully in a headgear of cloth. Gloves are rarely seen upon the dainty hands of the women, and shoes are worn only when out of doors.

The costume of the Japanese women was, and in great measure still is, marked by simplicity and sameness of cut. There is no variation of style--fond as the women of the country are of dress. In the material used and in the color, however, they have ample scope for the display of their exquisite taste, their individuality, and their wealth. The age of the woman may also be determined with considerable accuracy by her manner of dress, for a Japanese woman has no sensitiveness on this score. The girl baby is clothed "in the brightest colors, and largest of patterns, and looks like a gay butterfly or a tropical bird. As she grows older, colors become quieter, figures smaller, stripes narrower, until in old age she becomes a little gray moth, or a plain-colored sparrow." The hair and head ornaments also vary with the age of the wearer; so that one who is acquainted with the Japanese mode can read the age of his lady friend within a few years, at most. The V-neck is the uniform fashion in Japan, and when a woman of the better classes is properly clothed in her native costume she presents a most graceful and attractive appearance. When appropriate, she wears a sort of cloak fastened with a cord, and the familiar kimono made without any plaits, lapped over in front and confined with a broad sash which is looped in a big bunch at the back to conceal the plainness of the kimono. This sash, or obi, and the collar, or eri, are usually of the finest silk the women can afford, and are altogether the gayest portion of the habit. When a Japanese woman is at her best, she may be imagined to have just stepped from a group painted upon some artistic fan, especially when in the hands are the umbrella and the lantern. The women of the poorer classes, however, are often meagrely clad--sometimes too scantily so for decency. They peddle their wares or work in the fields, barefoot and almost naked. The shoes of a Japanese lady are so constructed that they may be easily taken off before entering the house, as is the custom. There is first put on a short stocking, or tabi, which reaches a little above the ankle and fastens in the back. This is made after the fashion of a mitten, that the great toe may be separate from the others; for a cord is to pass between the toes to hold in the geta, or "shoes." There are several styles of these; some are partly of leather, to cover the toes on rainy days; some are merely straw sandals; while others are of wood, which are clumsy and lift the feet quite above the ground, and when worn make much noise along the streets.

In Japan, the disgrace of not being married does not arrive so early in the young girl's life, as is the case in some countries of the East. And yet, even here it will not do for a woman to wait until the age of twenty-five without having made her peace with the god of matrimony. Usually, however, marriage, which to a Japanese woman is almost as much a matter of course as death itself, comes at the age of sixteen or eighteen. Here, too, the girl of the land of the Cherry Blossom is given more freedom of choice as respects the question who her life partner shall be than is generally true in the East; but marry she must. The inevitable Eastern "go-between" is of value here. The first steps in Japanese courting are undertaken by him in consultation with the parents of the girl who it is thought will make the inquiring young man happy. Opportunity is given, at the home of some mutual friend, for the couple to meet and pass upon each other's qualities. If there is mutual admiration, or, indeed, if the young people find no reason why they should not be joined in marriage, the engagement present, a piece of silk, used for the girdle by the groomsman, is given, and finally arrangements are made for the wedding.

[Illustration 6:WOMAN'S TASTE IN JAPAN After the water-color by Charles E. Fripp There is no variation of style--fond as the women are of dress. In the material used and in the color, however, they have ample scope for the display of their exquisite taste, their individuality, and their wealth. The age of the woman may also be determined with considerable accuracy by her manner of dress, for a Japanese woman has no sensitiveness on this score. The girl baby is "in the brightest colors. As she grows older, colors become quieter, figures smaller." The hair and head ornaments vary with the age of the wearer. The V-neck is the uniform fashion in Japan, and when a woman of the better classes is properly clothed in her native costume she presents a most graceful and attractive appearance.]

The marriage ceremony is not at the home of the bride, but at the house of the groom, to which the bride is taken, her belongings, such as her bureau, writing desk, bedding, trays, dining tables, chopsticks, etc., having gone before. The giving of presents is often profuse. But it is not the bride and groom alone who are remembered; the groom's family, from the oldest to the youngest, the servants, even the humblest, are presented with gifts by the members of the bride's family. The gifts to the newly wedded pair are often very practical, consisting of silk for clothing or of articles of household use; and it is not uncommon for a bride to receive dress goods enough to last her her lifetime. The ceremony itself is simple and impressive. Friends and relatives generally are not present. The bride and groom are there, of course; besides these are the go-betweens of the couple, and a young girl, whose duty it is to take the cup of sak? or native wine of Japan, and press it successively to the lips of the contracting parties, emblematic of the coming joys and sorrows of their common married life. The wedding guests, who have been waiting in the next room, now appear with their congratulations, and merriment and feasting follow. On the third day after the marriage, the bride's parents must give to the couple another wedding feast. At this the bride's relatives receive presents in return for the large number of gifts sent by them on the wedding day to the household of the groom. Announcement of the marriage is not sent out until two or three months later; it is then made in the form of an invitation, sent out by the bride and groom, to an entertainment at their house. Acknowledgments of the bridal presents sent by friends must, of course, be made. This is done in sending to those who remember the young pair gifts of kawam 閼 hi, or "red rice."

It will be seen that there is in the conduct of a wedding in Japan neither legal nor religious sanction. The only prescribed formality is the erasure of the bride's name from the register of her father's family and its insertion in that of the husband's. She is no longer a part of the genealogical tree. She lives with and is a part of the groom's household. The exception to the custom is found in the yoshii, or "young man," who becomes a part of his wife's family, taking her family name and repudiating his own. This is done when in a family there are no boys who may inherit the estate and name. Some youth is then found, usually a younger member of a household, who can be induced to leave his heritage and unite himself with a brotherless daughter of another house. He cuts himself off absolutely from his own people and raises up heirs for his wife's people. But he has not the standing and authority of the woman's husband, for he becomes the servant of his mother-in-law, and may be sent back to his people if he does not conduct himself in a way acceptable to his wife's family; or if they should weary of his presence. Ordinarily, children are scarcely regarded as of the mother at all--the blood is all the father's. The low social standing of the mother in no way impairs the rank or respectability of the children. The past few decades have witnessed many notable changes in Japan, and there is a reaching out after legislation that shall make the marriage relation more satisfactory and permanent, for divorces have been the frequent cause of great hardships, especially upon the women, who have little opportunity to earn an honorable living when once the marriage tie has been broken. Home life is kept comparatively pure in Japan, but the price is enormous. The abandoned woman carries on her business or has it carried on for her with shameless openness. The ideals of purity are far higher among the women than among the men. And yet, chastity is not regarded as the highest virtue among Japanese women as among northwestern people. Obedience to the will of the husband stands first in the list of virtues. Thus, Japanese women have often been known to sell their chastity in order that they might save their husbands from debt or disgrace, and they have received the plaudits of the public for what is styled their fidelity to their husbands' interest.

In few, if any, countries of the Orient do the women appear in public as the equals of their husbands. The Japanese women of the lower social classes, when they go out with their spouses, follow on behind, bearing whatever burden is to be borne. In trains or crowded rooms it is the women who stand, and not the men. Japanese gallantry is not shown in such public courtesies as are commonly offered to women in the United States. The wife does not begin her wedded life with the thought of equality with her husband; and, in law, he is greatly her superior unless, happily, her husband should be motherless. Next to her duties to her parents-in-law, the wife's great concern is to be a good housekeeper, rather than a companion for her husband. She must, with due self-control and even with smiling face, humor the whims and the vices of her lord and master, even though he bring another woman into the home. But it may be said that the Japanese husband extends to a legal wife comparative respect and even honor, if, as the mother of children, she fulfils well her duties. Third in line of demand upon a wife's care, stand the children. In them the Japanese mother takes delight; and here the self-control which she has learned almost from the cradle stands her in good stead and beautifully exhibits itself, for she seldom loses her temper or scolds her children. Even the wealthy women come in contact with their children and personally guide their lives. The training of the girls is almost entirely in the hands of the mother; and the domestic cares of routine life are under her skilful direction. In the rural districts the activities of women are enlarged by the part they take in the making of the crops, the running of the rice fields, the production of tea, the harvesting of grain, and the care of the silkworms, the bringing of products to market, and the like. But the freedom they thus enjoy makes amends, in a measure, for the more burdensome work of which their sisters of the city know nothing.

The geishas, or singing girls of Japan, are, physically speaking, among the most attractive examples of female grace. The word geishas means "accomplished persons," and these girls are trained in the art of making themselves agreeable. They are accomplished in music, singing, and playing the samisen, witty in conversation, and beautiful in figure. Theirs is a regular occupation, their services being sought on occasions when entertainment is the chief concern. While these girls do not come from the higher social circles, some of them marry well and become the mothers of reputable families, while many others, yielding to the strong temptations incident to their employment, become the concubines of some well-to-do citizen or lead lives even lower in the moral scale.

Among the special occupations of women may be mentioned that of acting; for there are women's theatres in which all the parts are performed by women. Men and women never appear on the same stage. In literature, two Japanese women have gained the distinction of having written the two greatest native works--works admittedly at the very acme of Japanese classics. One of these is Genji Monogatari, or "Romance of Genji," and the other Makura Zoshi, or "Book of the Pillow." The authoresses of the two masterpieces, both court ladies living in the eleventh century of our era, were Murasaki Shikibu and Seisho Nagon. To their names may be added that of a brilliant female contemporary Is?no Taiyu. The Emperor Ichijo, who reigned at that period, was a distinguished patron of letters. He gathered about him men and women of culture, and the more lasting literary monuments of his day are those written by women. The work of these gifted women is marked by ease and grace of movement, fluency of diction, and lightness of artistic touch.

Murasaki Shikibu was a lady of noble birth. She was, in her youth, maid of honor to the daughter of the prime minister of that day. This daughter, Jioto Monin, became wife of the Emperor Ichijo, and from this station of influence became a most valuable patroness of Murasaki, the talented authoress. She herself married a noble, and their daughter also became a writer of note, producing a work of fiction called Sagoromo, or "Narrow Sleeves."

The chief work of this noted Japanese authoress, Murasaki, is what may be called a historic novel, Genji Monogatari, or "The Romance of Genji." In this story the writer gives an accurate view of the conditions which surrounded court life in the tenth century of our era. From the romance of Gengi it may be seen, as a native Japanese critic has said, that "Society lost sight, to a great extent of true morality, and the effeminacy of the people constituted the chief feature of the age. Men were ready to carry on sentimental adventures whenever they found opportunities, and the ladies of the times were not disposed to discourage them. The court was the focus of society, the utmost ambition of ladies was to be introduced there."

In those early days of Japanese life, it was not an unknown occurrence for a woman when plunged into the depths of some disappointment or overwhelming grief to take the oath of a religious recluse. "Her conscience," says Sama-no-Kami, "when she takes the fatal vow may be pure and unsullied and nothing may seem able again to call her back to the world which she forsook. But as time rolls on, some household servant or aged nurse brings her tidings that the lover has been unable to cast her out of his heart, and his tears drop silently when he hears aught about her. Then, when she hears of his abiding affection and his constant heart and thinks of the uselessness of the sacrifice she has made voluntarily, she touches the hair on her forehead, and she becomes regretful. She may indeed do her best to persevere in her resolve; but if one single tear bedew her cheek, she is no longer strong in the sanctity of her vow. Weakness of this kind would be in the life of Buddha more sinful than those offences which are committed by those who never leave the lay circle at all, and she would eventually return to the world."

There are many short Japanese poems which breathe of love, and tell of womanly charm. These short poems are highly prized, and many of them are familiar to the majority of the people. Among the women who won distinction as writers of love poems was the Lady Sakanoe, who lived in the eighth century. She was a woman of high position, being the daughter of a prime minister and wife of the viceroy of the island of Skioku. Her poems are among the most popular in Japanese literature, and some of them reveal a high order of imaginative power.

Japanese poetry, which has been described as "the one original product of the Japanese mind," contains many references to woman, her loves, her laments, her passions, her ills. Sometimes the loyalty of a maiden's love is set forth--as in a poem by the Lady Sakanoe in the Manyoshu:

"Full oft he swore with accents true and tender, 'Though years roll by my love shall never wax old,' And so to him my heart I did surrender, Clear as a mirror of pure burnished gold."

A large number of the love poems are sensual; yet, pure love breathes in many others, as in A Maiden's Lament, a poem by the Lady Sakanoe, and in the Elegy written by Nibi upon his wife. The poet Sosei, also, has written words that speak to the heart:

"I asked my soul where springs the ill-crowned seed That bears the herb of dull forgetfulness; And answer straightway came; th' accursed weed, Grows in that heart which knows no tenderness."

The mutual regard of husband and wife in early Japanese life is beautifully expressed in an anonymous poem in the Manyoshu. A wife laments that while other women's husbands are seen riding along the road in proud array, her own husband trudges along the weary way afoot:

"Come, take the mirror and the veil, My mother's parting gifts to me; In barter they must sure avail, To buy a horse to carry thee."

To which self-denying love, the husband graciously replies:

"And I should purchase me a horse, Must not my wife still sadly walk? No, no, though stony is our course, We'll trudge along and sweetly talk."

There have been many able women in this land of the Cherry Blossom, and the Japanese people have not been blind to their claims to recognition as controlling forces. This is shown by the fact that no less than nine empresses have ruled the land. Some of them have been women of marked sagacity and influence. On the dim borderland of the mythical, for example, history shows us the heroic Empress Jingu Kogo, who, tradition says, was the conqueror of Corea, and the embodiment of all that is good and great in Japanese womanhood.

Among the women of Japanese legend is the Maiden of Unahi, the story of whose noble life and death has been often sung by the poets. Her tomb is to-day pointed out in the province of Settsu, between Kobe and Osaka. Such heroines of the earlier days have furnished inspiration for the women of Japan for many generations; and the ideals of domestic life are far higher than might be expected in a region of the world where women, as a rule, live out their round of life upon a general plane that is sorrowfully low.

The present generation in Japan has been truly blessed by the influence of an empress who is described as not only "charming, intellectual, refined, and lovely," but also "noble and beautiful in character." Haru Ko, born of noble parentage, became empress in the year 1868. Her husband had just come to the throne at the age of seventeen. This was the very year of the downfall of the Shogunate and the restoration of the imperial power. Though reared in seclusion at Kioto, the young empress began at once to measure up to the responsibilities which her position had in store for her. She proceeded to exert her influence in favor of the elevation of the women of her country. Without hesitancy, she mingled personally among the people, administering charity to them. Very early in her life as empress, in the year 1871, she gave a special audience to five little girls of the military class who were about to set out for America in order to study to prepare themselves for the larger life of womanhood in the new Japan. From the beginning of the school established for daughters of the nobility, who are expected to play an important part in the Japan that is to be, she has taken great interest in its progress.

The religious side of a Japanese woman's life, as has been intimated, is remarkably undeveloped. In the portico of a certain temple in the interior of Japan is found this inscription: "Neither horses, cattle, nor women admitted here." This may be taken as but one intimation of the fact that little in the way of religion is expected of the female sex. The introduction of Buddhism into Japan marked an epoch in the country's history; but Buddhism has done little for woman, for she does not occupy so exalted a position under it as under the more ancient religion. Shintoism has its priestesses and Buddhism its nuns, but neither of these religions has brought any noteworthy blessing to the women of the kingdom. The ancient religions still influence their lives. The multitude of temples still claim the veneration of the people. Kioto retains its eminence as the chief seat of ecclesiastical learning, but the Western spirit has found an entrance into the land of the Cherry Blossom; traditional customs are yielding to its influence, and inveterate prejudices are bending before it.

The progress of Christian ideals has in recent years been rapid, and Western religious teaching has advanced with giant strides. Recent legislation has done something to increase the stability of the home by making divorce less easy. The putting of concubinage under the ban by not allowing the children of concubines to inherit a noble title, making this law apply even to the son of the emperor himself, who must also hereafter be son of the empress if he would inherit the throne, will also mean much for the elevation of womanhood in the land of the cherry and the japonica.

XIV

WOMEN OF THE BACKWARD RACES OF THE EAST

No volume upon the women of the Orient could be deemed complete without some account of those women whose lives have been developed remote from the larger movements of civilization,--the women of the backward races, and those whose sphere has been contracted, not by social ideals simply, but by virtue of the lack of that larger opportunity of world contact which has given to some peoples a far more powerful impulse to progress than has been the privilege of others. As representatives of this class we may choose the women of the South Seas and of some of the African tribes. These will furnish us typical examples.

George Eliot has declared that "the happiest women, like the happiest nations, have no history." In the advance of the world's civilization from crude savagery to high culture, woman's part, though of incalculable value, has, generally speaking, been unheralded. Bearing the brunt of the downward burden, while man's shoulder presses upward, woman, from the beginning, has had a minor place in written history. But even among the obscurer races she has managed to bear her part with marked happiness. This seems to be notably true among the island women of the world. The peoples of the seas, removed from many of the pressing conditions and harsh frictions which are present in the larger countries of the continent, exhibit a freedom, if the term may be justly applied to undeveloped races, which is not the possession of many of the larger and older nations of men. One is prepared, of course, for great variety of blood, custom, and development among the peoples who inhabit the islands and the lands that lie out of the beaten track of travel and commerce. There is probably no part of the world where the races of mankind have become more mixed than in the South Seas.

The women of the Indo-Pacific area belong to certain great classes or groups of humanity. First, the Australian, inhabiting the great island continent that seems to be the southeastern extension of Asia; they are considered the lowest among the races of mankind, have black skins, but not woolly hair, and are looked upon as a distinct race. Second, come the Papuan women, who are in every respect negroes, resembling their kindred in Africa in the variety of their types, including the tall, very woolly-headed people of New Guinea, who have black skins and comely bodies. Of the same race, but differing greatly in ethnic characteristics, are the pigmy people of the Andaman Islands, of the Malay Peninsula, and of the Philippines. Third, the brown Polynesians, who are among the finest looking people on the face of the earth; they inhabit the groups of small islands all about the Pacific Ocean, from Hawaii to

New Zealand, and from Easter Island to Samoa. Fourth and finally, the Malays proper, who are a small, wiry, energetic people of southeastern Asia and the great islands lying around Java, Sumatra, Borneo, and the Philippines. The eight million people (called Filipinos) in the last-named islands are, as will be seen later, of mixed blood, a compound of all the sub-species of humanity, brown, black, yellow, and white, even a small sprinkling of American Indian blood being there. Women of so great admixture of blood must necessarily exhibit wide differences of personal appearance and of inherited as well as acquired traits.

It would be highly instructive to take up the women of these several races and consider them one by one in the various experiences of their lives, from birth to burial, in childhood and name, in girlhood and marriage, in family life and social standing, in religion and the last act; for interest in this study extends far beyond the lives and activities of those to whom it is directed. The whole human species are one, and it is not a violation of good reasoning to suppose that the activities and social life of these lowly women may, in a certain general way, represent the standing of members of our own race in the early stages of their progress. It is true, however, that in the Indo-Pacific area we are more or less in the suburbs of the world. Caution, therefore, must be exercised in forming conclusions that the abject conditions of the Australians, for instance, is a correct picture of a previous condition of the Caucasian race. These races have lagged in the progress of the world, and in all the centuries of their isolation have rather retrograded than advanced. They are in possession of arts and practise social customs that are evidently the survival of a more advanced state, as will be seen in the separate study of each race.

Further interest is added to the study of these tribes in that, despite the fact that they are the lowest of the world's peoples, they each lead a rounded existence. Industries, fine art, speech, social forms and usages, the explanation of things, creed and cult, all fit together harmoniously. To the civilized woman, almost every act in the life of her sex among the people named would be intolerable, but to the woman there, these actions are the things to be done and any contrary course would never enter her thoughts. The joys of life come from obedience to the present order and to the venerable customs and traditions that have come down from mothers for many generations.

In height, Australian women average about five feet two inches, the tallest not exceeding five feet five inches. They have small feet and hands, the widest span being six inches. The color of the skin is dark chocolate, the lips are thick, the nose is broad and incurved, the head long, the hair black, but not woolly, and is generally worn short. Some of the young girls are pretty, and from carrying burdens on the head they have an erect pose; the Australians, however, are an unhandsome race, and at thirty, if she lives so long, the woman is an old hag, the acme of indescribable ugliness intensified by following the habit of knocking out the front teeth for the sake of fashion.

The girl-child born in Australia has little care beyond what is necessary to preserve her life. The almost deserted mother is placed apart in a brush shelter and is attended by some old woman of her clan. The birthplace of the little girl is amid the greatest squalor. On rare occasions mothers practise infanticide. The child is killed as soon as born, in the belief (in the words of Nicodemus) that it can enter a second time into the mother's womb and be reborn. As infants are suckled several years, the chief cause of this unnatural act is the inability of the mother to add another ounce to life's burdens. Being considered uncanny, twins are immediately killed; and once in a while a healthy child meets with a like fate, in order that its vigor may go into a weaker one.

The baby's name is inherited from her mother, or perhaps from her father. It is merely a class title, for every tribe in Australia is separated into classes with names. If descent be in the female line, then everyone in a class has the same name from the mothers; if it be in the male line, all whose fathers are in the same class are named alike. In all Australia there is no such title as "mother," in our sense of the word. Of the girl-child here considered, there are as many mothers as there are females in that class belonging to the same generation.

If the reader were an Australian girl, she would, then, have several or many mothers; there would be her own mother, her maternal aunts, and all collateral female kin of that generation and of the mother's class. For example, suppose a tribe in which the two moieties were named Brown and Smith. Every Brown man would have to marry a Smith woman and vice versa. A Smith would not and dare not marry a Smith, or a Brown marry a Brown. Now, if the mother-right prevailed, all the children of the Brown mothers would be Browns, of the Smith mothers would be Smiths; but if father-right prevailed, then all the children of Brown mothers would be Smiths, and those of the Smith mothers would be Browns. The marriage tie is so loose in Australia that the family exists only in the group, and the little girl is not "Miss Brown," but a Brown--one of the Browns. The principle is as here stated, but the practice in detail is most bewildering. The little newborn girl is not merely "Miss S." or "Miss B." Her tribe, with its two moieties or classes, may have six totems in each. In that case, her father and her mother will have totem names. Take the Urabrinna tribe with its two classes, Matthurie and Kirarwa. If the father be a Dingo Matthurie and the mother be a Water Hen Kirarwa, our little girl will bear her mother's name, so will all other girls of Water Hen mothers and, also, their children to remotest posterity.

The girls of this generation are, in fact, sisters and look upon the whole generation that gave them birth as a class of mothers; it is the best they can do.

In some tribes the classification takes this quaint form: every man belongs to one of a number of families or classes, which we may mark, for convenience, A, B, C, and D. Every woman belongs, also, to one of a number of named classes, which we may call E, F, G, and H. Now, all the men in the A class are compelled to marry one of the four classes of women, and their children are classified by rule under the other letters in the most confusing but interesting fashion. The system is far more intricate than that of the American Indians.

Besides these class or totem names, each little Australian girl has a personal name by which she is freely addressed by all excepting such of the opposite sex as are tabooed by custom. She may also have nicknames like the American Indian girls, and finally, every girl of the tribe has her secret name which may be that of some celebrated woman handed down by tradition. It is never uttered except upon most solemn occasions, and is known to those only who are initiated. When mentioned at all, it is in a whisper. If a stranger should know one's name, he would have a special chance to work her ill by ways of magic.

At a very early age, the Australian girl has graduated in all the hardening processes which result in the survival of the fittest, and is ready to take her place among women. The rites by which she is initiated into womanhood lessen her vitality, if they do not destroy it. No sooner does the little girl get upon her feet than her education begins. Her play is imitation of her mother's labors and enjoyments. A group of girls will amuse themselves by the hour, playing little dramas with the hands. Many of these games are to be found among civilized peoples. Your meaningless piling of fists in the play: "Take it off, or I'll knock it off," is part of a game which represents the entire operation of finding a honey tree, cutting it down, gathering the honey, mixing it with water, and eating it.

The marriage tie of Australian women cannot be likened to that existing among Christian nations, nor is it similar to the polygamy of Mohammedan peoples, but is a modified form of group marriage.

The Australian man obtains his wife in one of four different ways. His father secures her for him by an arrangement with the girl's father; he charms his intended by magic; he captures her as he would an enemy in battle; or she elopes with him. It is to be understood, of course, that the woman belongs to the proper class by descent. The Australians are very particular in this regard. The first and most usual method of taking a wife is connected with the law which makes every woman the possible wife of some man. There is little or no ceremony in connection with the rite of matrimony. When a man has secured a wife, she becomes his private property.

Let us imagine, therefore, that a man has set his heart upon a woman of the proper group. There are several ways of practising magic to procure a wife. Spencer and Gillan, the greatest authorities in this line of study, say, that when a man is desirous of securing a woman for his wife,--it makes no difference whether or not she be already assigned to some other man,--he takes a small strip of wood, attached at one end to a string, and marks it with the design of his totem, and with this instrument (called by the American boy a "buzzer") he goes into the bush accompanied by his friends. All night long the men keep up a low singing and chanting of amorous phrases. At daylight, the man stands up alone and swings his roarer. The sound of the instrument and the singing of the air is carried to the ear of the woman by magic, and it has the power of compelling her affections. It is asserted that women have been known to come fifty miles in order to marry the man who had bewitched them. There are other ways of charming a woman upon whom the lover has set his heart,--such as the charm of the gaudy headband worn on a public occasion, the charm of blowing the horn, and more. Elopement is only another form of magic. The third method of obtaining a wife, by capture, has been described as universal among the Australians, but the latest writers affirm that it is the rarest way in which the central Australian secures his wife.

Among the Australians, Polynesians, Malays, and many others of the lower races, descent has been primarily and uniformly through the mother. It was not until tribes became sedentary and property was held by individuals that inheritance passed to the male members of the family. The so-called mother-right is based upon the belief that individuals forming a certain clan or group, by whatever name they may be called, are the offspring of a woman who lived long ago. The term mutterrecht, by which this custom is called, is of course a sort of legal fiction; for men have always governed the world. Two benefits grew out of this form of descent. One was the certainty of motherhood. The other was the assurance, to every individual, of family support, as the children of a number of sisters were not cousins to one another, but all were brothers and sisters. So long as there were provisions with any one of this group, the rest were sure of a meal. This plan of descent through the mother has survived in many curious ways. It is found among many African tribes. Even to-day the Spaniards, who have a great deal of Moorish blood in their veins, have the custom of adding the mother's name to the father's to show that the descent is legitimate. It may be of interest to know, in passing, that James Smithson, the founder of the Smithsonian Institution, was required by his father, the Duke of Northumberland, to be known by his mother's name until he was of age, when he was allowed to assume the family name of the duke, which was Smithson. This is but a modern instance of how persistent the ancient custom has been. As soon as sedentary life and settled ownership of property took the place of nomadic life and communal ownership, mother-right or matriarchy passed gradually into patriarchy. It is curious to know that among the American Indians at the time they were discovered one could find all degrees of this transition. We must be careful, too, to discriminate between the tribe and the clan, or gens, for all savage tribes are exogamous with respect to the clans and endogamous with respect to the tribes. When the people develop the tendency to marriage within the tribe, it is evident that they have passed out of the earlier stages of clan grouping into the stage of property grouping. Marrying in the tribes was necessary, in order, as we might put it, to "keep the money in the family." Among many of the lowest as well of the highest civilization, the practice is against marrying a girl who is akin; and it is always a subject of humor when a young woman in our own country marries without changing her name, a quiet recognition of the old practice of the exogamous marriage between clan members.

Clothing for warmth or protection is not worn by Australian women; even the apron is not universal. The sense of beauty, however, has been awakened in these savage breasts, and expresses itself in pretty headbands, necklaces, and breast ornaments of seeds, teeth, and strings colored with ochre. The men, too, are but little better attired; but one indispensable article of their costumes must not be omitted in this connection, namely, the knout, or coil of twine, with which they thrash the women.

The home of the Australian woman, where she and her co-wives and their children live, is nothing more than a brush shelter, so faced as to protect the occupants from the prevailing wind. In front of this, or under it, they work, eat, sleep, and hold social intercourse. In the morning, they go forth with their digging sticks and wooden troughs to gather small animals. They take no thought of what they shall eat, the problem being to have anything to eat. When the men hunt the small kangaroo, the women surround the game and drive it toward the ambush. Every edible thing is known and is used for food. The women are the gleaners also, gathering large quantities of seeds, throwing them from one trough to another so that the wind may blow away the chaff, grinding them on one stone with another, and cooking in hot ashes the dough made from the meal. The cooking of flesh food is done by men, as that prepared by females may not be eaten by them; the women attend to the vegetable diet. In many places, females over a certain age take their meals apart; this rule, however, is not uniform.

Should the Australian woman allow her child to live past the earliest stages of infancy, she is usually a devoted mother. She often bears her child about on her shoulders as she attends upon her tasks, even after the child has become five or six years old. And should the little one die, she will continue to bear the dear body with her, apparently not noting the decomposition, which soon sets in. Mothers have been known to carry the body of a dead child for weeks.

From earliest childhood, girls as well as boys are trained to note the tracks of every living thing. For amusement, skilful women imitate, in the sand, the tracks of animals; and they know one another's footsteps. Spencer and Gillan say that every woman has her pitchi, or "wooden trough," from one to three feet long, in which she carries everything, even the baby, for she is both pack and passenger beast; when she is hunting, it will very often be used as a scoop-shovel to clear out earth. Her only other implement is her digging stick, the primitive pick-plow excavator. It is a straight staff, pointed at the end. When at work requiring its use, the owner loosens the earth with the digging stick, held in the right hand, while her left hand plays the part of shovel. Acre after acre of the soil wherein lives the honey ant is dug over for this toothsome mite. Little girls go out with their mothers; and while the latter are digging up vermin and insects, the toddlers, with little picks, will be taking their first lesson in what will be their chief lifework.

Among savages, the textile art--woman's peculiar industry--is little encouraged. The spindle used in Australia before the discovery of the island-continent in 1606, and which is still in use among the wild tribes, is the most primitive conceivable, for it is merely a little switch with a hooked end. The women make string for tying, as well as for bags and network, out of human, opossum, and kangaroo hair, from sinew, like the Eskimo, and from vegetable fibre. They sit upon the ground, use the left hand for a distaff, and with the right hand roll the spindle dexterously on the naked thigh. When a foot or so of string is finished, it is rolled about the hook of the spindle for a bobbin. When two of these are completed, a stick is driven into the ground, and a rude rope or twine walk is set up. The women know the dyes in many plants and use them. With the strings they make basketry, nets, bags, plaiting, and many ornamental forms of simple lacework and borders. Indeed, the Australian aborigines are at the bottom of the textile ladder, where human fingers perform all spinning, netting, and weaving.

In lieu of the gaudy costumes and of the tattooed tooth patterns etched upon the skin among other Indo-Pacific tribes, Australian women decorate their breasts and other parts with horrid scars. They cut the skin with flint or glass, and rub ashes or down into the open wounds in order that the cicatrices may be large and prominent. They submit to these tortures with the greatest satisfaction, and add more from time to time as memorials of personal experiences or in honor of the dead.

The Australian women are fond of games and sports. Dr. Roth, the Northern Protector of Aborigines in Queensland, says that with a fair length of twine adult women will amuse themselves for hours at a time. The twine is used in the form of an endless string, known to Europeans as "cat's cradle" or "catch cradle." Hundreds of the most intricate and bewildering designs are made, in the formation of which the mouth, the knees, and the toes cooperate with the hand. Some of the figures are extremely complicated. Dr. Roth gives the plates of the finished patterns, which certainly are as fascinating as any work of savage hands.

Australian women are described as cheerful and light-hearted, but, on occasion, they fight with their digging sticks most furiously, giving and taking blows like men. The testimony of the best observers is to the effect that, in most tribes, women are not treated with excessive cruelty, which would be quickly fatal to the tribe in longevity, fecundity, and service. Women receive their share of the resources, be they abundant or meagre. What seems to be cruelty is only custom or, as one would say, fashion; and in Australia, even more so than in Paris, you had as well be out of the world as out of the fashion.

All her life, the Australian woman is in the most abject social state; her connection with the rites and ceremonies of her tribes is only as an assistant or attendant. She is charged with all the industrial occupations of food getting, and is not allowed to venture near the sacred places on in of death. She is bound hand and foot by custom.

No Australian woman is believed to die a natural death. All are killed by magic--it may be a personal enemy near at hand or by a great sorcerer far away. Their life, so remote from ours, is, however, less sensitive, and it would be untrue to say that they are a melancholy set, living in perpetual dread.

When an Australian woman dies, she is at once placed in a sitting posture, with the knees doubled up against the chin. The body thus prepared is deposited in a round hole at once or is placed on a platform, made of boughs, until some of the flesh disappears, after which the bones are put into a grave. Nothing whatever is deposited with her, and the earth is piled directly upon the body so as to form a low mound with a depression on the side toward the camp ground. As soon as the burial is over, her camp is burnt utterly and her group remove to another place. Those who stood in certain kinship to her may never mention her name again or go near her grave after the last act of quieting the spirit has been performed. This ceremony occurs about a year after the death of a woman, and consists of trampling on her grave. Her mother and the nearest clan kin paint themselves with kaolin and visit her grave, accompanied by certain of her tribal brothers. On the way, the actual mother throws herself on the ground and is only prevented from frightfully cutting herself by watchful attendants. At the grave, the blood flows copiously from self-inflicted wounds upon all the mourners. After this blood letting, charms are planted upon the grave mound, the blood stained pipe clay, with which the half dead mother has smeared herself, is rubbed off and the grave is smoothed over. All this is done cheerfully, as it is the custom of the country.

The widow (or widows) of a deceased man smears her hair, face, and breast with white pipe clay, and remains silent during a long time, perhaps a year, communicating by means of gesture language. She remains in camp, performing assiduously the ceremonies for the dead; indeed, should she venture forth on her old avocations, a younger brother of her husband, on meeting her, might run her through with his spear. When the time comes to have the ban of silence removed, she smears herself afresh with kaolin, prepares a large tray full of food, and accompanied by female friends walks to the dividing line of her camp. They are joined by the proper kindred of the deceased, who, after an elaborate ceremony, release her from her vows, and certify to her having done her whole widowly duties. At the ceremony of trampling on the grave of the dead man, in which certain women take part, and especially the widow, who scrapes the kaolin from her body, showing that her mourning is ended.

When a child dies, not only does the actual mia, or "mother," cut herself, but all the sisters of the latter perform a like ceremony. On the death of relatives, women gash themselves. The scars thus made have naught to do with the decorative cicatrices across the breast, before mentioned. They are specially proud of these self-inflicted wounds, since they are the permanent record of their faithfulness to their dead.

Let us turn our attention to the smallest women of the world. History, ethnology, and classic myth have united to make the Eastern pigmies the most interesting people in the world. Though they are a little people, and have been hard pressed by larger and stronger races, they have survived for centuries. They are to be found in Asia, Africa, and the islands of the sea. Africa was doubtless their aboriginal home; but this negrito type has spread eastward, probably in their canoes in the early days, till the islands of the South Seas have become their home.

The women among these little people are even smaller than the men. The Mincopies of the Andaman Islands are among the most interesting of the negritos. Because of their roving nature, they live in huts which are rather temporary in character. These are put up by the women, though when a sojourn in a given locality is to be of longer duration the men build huts that are more permanent. The boys and girls do not sleep in the same huts with the married people, but in huts specially constructed for them. The women often become quite expert in the manufacture of pottery by hand, the vessels having rounded bottoms, and being decorated with wavy lines, or lines made by a wooden style.

Both boys and girls in the first few years of life are left entirely nude. At about six years the little girl has placed upon her an apron of leaves. This is her sole garment. Later in life, the womanly instinct for ornament shows itself however, so that necklaces and girdles are added. There is a certain kind of girdle, made from the pandanus leaves, which is the peculiar possession of the married women. The women, as well as the men, tattoo their entire bodies. This art of tattooing is practised almost entirely by the women. They use a piece of quartz or glass, making horizontal and vertical incisions in alternating series. There was probably some religious significance originally in this practice, since the men begin the process by making incisions with an arrow used in hunting the wild pig, and while the wounds are still fresh the man must refrain from using the flesh of this animal. The bodies of the women are usually quite shapely, though their faces are not beautiful. With the women as well as the men, the body is of nearly uniform width, there being scarcely any enlargement at the hips. Since the race is comparatively pure, marrying among themselves, the type is very uniform; and since, as Quatrefages says, the occupations of men and women vary little, the difference in the development of female as contrasted with masculine characteristics is exceedingly small.

The young girl enjoys equal freedom with her brother, but preserves her modesty with commendable strictness. An official, "the guardian of youth," scrutinizes the conduct of the young people with much care and attempts to see that wrongs against modesty and chastity are, as far as possible, righted. The marriage relation is well guarded; bigamy and polygamy are rigidly prohibited; and betrothals, which are often made for the little ones at a very tender age, are held as inviolate, a betrothal being regarded as quite as binding as actual marriage. The young couple to be married never take the initiative for themselves, this duty falls to the "guardian of youth," whose watchful eye is expected to discern the eternal fitness of things in this important field of human interest.

The marriage contract is a purely civil one, being celebrated at the hut of the chieftain of the tribe. The bride remains seated. By her side is one or more women; the groom stands surrounded by the young men. The chief approaches him and leads him to the young girl, whose legs are held by several women. After some pretended resistance on the part of both, the groom sits down on the knees of his bride. The torches are lighted so that all present can attest that the ceremony has been regularly carried out. Finally the chief declares the young people duly married, and they retire to a hut prepared in advance. Then they are said to spend several days silently, without so much as looking at each other, during which period they receive from friends presents of a very practical nature, such as provisions and equipments for housekeeping. After this silent but profitable function is over, a wedding dance is given in which the whole community joins, except the two who are most concerned in the festivities.

"It is incorrect to say that among the Andamese marriage is nothing more than taking a female slave, for one of the striking features of their social relation is the marked equality and affection which subsists between husband and wife. Careful observations extended over many years prove that not only is the husband's authority more or less nominal, but that it is not at all an uncommon occurrence for Andamese Benedicts to be considerably at the beck and call of their better halves."

A writer upon the Andamese islanders has this significant utterance concerning woman's moral influence even among these uncivilized peoples: "Experience has taught us that one of the most effective means of inspiring confidence when endeavoring to make acquaintance with these savages is to show that we are accompanied by women, for they at once infer that, whatever may be our intentions, they are at least not hostile."

As a rule, marriage life among these Andamese islanders is said to be very happy. The women are constant and faithful; the husbands also exercise marked fidelity. The spirit of equality and reciprocity prevails to an exceptional degree when compared with many other uncivilized peoples, and indeed with many civilized people.

Even before the mother gives birth to the child, the little one receives a name with a qualitative, according to sex. This it bears for two or three years. It is then replaced by another qualitative which the boy bears till his initiation into the rites of manhood, and the girl till the appearance of signs of puberty. This name corresponds to some tree or flower. When the girl marries she drops her "flower name."

Mothers, too, have great fondness for their children, nursing them as long as there is milk for them, and it is not uncommon for three children to feed at the same maternal breast. A peculiar custom prevails, however, by which most of the children are by the fifth or sixth year taken from their parents, and become parts of another household. This custom of adoption is a method by which friends express and cement their friendships for one another. As Quatrefages says: "Every married man received into a family regards as an expression of gratitude and proof of friendship, the privilege of adopting one of the children of the family." The parents rarely see children that have been adopted. They may pay them visits, but they never take them back permanently to their homes, and temporarily only by permission. The foster-father may, strangely enough, pass his adopted child on to some friend of his, as freely as he might one of his own.

The modesty of the scantily clothed women is noteworthy. Man, who has written so minutely upon the Andamese, says that when a woman has occasion to remove one of her girdles in order to make it a present to a friend, she does so with a shyness that amounts almost to prudery; and she never changes her apron before a companion, but retires to some secret place. Even within the same family circle, the bearing of the sexes toward each other is modest and delicate. The man will observe the greatest care in his attitude toward the wife of a cousin or of a younger brother, only addressing her through a third person. The wife of an elder brother receives the respect accorded to a mother.

The negritos of Luzon in the Philippines are also found to be very correct in their ideas upon the relations of the sexes. Adultery is very rare, and is punished, as are theft and murder, by death. The manners of the young girls are very correct, for any suspicion of their chastity might prevent their marriage, for the young men are particular that their wives should be without stain or even an imputation of it. When a young man is ready to marry and has found the girl of his choice, he lets her parents know of his heart's wish. They are said never to refuse. They do not turn her formally or informally over to her suitor, however, but they send her out into the forest, where, early in the morning, before even the sun has risen, she conceals herself. It is the young man's business to find this pearl of great price, or else he cannot claim to be worthy of her and must forever relinquish all right in her. This, it will be readily seen, is but another way of leaving the whole matter in the hands of the girl, who may not seek the thickest jungles for a hiding place. The day for the marriage has come. The lovers climb two young trees which are adjacent one to the other and may be easily bent together. An aged man comes, and presses the boughs of the trees toward each other till the heads of the young couple touch. They are then husband and wife. Feasting and dancing follow, and then the pair settle down to life's realities in earnest. The husband gives his father-in-law a present, a custom surviving from a day when wives were purchased; and the father presents his daughter with a present as dowry, which becomes her own personal property. The A 雌 a has but one wife. If he should die after his children are grown, the family home is continued; should the children be yet very young, the mother usually takes them and returns to the home of her own people.

Among some of the negrito tribes there has been found an incipient literature. The following are words of a love song which Montano found among the A 雌 as. It has thus been translated:

"I leave, oh, my loved one, Be very prudent, thou loved one. Ah! I go very far, my loved one, While thou remainest in dwelling thine, Never the village will be forgotten by me."

In contrast with these pigmies of probably African origin, there may come to our minds the ancient tradition of African Amazons. For the poetical allusions among the Greek authors to such a community of female warriors there was doubtless some basis in fact, and this even when all due allowance is made for the imaginative element in the tale. According to the tradition, these African Amazons, an army of powerful women, under the leadership of their Queen Myrina, marched against the Gorgons and Atlantes and subdued them, and at last marched through Egypt and Arabia and founded their capital on Lake Tritonis, where they were finally annihilated by Hercules. The truth in these Amazon stories lies doubtless in the fact that it is not an unknown custom for African women, strong of body and brave of spirit, to enlist as soldiers in companies or armies, commanded by officers of their own sex, and to become very powerful in regulating the life of some communities.

Among the Dahomeys, women captives are often enrolled in the king's army of "amazons." These are said to have a perfect passion for fighting. They are bound to perpetual celibacy and chastity, under the penalty of death. They are described as famous in battle, but their chief utility is to prevent rebellion among the male soldiers. They have separate organizations and are commanded by officers of their own sex, and are most loyal to their king.

The world has long known of the Hottentots of South Africa. Their women are taller and larger than those of the neighboring Bushmen, who are the South African pigmies. Among these Hottentots woman often occupies a place of considerable power; this is notably in the home, where she reigns supreme. The husband may lord it over her outside of the house, and often does, making almost a slave of his spouse; but when he enters the house, he abdicates his authority. Without her permission, the husband cannot take a bit of meat or a drop of milk. If he attempts to infringe the law, the neighbors take up his case; he is amerced, often to the extent of several sheep or cows, and these become the absolute property of the wife. Should the chief of a tribe die, his wife takes his place and authority and becomes "queen of the tribe," unless her son is of age. And it is said that some of these women chieftains have left for themselves names of honor in the traditions of their people.

It is a custom among the Hottentots to call their children by the names of their parents, but by a sort of exchange, the girls assuming that of their father, the boys that of the mother--a syllabic suffix indicating the sex. To the oldest daughter are accorded especial authority and honor; for it is she who milks the cows and, in a way, has them under her control. Requests for milk must be made to her, reminding us of the Aryan wood-daughter, who was once the milkmaid.

No extraordinary claims can be made for the beauty of the Hottentot women. They have the knotty hair that characterizes the negro races, and the flat noses, thick lips, and prominent cheekbones. While their faces have no especial beauty, their figures, when maidens, are regular, plump and attractive; but after the first years of womanhood are past, the roundness of youth yields to the wrinkles of age, and all attractiveness disappears, the woman either becoming withered and haggard, or manifesting that peculiar development said to be so much admired among the Hottentots, known to science as steatopyga. The famous "Hottentot Venus" furnishes an example of this type of beauty. The back is given a most remarkable contour by the enormous growth of fat about the hips, which, though hard and firm, shakes like jelly when our Venus walks. This extraordinary development has to the Hottentot lady not only an aesthetic but also a utilitarian value, in case she cares to support her infant upon it.

The less cultured a people, the greater the place given by it to ornament. Among many uncivilized peoples the men as well as the women exhibit a fondness for decoration; but ornamentation is pre 雖 inently the weakness of women. Although the savage lady regards clothing as altogether an unnecessary burden, she must have her ornaments. One of the methods of ornamentation is that of tattooing the body. Among some tribes almost the whole body is covered with more or less artistic designs, while others mark only parts of the body, as by rings around the arms, or, as among the aboriginal New Zealand women, by puncture of the lips. The use of shells, metal rings, bands, beads, feathers, mats, and so on ad infinitum, is one of the marks of savagery.

A traveller has given the following description of a Kaffir's marriage ceremony witnessed by him. The occasion was the marriage of a Kaffir chief to his fourteenth wife, "a fat good-natured girl--obesity is at a premium among African tribes--wrapped round and round with black glazed calico, and decked from head to foot with flowers, beads, and feathers. Once within the kraal, the ladies formed two lines, with the bride in the centre, and struck up a lively air; whereupon the whole body of armed Kaffirs rushed from all parts of the kraal, beating their shields and uttering demonic yells, as they charged headlong at the smiling girls, who joined with the stalwart warriors in cutting capers, and singing lustily, until the whole kraal was one confused mass of demons, roaring out hoarse war songs and shrill love ditties. After an hour dancing ceased and joila (Kaffir beer) was served around, while the lovely bride stood in the midst of the ring alone, stared at by all and staring in turn at all, until she brought her eyes to bear upon her admiring lord. When advancing leisurely, she danced before him amid the shouts of the bystanders, singing at the top of her voice and brandishing a huge carving-knife, with which she scraped big drops of perspiration from her heated head, produced by the violent exercise she was performing."

Among African tribes, generally, the value of a woman is rated in terms of the cow. While in India the cow is more sacred than the woman, in Africa, a woman sometimes brings several cows in a trade. When a man wishes a wife there is usually little trouble in obtaining her, either by purchase, theft, or in some rather more sentimental manner. Among some tribes female go-betweens are made use of, while genuine courtship prevails among other tribes. The courtship, however, is seldom of long duration.

The matter of marriage is more completely guarded among the tribes of Africa and the Indo-Pacific than we might expect of the people of their grade of culture. While tribes vary much in marriage customs, purity of life is, as a rule, rigidly expected of married women, and most women marry at an early age. Lewdness, however, is not generally regarded as so great a crime as marital infidelity, which is often punished with death. Betrothals are looked upon as much more sacred and binding than they are among more cultivated peoples.

In Tahiti, so careful have been the natives in this matter of betrothal, that the betrothed young lady was compelled to live upon a platform of considerable elevation, built in her father's house. The parents or some members of the family attended to her wants here, night and day, and she never left her high abode without permission of her parents and accompanied by them.

In the Yomba country courtship is carried on usually through female rather than male relatives, and either sex may make the first advances toward a minor. Among all uncivilized peoples, as indeed among many that are advanced in civilization, the early marriage is one of the most important elements in the backward condition of the people, if not indeed the most serious cause of deterioration. Women are forced into the arduous duties of motherhood at an age when they are neither physically nor in any other sense prepared for such an obligation. Children born of immature mothers can scarcely expect to be robust either in body or mind.

The Kroomen, one of the native tribes of Liberia, hold marriage to be the highest ambition of life. They will marry as many wives as they can pay for, often leaving their homes in search of means whereby they may accumulate wealth enough to buy another wife. Enjoying for a few months the new relation, the ambitious husband goes off to seek again his fortune, returns, buys another companion, the marriage is again celebrated, and so the number of women who perform the drudgeries of life increases. At about middle life, usually, the Krooman has accumulated a sufficient fortune in the form of wives to enable him to retire from active labor. He now settles down to live upon the labor of his wives, who willingly support him. He is now known as a "big man," and enjoys not only the ease, but also the reputation and honor of one who has come into possession of a well-earned retirement. Another characteristic which marks woman's career among the lower races is the fact of her early and rapid physical deterioration after marriage. This is true not only of the women of Polynesia, but of the African tribes, with which they have much in common. At the age when European and American women are at the prime of their vigor and physical beauty, these women have not only seen their best days, but are broken, unsightly, and withered.

This deterioration is chiefly due to two causes; one is the uniform early marriages among these races, and the other is the hard life which is early thrust upon the woman. For she not only becomes the childbearer, but the beast of burden, the farmer, too, it may be, and the mechanic and the "general utility man."

It is true, especially where polygamy prevails, that there is a division of labor, but the labor is divided among the women; the men do only the lighter work. The several wives of the household take their servitude as a matter of course, and usually, especially in Kaffir land, they are so brought up that they regard a husband as degraded and effeminate if he takes any part in the ordinary labors of domestic life. The women are, generally, quite reconciled also to the polygamous relation, because a husband is regarded as possessing dignity and respectability in proportion as he is much or little married.

The less developed a race is, the less specialized is woman's sphere. Among the barbarous and savage peoples woman is the "maid of all work." She is weaver, potter, basketmaker, cook, agriculturist, water bearer, beast of burden, everything. Men hunt and fish, eat and sleep. In general, it may be said, that among the barbarous races there is a greater relative disparity between the size and attractiveness of men and women. This is doubtless to be accounted for by the fact that very early the female is set to hard tasks of menial service and her body is accordingly abused and stunted.

While the physical and social status of woman is one of acknowledged inferiority, there are not wanting among the African tribes instances in which woman exerts no small influence and exhibits no little power. This we have noted in mentioning the tribes dominated by warlike women. It is more particularly true of her influence within the precints of her domestic life, as was seen in the case of the pigmy women of the Andamese Islands. Mothers, and more especially mothers-in-law, exert noteworthy power, but this is always by virtue of station rather than of any inherent respect due to the sex itself. There are isolated examples of a more active power exerted by woman.

As a rule, women of the inferior races have no part in the government of their tribes. There are some exceptions, however. In the Sandwich Islands, as is well-known, the hereditary right of rule might fall to a woman as well as to a man, and there have been, in these islands, a number of queens. Our own country took some part, as will be readily remembered, in deposing the last of them from her throne.

Every student of what has come to be called "woman's sphere," especially among the uncultivated races, must be led to the conclusion that the condition of the female sex, the sphere of her activity and influence in any race, is one of the very best indexes of the civilization of that people. The view of Havelock Ellis, in his Man and Woman, is that it is the latter who is leading in the evolution of the race, in the sense not only that the traits that more distinctively belong to her are those that characterize the advance of society, but that she registers more accurately the advances. "What is civilization?" asked Emerson; and answers, "The power of good women."

Among the deplorable traits of women of uncivilized races is that of infanticide. Among some of the Pacific islanders and in some parts of Africa, the regular and systematic sacrifice of children is among the most remarkable and cruel features of the social life of the people. This is more particularly true of female infants.

War plays a very large part in the life of uncivilized races, and the presence of women is a source of weakness rather than strength, since usually they are not bearers of arms, and are among the most envied prizes for which war is waged.

Ellis, in his Polynesian Researches, draws this gloomy picture of unnatural motherhood among peoples of the Pacific islands: "In Tahiti, human victims were frequently immolated. Yet the amount of all these and other murders did not equal that of infanticide alone. No sense of irresolution or horror appeared to exist in the bosoms of those parents, who deliberately resolved on the deed before the child was born. They often visited the dwellings of the foreigners, and spoke with perfect complacency of their cruel purpose. On these occasions the missionaries employed every inducement to dissuade them from executing their intention, warning them in the name of the living God, urging them by every consideration of maternal tenderness, and always offering to provide the little stranger with a home, and the means of education. The only answer they generally received was, that it was the custom of the country; and the only result of their efforts was the distressing conviction of the inefficacy of their humane endeavors. The murderous parents often came to their houses almost before their hands were cleansed from their children's blood, and spoke of the deed with worse than brutal insensibility, or with vaunting satisfaction at the triumph of their customs over the persuasions of their teachers." It is thought that not less than two-thirds of all the children born were murdered by their own parents.

"The first three infants," says Ellis, "were frequently killed; and in the event of twins being born, both were rarely permitted to live. In the largest families, more than two or three children were seldom spared, while the numbers that were killed were incredible. The very circumstance of their destroying, instead of nursing, their offspring rendered their offspring more numerous than it would otherwise have been. We have been acquainted with a number of parents, who, according to their own confessions, or the united testimony of their friends and neighbors, had inhumanly consigned to an untimely grave, four, or six, or eight, or ten children, and some even a greater number."

But changes have taken place since the writing of these lines; it seems certain that a generation ago nearly if not quite two-thirds of the children were slain by their mothers, and few mothers were guiltless of the blood of their own offspring. The explanation of the prevalence of this species of massacre is readily discernible in the following paragraph from Ellis's Researches: "During the whole of their lives the females were subject to the most abasing degradation; and their sex was often, at their birth, the cause of their destruction. If the purpose of the unnatural parents had not been fully matured before, the circumstance of its being a female child was often sufficient to fix their determination on its death. Whenever we have asked them what could induce them to make a distinction so invidious, they have generally answered,--that the fisheries, the service of the temple, and especially war, were the only purposes for which they thought it desirable to rear children; that in these pursuits women were comparatively useless; and therefore female children were frequently not suffered to live. Facts fully confirm these statements."

Dense superstition, too, has sometimes played a part in this murder of children. In Central Africa, for example, it is held with religious scrupulosity that twin children should never be allowed to live. When children are born with a deformity, they are despatched as a matter of course. And yet, notwithstanding all these horrors, the instinct, even of the most debased mothers, is toward the love and preservation of their offspring. From the earliest days, this care for the infant, the helpless, and the weak has been the most powerful counterpoise to abnormal self-seeking. These two characteristics, self-giving and self-seeking, are among the most potent factors in the development of all the races of mankind.

The Filipino woman has lately had for us fresh interest. Indeed, the women of the Philippine Islands are among the most interesting in the world. In the mountains of Luzon and in the other out-of-the-way places are the negritos, or little negroes, of whom we have written in an earlier portion of this chapter. These little people are shoved away into the mountain regions, where the resources of life are as meagre as they can be if existence is to endure. In the lower parts of the archipelago, which are more accessible to the coast, will be found the descendants of an old Malayo-Polynesian race; these are characterized by their primitive industrial life. A later immigration of the same stock brought people to the island who have developed alphabets, metallurgic arts carried on by the men, and weaving and needlework done by the women. Closely following these, and because there were opportunities for commerce, came the more cultivated races of Eastern Asia, Chinese, Japanese, Siamese, and even Hindoos, to mingle their blood with these more primitive stocks. In the twelfth century of our era, Mohammedanized Malays took possession of the southern part of the archipelago. These people are called Moros, or Moors. Leaving out the negritos, who are only a little mixed with the other races, the other peoples we have mentioned have mingled their blood with the modern population, the Spanish and Portuguese, who have come in since the sixteenth century. The commingling of blood has been favorable to the modern Filipinos, and many regard their women as worthy of being admired for their grace and beauty. Notwithstanding their great variety of racial stocks, the women of Manila have a certain common physiognomy, the Malay type being the strongest element in their composite face. Features that mark the yellow races are also quite prominent in many of the Filipino women.

As in other races of the same grade of culture, the marriage tie is a part of the social system. Clan relationship, by whatever name it may be called, governs the selection of a spouse. The bond has been a very loose one in the islands, and it has not been an uncommon thing for men and women to break up their relationships unceremoniously and form new ones. Among a people composed of so many elements, wide differences may be expected in the matter of marriage. The Igorrotes, or wild inhabitants of Luzon, though primitive in development, are monogamous. The clan system is broken down and a young man is allowed to take the woman of his choice with little ceremony, and they become man and wife. Many astonishing customs are, of course, found among these people. For example, Alfred Marche calls attention to a form of voluntary slavery.

It is that of a young man who wants to marry. In many places, he is bound to work for two or three years as a simple domestic in the house of the father of his fianc 閑. During this time he is fed, but never takes his place at the same table with the young girl. He is allowed to walk with her and to sleep under the same roof, but he may not eat with her.

When the young man has passed this stage, he must, before the ceremony of marriage, build a house and make certain indispensable purchases. He must also pay all the expenses of the marriage. The affair does not always terminate as regularly as one could wish. The father sometimes seeks a quarrel with his future son-in-law at the moment when the ceremony is about to take place, and admits a new aspirant for his daughter's hand. The newcomer undertakes to work for him without any scruples. The house, which is of little value, is all that remains to the late fianc?as a consolation.

De Morgan, who travelled in the Philippine Islands for the Spanish government and published his account, in the City of Mexico, in 1609, gives an account of the native women three hundred years ago.

The women of Luzon are described as wearing sleeves of all colors which they call baros. White cotton stuffs were wrapped or folded from the waist downward to the feet, and over these sometimes was a thin cloak folded gracefully. The people of the highest rank substituted silk or fine native fabrics for the cotton, and added gold chains, bracelets, and earrings, and rings on their fingers. Their hair, which is exceedingly black, was tied gracefully in a knot on the back of their head. Many of these characteristics noted by De Morgan may still be seen among the women of the islands. The closer contact of the Philippine Islands with the mainland and more particularly with western commerce and civilization is destined to work many and possibly rapid changes even in the customs and ideals of the women whose native conservatism has held them for many centuries very much in the same groove of life and daily routine.

The women of Luzon have always been cleanly and elegant in their persons, and they are attractive and graceful. Much time is spent on their hair, which is frequently washed and anointed with the oil of sesame prepared with musk. They spend much time on their teeth, and formerly began at a tender age to file them into the shape demanded by the customs of the country. They also dyed their teeth black. Like the Moorish women, the Filipinos are fond of the bath; they frequent the rivers and creeks and bathe throughout the entire year, the genial climate allowing such pastime.

As in other countries below the grade of civilization, the industrial employments of the Philippines are largely for the women. To them is the task of spinning and weaving the exceptionally delicate fabric of the archipelago into the finest cloth. They also are the food purveyors, assisting in gathering food material, pounding it in their simple mills and serving it. In their cuisine are such vegetables as sweet potatoes, beans, plantains, guavas, pineapples, and oranges. The women rear fowls and domestic animals, and take upon themselves the entire care of the family and household.

While the women of all countries have always been the natural and most persistent conservers of ancient ideals and racial customs, yet it may be predicted that the throwing of the Filipino tribes into contact with New World politics, trade, and customs will, at length, bring about marked social changes. These must eventually give to the women of the Filipinos a wider outlook upon life and a new power to carry its burdens.

CONTENTS